The editors

from science fiction to women's and ge
this time that she joined the RNA. She w
for her first major novel, *The Marigold Field*, and was still with them
when her bestselling *Csardas* was published, a breakthrough novel
in which she covered 40 years of Hungarian history told through
the eyes of two families. With the publication of *Csardas* she was
created a Vice President of the RNA. This was followed by *The
Summer of the Barshinskys*, which also became a bestseller on both sides
of the Atlantic. Since then she has published *Voices of Summer*, set
in the world of opera and operetta, of which she is a great fan. She is
the author of many short stories, primarily for the women's market.
She was invited to be President of the RNA in 1987, and was delighted
to accept. She has enjoyed every moment of her role.

*

Jenny Haddon read English at St Hugh's College Oxford, ran away to
Ireland to write her Great Work, realised it was terrible and went
out to work.

Meanwhile an agent steered her towards Harlequin Mills & Boon,
with the cheering words, 'Your writing is great, I love your hero,
your dialogue makes me laugh, your plotting stinks. Go and learn
from the best.' She meant Alan Boon.

It was the start of a double life—the day jobs and the books
her alter ego, Sophie Weston, could weave out of them for Mills &
Boon. At various times she edited press releases for a Latin American
embassy in London (*The Latin Affair*); lectured in the Arabian Gulf
(*The Sheikh's Bride*); waitressed in Paris (*Midnight Wedding*); and made
herself hated as a consultant by getting under people's feet asking
stupid questions all over the world (*The Millionaire's Daughter*). So far
she has written 44 novels for Harlequin Mills & Boon. They are
published in 26 languages and over 100 international outlets.

Over time, the day job embraced the Bank of England where
she ended as a bank regulator (figures tell stories; great job) and

the International Monetary Fund, World Bank and other financial institutions. She was a member of the Gibraltar Financial Services Commission for three years.

With fellow RNA Member Elizabeth Hawksley, Jenny has written *Getting the Point, A Panic-Free Guide to English Punctuation for Adults*, published by Floris Books, 2006. (The working title was *Punctuation for the Petrified.*)

She has served on the RNA Committee as Conference Organiser, Vice Chairman, Chairman and now Treasurer—which is having a very bad effect on her character, incidentally. These days Scrooge could take her correspondence course.

Fabulous at Fifty

RECOLLECTIONS OF
THE ROMANTIC NOVELISTS' ASSOCIATION
1960 –2010

EDITED BY
JENNY HADDON & DIANE PEARSON

RNA

THE ROMANTIC NOVELISTS' ASSOCIATION

First published in Great Britain 2010
by the Romantic Novelists' Association
www.romanticnovelistsassociation.org

© The Romantic Novelists' Association 2010

Designed by Jenny Carter Communications

Cover image istock photos ©aleksandarvelasevic

Printed and bound in Great Britain by Welshpool Printing Group, Powys

ISBN 978-0-9566957-0-3

This book is dedicated with gratitude,
respect and affection to

ELIZABETH FANCOURT HARRISON
1921-2008

Author, RNA Chairman
and generous benefactor

Acknowledgements

Special thanks to Mike Legat, who gave us permission to quote as much as we liked from his autobiography *They Read Books and go to Cocktail Parties*; to Claire Lorrimer, Denise Robins's daughter, who gave us permission to quote from her mother's book *Stranger Than Life*; and to Ida Pollock for permission to quote from her memoir, *Starlight*.

We are grateful to Mira Books for permission to quote from *Safe Passage* by Ida Cook (Mary Burchell); to Transworld Publishers for permission to quote from *No Time for Romance* by Lucilla Andrews; and to the *Daily Mirror* for permission to quote the Marje Proops article.

Where we have quoted from other work, every effort has been made to trace the copyright owner. Where we have failed, however, anyone claiming copyright should get in touch with the RNA.

Contents

The editors

Diane Pearson began her career in publishing at the age of sixteen when she went to work in the Production Department of Jonathan Cape Ltd, at the time still a privately owned company. It was a lowly job, but she did have instant access to a huge range of books and read voraciously and indiscriminately through *Seven Pillars of Wisdom*, the works of Beverly Nichols, Arthur Ransome and Ernest Hemingway (considered very raunchy in those days and taken home with a Doctor Dolittle dustjacket wrapped round the volume in case her mother saw what she was reading), the essential Proust (difficult), the first Barbara Pym (lovely!) and the early James Bonds.

After a spell in local government, she went to work in the Advertisement Department of Purnell's on several magazines, and then joined Transworld Publishers, Corgi as it was more generally known in those days, as a junior editor. She remained at Transworld for 38 years, finally becoming Senior Editor, and working with a large stable of writers including Kate Atkinson, Jilly Cooper, Frederick Forsyth, Terry Pratchett and Joanna Trollope.

She had been writing since she was 16 (well, six really—a blood-thirsty story called 'Murder in the Lighthouse', never published) and in her thirties began to get some of her science fiction stories accepted. Also in her thirties she finally had a novel accepted, a gothic called *Loom of Tancred*, and from then on changed direction—away

Introduction by the President

Fifty years is a long time in a writing organisation and our golden anniversary is one of which we can justly be proud. We have celebrated magnificently, beginning the year with the publication of our volume of short stories written by members, *Loves Me, Loves Me Not*, enjoyed one of the most memorable conferences we have ever had at the Royal Palace at Greenwich (which coincided with one of the hottest weekends of the summer), organised a poll in association with *Woman's Weekly* to name the most popular romantic novel of the last 50 years, and in addition have participated in our regular parties and a particularly glittering Romantic Novel of the Year Awards luncheon. We have come a long way from 1960, as the following pages illustrate. In the beginning the members were mostly 'romance' writers—that is, short books dealing mainly with one-on-one relationships and with small canvasses. Now we cover an enormous range of women's fiction from Mills & Boon through to operatic-sized epics, taking in on the way, sagas, chick-lit, contemporary situation novels (how I hate the term Aga sagas), historicals, paranormal, and whatever the next fashion is going to be.

This book is not a history—Jenny Haddon and I decided that might prove rather dull, containing 50 years' details of committee meetings etc—factual but not much fun. So although we have included many facts from the archives (Jenny has done a brilliant job digging around in old files and selecting and presenting the important developments of the times) we have also included first-hand memories from journals and early members. Sometimes there are anomalies—50 years is a long time and not everyone remembers things the same way—but we have left the 'memories' as they are.

Our thanks to all those who contributed to this book, especially Jay Dixon who co-authored the chapter on Mills & Boon; to Jenny Harper without whose design and production expertise this book would not exist; to Jane McCarten for the index; to Evelyn Ryle for her eagle-eyed proof reading; and to Joanna Trollope, whose thoughtful remarks on romantic fiction close this memoir.

There are quite a few biographies along the way of those who were, and are, important to the organisation and we have endeavoured to cover every aspect of our hugely comprehensive and efficient Association. If we have left anything or anybody out it is because, in spite of searching, we have been unable to find out the necessary facts.

While writing and editing this book, two things have become increasingly clear. Our very title suggests a pleasant group of middle-aged, middle-England, mild-mannered ladies, but in fact we have had more than our share of 'characters', not to say eccentrics over the years. And the other fact that has emerged is what a very supportive organisation ours has been, constantly helping and encouraging each other and new young writers to achieve success. I can think of no other writing group (and I've belonged to quite a few in my time) where so much help, information, and assistance has been so generously given. Where we shall go in the next 50 years it is difficult to say, but I hope and believe this one aspect of the RNA will always prevail.

Diane Pearson, President

In the beginning

The Romantic Novelists' Association was brought into being by two highly individual characters: Denise Robins, who was glamorous, forceful, romantic, and Alex (sometimes Vivian) Stuart, perhaps a touch eccentric, also forceful and enormous fun.

First meeting

The inaugural meeting took place on 12th January 1960 at the Royal Overseas Club, chaired by Alex Stuart under the Presidency of Denise Robins. They were supported, as *The Bookseller* reported, by two Vice Presidents, Miss Barbara Cartland and Miss Netta Muskett.

The Woman Journalist, the magazine of The Society of Women Writers and Journalists, also reported that both Miss Robins and Miss Cartland paid tribute to Alex Stuart, who had seen the need for an association. Then Miss Robins made a fighting speech declaring that although, according to the libraries, romantic novels gave the most pleasure to the most people, the writers almost had to apologise for what they did. It had got to stop!

Barbara Cartland, the ultimate apostle of the happy ending, thought romantic novels were popular because they had an enthusiasm for life. Netta Muskett thought they emphasised the *good* and said she received letters from readers thanking her for providing short periods of forgetfulness.

Alex Stuart reported that the RNA already had 115 members. It was going to award an Oscar for the best romantic novel of the year and mount a touring exhibition of romantic novels in conjunction with the Book League. (The Book League would display 150 romantic novels published before 1900 and the RNA would nominate between 250 and 300 subsequent novels.) The RNA would also award two scholarships to probationer members—that is, those without a full length novel yet published.

Founders

Alex Stuart

Alex Stuart was obviously the brains behind the formation of the RNA. It was she who gathered together the original members and became the first Chairman. She had begun her writing career in the fifties, as a serial writer, producing an average of four commissioned serials a year. These were subsequently adapted and published as novels by Mills & Boon, Robert Hale, and Herbert Jenkins under several pen names.

Mike Legat (publisher, author and Associate Vice President of the RNA from its earliest days) knew her well and gives us a portrait of this colourful character:

'She had an Eton crop, no make-up, always wore trousers, and had a rather gruff voice which was probably due to her heavy smoking which eventually led to her death from cancer. Anyone who would have hazarded a guess as to her sexuality from the mannish appearance and the sometimes masculine style of writing would have jumped to the wrong conclusion. She was married twice and had children and grandchildren. She had had quite a distinguished war, in Burma I think, in some kind of medical capacity.

'Vivian had a great sense of humour and enjoyed life hugely, especially when doing something quite childish; for instance, at the Swanwick Summer School (which she adored—she did a stint as Chairman and was a permanent fixture on the committee). When dishing out sausages at breakfast on the committee and speakers' table, she would save some sausages, wrap them in a paper napkin and give them to Nancy Martin to put in her handbag. (I don't think she had a handbag of her own.) She would also steal some bread and butter, and these goodies would be produced at the end of the evening in Room X (the committee room) for what she liked to call 'our midnight feast'. And stern Vivian (and she could be formidable when she wanted) would be giggling like a schoolgirl.'

After the Great Walk Out, Alex Stuart was the only one of the founding team to maintain a relationship with the RNA. She retained her Life Membership and would often send chatty pieces in to the *RNA News*. For instance in 1974, she posted that, as VA Stuart, author of 12 military and naval historical novels published by Pinnacle Books Inc. of New York, she had been invited to tour the USA (including Washington DC, San Francisco and El Paso) ending with an address to the creative writing students at the University of Texas at El Paso. The downside, she records ruefully, is that she 'will have to reveal the guilty secret that she had kept dark for so long ... that she is not a man but a woman and, far from being (as Pinnacle once claimed by a slip of the typewriter) a Lieutenant Colonel retired, she had only attained the rank of Second Lieutenant when her service in Burma with XIV Army terminated.' Her Sheridan (army) and Hazard (navy) series had just been reprinted in the USA and sales topped 80,000 copies.

She also continued to bat for romantic novelists in public fora. In the summer of 1974 she entered into brisk correspondence with the then Literature Director of the Arts Council, who de-listed her from the Writers in Schools scheme. He explained that the intention of the scheme was 'to introduce creative and imaginative writers (that is, poets, novelists) into schools to talk to older children.' It was not intended to involve the general writer, critic, specialised or technical writer or romantic novelists. He said the Arts Council had been in error to include her in the past and—without a word of thanks for her three years of work for the scheme—said he would be deleting her name from the next edition of the list. Stuart was outraged that 'the Arts Council refuses to concede to romantic novelists the title of novelist or to accept that they are creative and imaginative,' and responded accordingly, with copies to Victor Bonham Carter at the Society of Authors. (She was always urging RNA members to join.) However, when she learned that the Society's then Joint Chairman, children's author Nancy Martin, had also been de-listed by the Arts Council, she gave up the fight. 'I am left wondering,' she commented tartly in the *RNA News*, 'what sort of novelist the Arts Council does consider sufficiently "creative" to be permitted to address schools under their auspices.'

The RNA was a lifetime commitment for her. In spring 1986, when inflation was producing real financial difficulties for the organisation, the committee thanked Alex Stuart for a donation; she died that August.

Denise Robins

If the idea of the RNA originated with Alex Stuart, much of the inspiration and glamour were provided by Denise Robins, famous author of over 200 books and an autobiography, *Stranger Than Fiction*. Her last book was published only two years before her death at the age of 87. She was a true romantic with what she described to the Society of Women Writers and Journalists as an urge to dramatise her emotions and romantic beliefs and 'write for the many who love, have loved, or want to be loved.'

Her daughter, Claire Lorrimer, a fellow author, writes about her mother:

'The career Denise would have chosen was that of an actress but of course, in those days, such an occupation was considered socially unacceptable for a girl of her background. She therefore followed her mother, herself an authoress, into a writing career. Her love of the stage stayed with her and as a result, she was always impeccably turned out, her good taste ensuring she was always noticeably elegant. For instance, she did not "go into" the Ivy restaurant but made an entrance, sometimes with her three small daughters behind her looking shy and highly embarrassed by the attention their glamorous mother was receiving.

'Denise's attention to her appearance once prompted her to ask her friend, Barbara Cartland, why she chose to dress like a Christmas tree. Barbara's answer was that she was a romantic novelist and her fans expected her to look romantic! Denise, meanwhile, was doing her utmost to resemble her look-alike, Marlene Dietrich, and indeed, in one of her beautiful evening gowns with her jewellery and furs, she did bear a striking resemblance to the film star. To complete her image, she finally bought a magnificent full-length mink coat, which nearly sank beneath the waves on a disastrous seaplane trip to Egypt when the plane made an emergency landing in a Sicilian bay. Orders were given to evacuate the plane immediately, leaving everything behind. Not Denise's precious new mink, which made its way with her on to the escape launch! Typical of her thoughtfulness, she used it to keep a baby warm as there was a violent thunderstorm in progress and no shelter on the launch.

'Denise hated the thought of old age and refused to acknowledge it. On one occasion she asked one of her daughters to assist her as she was giving a tea party in her garden for "the poor old people" from the nearby retirement home and would need help. As it turned out, she was at least ten years older than the youngest of them but having danced attendance upon them, still referred to them as "the poor old dears" having enjoyed themselves.

'Denise's love of the stage manifested itself by way of the friends she made amongst the famous actors, actresses, playwrights and musicians of the times, many of whom she had met when she co-wrote a play with Roland Pertwee. He was among many famous people who were frequent weekend house party guests at the lovely Queen Anne house in Sussex, where inevitably charades were part of the entertainment. Denise herself was an enthusiastic performer! Jack Strachey (composer of 'These Foolish Things') would perform on the piano; George Sanders would play and sing to his guitar; Phyllis Neilson-Terry, Gwen Ffrangcon-Davies, Diana Wynyard, Flora Robson, Edna Best, were all visitors, as were writers such as Noel Streatfeild, Ernest Raymond, Ruby M Ayres and editresses including Joan Werner Laurie, and Nancy Spain and Phyllis Panting, wife of Digby Morton, the dress designer of the day, who made so many of Denise's striking outfits.

'Her children, having paid their respects, were thankfully confined to the schoolroom having quickly sussed out that they were very much surplus to requirements by all these important thespians. Although the house was not particularly large, Denise had an extension added to the drawing room which now had a raised dais at one end of the room, with a room leading off it, which made it a perfect "stage" for these weekend theatricals.

'At the height of her career, Denise had truly achieved the fame she wanted and had entrée anywhere she wished. She was on intimate terms with Noel Coward, one of whose plays she rewrote as a novel. John Gielgud welcomed her backstage after one of his performances; she dined with Gerald du Maurier at the Garrick Club. As a long-time friend of the playwright Roland Pertwee, she was often at his house, where she even played charades with a young Laurence Olivier. She became a great friend of Sir Patrick Hastings, the famous barrister, and of Christina Foyle, Godfrey Winn—really anyone who was anyone! She greatly enjoyed speaking—opening bazaars, at literary lunches, on radio and, after the war, on television. Yet with all her success and fame, she remained remarkably modest. "I may not be a great literary writer," she said, "but I tell a cracking good story, and that is what my readers want."

'A quarter of a century after her death in 1985, Denise's "good stories" are still being read by no less than forty thousand women every year. Small wonder therefore that she campaigned so vigorously to have the romantic novel suitably acknowledged. For many years she had complained bitterly that book reviewers either ignored or denigrated light romantic fiction, until finally in 1960 Denise and Alex Stuart founded the RNA.'

Denise herself wrote of it in her autobiography *Stranger than Fiction*:

'In 1961 [sic] Alex Stuart, well-known writer of light fiction, and I, founded the Romantic Novelists' Association. I was elected

President. Barbara Cartland was one of the Vice Presidents. She is a great friend of mine. We have now both resigned, but I often meet the glittering, glamorous Barbara. While I was President, AP Herbert was my Guest of Honour at my very first dinner. He spoke to us as the great champion he is of the rights of novelists who, unlike the composers of songs, receive not a penny from the libraries who handle so many millions of their books. In 1964 we had the late Ian Fleming as our Guest of Honour, the great James Bond himself! He told me that he felt a bit out of place among all the "romantic ladies", but I assured him (as I have done so many of those who criticise) that the word romance does not necessarily stand only for sentimental love but for deeds of chivalry, and for all kinds of adventure, an atmosphere which might be found even in an Ian Fleming thriller.'

Vice Presidents

Netta Muskett and Barbara Cartland were the first Vice Presidents. Netta Muskett is not so well remembered today, although she was a very big name when the Association began. By contrast, Barbara Cartland was a unique figure and there are still a great many people who remember her.

Netta Muskett

Netta Muskett was one of the major names to join the RNA as a founder member. She does not seem to have started to write until her marriage broke up in 1928 (almost unheard of then) when she was 40. She told an RNA member, 'I had crawled out from my marriage with two children in each hand, a cat, a dog, a sewing machine and my old typewriter.' Times were very hard until she got a body of work behind her, and she often recalled giving her characters wonderful food as she added another onion to the thin family stew. She told the inaugural meeting of the RNA that in writing her novels she herself had escaped from drab surroundings, particularly in the early days. No heroine of hers ever had to endure the deprivations she had known!

When the debate about a change of name for the RNA arose

in 1965 she was already ill, but she wrote to the *RNA News* saying, with considerable justification, that she did not think her own books were very romantic. By then she had written over 50 books for publishers who were accustomed to marketing them as romantic novels. Yet often the protagonists not only ended unhappily but also lurched through a range of disasters and moral degradation along the way. Unlike the put-upon but impeccably upright heroines of Cartland, Robins and, indeed, most of the original RNA membership, Muskett's protagonists contribute enthusiastically to their own downfall and learn painful moral lessons in doing so.

Most of the trouble comes from sex, or, interestingly, lack of it. Men who marry empty-headed socialites (*Light from One Star*); girls pushed by their mothers to marry the handsome but chilly lord of the manor and finding they are limited to sexual congress once every three months (*Philippa*); ambitious men who, for the sake of fame and advancement, spurn simple wives who only want a baby (*The Shadow Market*); they all have to pay for their sins. Her blurbs regularly referred to 'griefs and trials' and she seemed to specialise in giving her characters particularly intractable difficulties.

Yet Netta Muskett's tortured heroines and gloomy endings did not prevent her from being one of the most successful authors of the mid-century. Why? Well, sex. On the back of some of her books is a quote from Robert Pitman of the *Sunday Express*: 'Like all the best romance women, she feels for her slim heroines and bronzed heroes. But she brings in someone else as well. Freud. While most other books on the romance shelf are stronger on sentiment than sex, you can be certain of realism every time you pick up a Muskett.' Indeed you could. As the late founder member Anne Weale recalled, 'I remember grown-ups talking about her novels in the thirties, their tones of voice suggesting she was regarded as rather daring/spicy.' Fellow author and RNA-er Daphne Clair confirms this: 'I have a number of her books; she was a favourite of my mother. Very racy in her day, and one of those covers—on her last book *Cloudbreak*—would probably raise eyebrows in some circles even today. My mother wouldn't allow me to read them!' Anne Weale, one of the youngest founder members, was disappointed to find that in person the daring Netta Muskett 'was overshadowed by Denise R, Barbara C and Alex S'.

By today's standards, the books are unexceptional. Sexual activity takes place off the page and, though it has clearly happened, is referred to only in the most delicate terms, generally indicating regret, guilt, or—and this was genuinely an innovation at the time— disappointment on the heroine's part. Even so, mothers, teachers and librarians were all heard to warn against Netta Muskett's books. So it is easy to see why President Denise Robins worded her tribute so carefully after Netta Muskett died in May 1963: 'She wrote in the true romantic vein without too many restrictions and yet always preserving the delicacy and tact that are essential. Her sales were prolific.'

In recognition of her support and friendship, the committee decided, the following year, to name the award for a probationer writer after her. It remained the Netta Muskett Award for many years.

Barbara Cartland

Barbara Cartland is the epitome of the romantic novelist for most people. Quite apart from her 700+ books, there is the energy, the over-the-top style, the pronouncements on everything from sex to politics, the love affair with the media to the day she died.

Yet when she helped to found the Romantic Novelists' Association, the Queen of Romance was not Cartland but her good friend Denise Robins. Nor had she hit her legendary prolific stride—she did not reach her hundredth book until 1963, which was noted in the *RNA News*. But, energetic and highly visible, she had two qualities way ahead of her time that were a real plus for the fledgling organisation: she was an ace networker and she knew the importance of publicity and how to attract it. It is probably fair to say that, if Denise Robins and Alex Stuart wanted more respect for the genre in which they wrote, Barbara Cartland just wanted it to get more headlines.

She was born in 1901, the product of a marriage between gentry (her mother) and trade (her father). However, only a year after she was born, her paternal grandfather shot himself when banks called in their loans on a railway he had financed. Her parents had to leave the mansion, with its 12 servants, and move to a rented cottage in Pershore. Finances were squeezed further when her father was killed in action in May 1918. The family could not afford mourning clothes and Barbara had to have a coat and skirt dyed black. Their mother, Polly, moved the family to London and set up a dress shop in Kensington. Extreme money troubles and families trying to keep up appearances haunt Barbara Cartland's heroines, especially in the later stories. So do absent or feckless fathers.

With the practical resilience that characterised her, Cartland managed to join in the Season (her heroines often manage their wardrobes on a shoestring, too) and earned some cash from contributing paragraphs to the *Daily Express*'s society columns, from which she progressed to writing features. She afterwards said that it was the proprietor, Lord Beaverbrook, who taught her to write the short, punchy narrative that later became her trademark. In her book of memoirs, *We Danced All Night 1919-1929* (1970), Cartland is typically upbeat: all the wartime restrictions were ended. She was out! She was grown-up! She was expected overnight to be amusing, gay, and attractive to men. And, incredible though it seemed to her, she was!

She was a great fan of Elinor Glyn and claims to have started her first novel at 20, inspired by Glyn, who later became a friend. She was to condense several of Glyn's books for her own Library of Love in the seventies. However, Cartland's own first published novel, *Jigsaw* (1923), was much closer to her own experience than Glyn's high octane melodrama—one reviewer said it was Mayfair with the lid off—and was a success on both sides of the Atlantic.

She continued to write novels in a variety of styles, contemporary and historical—often echoing her favourites, Glyn, Ethel M Dell, Anthony Hope, and even her contemporary Georgette Heyer, whose plots she plundered shamelessly—at the same time as leading a packed private and public life.

After World War II, Barbara Cartland increasingly turned away from contemporary stories to concentrate on historicals. Indeed, as Vice President of the RNA, she presented an annual award to the historical novel which she personally chose from among those submitted for the Romantic Novel of the Year award. Miss Cartland's Prize, as it was called, was discontinued after she resigned. Heyer had made Regencies very popular, of course, but Cartland experimented with other eras as well, including Victorian, Restoration and, probably her favourite, the Edwardian *belle époque*.

Once she had done her research, it was often pressed into service many times. She was particularly taken with Empress Elizabeth of Austria, for instance, and used her story (and the famous Winterhalter portrait) in the novel *Stars in My Heart* (1952) as well as *The Private Life of Elizabeth of Austria* (1959) and as background to several other novels.

It was only after she resigned from the RNA that Cartland's output became truly prodigious, earning her an entry in the *Guinness Book of Records* for her 723 books. As well as fiction, she wrote a number of biographies, whose titles reflect the author's approach—for example, *Metternich, the Passionate Diplomat, The Outrageous Queen* (Queen Christina of Sweden); books of advice and cookery; several books of autobiography and reminiscence, as well as biographies of her mother and her brother Ronald, who died at Dunkirk, the first MP to be killed in the War, and to whom she was always close.

She worked as hard at self-promotion as she did at her novels, embarking on international tours and always ready with a quotable remark if a journalist rang her up. She had the concept of branding to her fingertips: glittery dresses and diamonds, or chiffon and feathers; often a fur wrap; generally a Pekingese (a genuine friend to whom she was devoted but also, with his huge eyes, a useful addition to the image); lashings of make-up; and pink on every possible occasion.

The image was so consistent and forceful, especially as she got older, that cynics started to ask whether it was wholly contrived and she did not believe a word of her own trumpeted precepts. Clearly, there was an element of performance and not a lot of personal revelation.

She was, anyway, of the generation that thought it bad form to make a song and dance about your private griefs. Psychiatrist Anthony Clare, who regularly reduced his subjects to silent tears in his in-depth radio interviews, *In the Psychiatrist's Chair*, was driven back into asking her whether the class system had been eroded. (Splendidly, she said of course it had, or she wouldn't be there talking to him.)

So did she jump on a convenient bandwagon, and then decorate it to within an inch of its life? Or was she, like Denise Robins, a genuine romantic? A startled Andrew Billen, in a humane but realistic profile towards the end of her life (*Observer*, 9th July 1996), thought she was the real thing.

Barbara Cartland was the biggest personality ever in the Romantic Novelists' Association, even though she was only a member for six years. She was undoubtedly a major force in getting it off the ground and recruiting founder members. But over the years she has also presented a problem, with which the Association still grapples today: that carefully crafted image of hers has been accepted universally as the archetypal romantic novelist. Of course, it was not true in 1960, but so much the more is it wide of the mark today. Cartland was fabulous, romantic, and a model of industry, but she was not typical. Even now, ten years after her death, when hearing what some RNA member writes, people will say, 'You mean, like Barbara Cartland?'

No. We don't. There was, and will only ever be, one Barbara Cartland.
Jenny Haddon

Diane Pearson writes:
I have a few memories of my own of Barbara as I was her editor for many years—actually 'editor' was a bit of a misnomer as she paid a private editor to do any preliminary work and the actual publisher wasn't allowed to do very much. I was really more of a PA at the publishing office. At first, when I was a young editor, she terrified me and every time the phone rang (often) and a voice said, 'Miss Cartland on the phone for you,' I would brace myself

for complaints, commands and peremptory orders and frequently a ticking-off. Over the years we worked out a *modus operandi* and I became increasingly fond of her. She was kind, generous, and I was able (sometimes) to make her laugh. Once I got the measure of her we got on very well. As all editors are supposed to do, I suggested taking her out to lunch and was told, brusquely, 'I never lunch with women.' When one of my books, *Csardas*, got on the bestseller list she told me to send a copy along as she would read it. Her verdict, 'Very good, dear, but you've been very stupid. You had plots for at least eight books there and you've used them all up in one.'

She was immensely professional. I recall one occasion when she was on *Parkinson* which went out about 10pm on Saturday night. This particular programme was recorded at 10am and she arrived at White City in full regalia, sequinned pink evening dress, white fur stole, the famous aquamarines, the lot. As she swept through reception at around 9.30am, everyone sniggered. And of course, when the programme went out in the evening she was the only one dressed for the occasion and who looked right.

Eventually she was taken up by America and became hugely successful there, so much so that she was asked to go on a publicity tour complete with white Rolls Royce. This was almost my busiest time as I was constantly receiving instructions for the tour, which I had to fax over to New York. They ranged from ensuring every hotel had a bottle of cider vinegar and a jar of honey by her bed, to the hiring of a stuffed Pekingese as, because of quarantine, she couldn't take the real one with her.

I liked her and admired her professionalism. When I had a long illness she was kindness itself and sent me ginseng and masses of vitamin pills. She was unique in that, outrageous as she might be, she was never boring. I have wonderful memories of some of the comments which I couldn't possibly repeat in these days of political correctness but which still make me chuckle. She was certainly one of the greatest 'characters' of the romantic fiction world.

Henriette Gyland, Translator, RNA New Writers' Scheme:
I first started reading Barbara Cartland to annoy my father.

My younger sister was already a fan, but I was still scoffing, no doubt influenced by my parents' reading tastes. I was on my way to the orthodontist with my lunch money jingling in my pocket, despite my mother's pleas that I must eat something at school (not easy with braces), when on a revolving newspaper stand at a railway station in Northern Denmark I chanced upon the first Barbara Cartland title I ever bought, *The Black Panther* (1939). The cover was of a young woman gazing adoringly up at a raven-haired, square-jawed man, and, in a moment of epiphany, and seeing a chance to rebel at the same time, I knew I had to have it.

Or rather, I had to have him. The hero. Despite my gawky, knobbly-kneed and flat-chested exterior, I was growing up and, from that moment on, it was no longer the boy with the coolest bicycle who set my heart a-flutter. But Lord This and the Marquis of That ... real men, albeit fictitious. A safe way to be interested in the opposite sex.

I grew up in a household with bookshelves populated by authors such as Erica Jong, Fay Weldon, and Germaine Greer, as well as William Faulkner, Eugene O'Neill, Tennessee Williams and, incongruously, Raymond Chandler. This was undoubtedly a treasure trove for the discerning reader but not very accessible to an adolescent. Barbara Cartland was for me an escape into a fantasy world, enabling me to visit another time—many of her novels were set in the Regency period—to experience different customs and cultures. There was often a history lesson thrown in as well.

She also offered beauty tips and advice to young girls, featured on the inside covers of her novella magazines, as well as in her book *Barbara Cartland's Book of Beauty and Health* (1972), which I found in the library of my comprehensive school, and which my friend and I fought over. She taught me how to henna my hair and take brewer's yeast against spots. I learned about healthy eating, how to respond when asked out on a date, even how to apply make-up! It was on her chiffon-clad arm that I made my debut into the adult world.

I can't imagine anyone writing like her now. Her tendency to pair very young women with men in their thirties wouldn't wash with today's audience. Perhaps more significantly, she was of an entirely different era, writing her novels in a century when the role of women went through momentous changes, from the flappers with their short hair and skirts and the female munitions workers of WWII, through the sexual revolution, the birth of Women's Lib, and beyond.

Despite the criticism levelled at her for giving young women unrealistic expectations about romantic relationships, she gave me enormous reading pleasure. In the two years following my discovery, I devoured every single title I could beg, borrow or steal, in total more than 40 novels and novellas, which was only a fraction of her output.

My father, at this point, was still despairing over the 'romantic nonsense' I was reading, but he grudgingly introduced me to *Gone With The Wind*. Then followed the Brontës, Jane Austen, Charles Dickens, and I slowly graduated to a wider reading world.

Aside from the enjoyment I drew from her books, by going through my 'Cartland phase' and growing out of it at my own pace, I learned an important lesson: to always make up my own mind about things and not be influenced by the opinions of others.

Melanie Hilton, who writes as Louise Allen, remembers:
Many years ago I worked in the reference section of the nearest large library to Barbara Cartland's home and phone calls from Camfield Place were not uncommon. Usually, the secretary would put Miss Cartland on to speak to the male Reference Librarian— she very clearly preferred talking to men—and a stack of books or photocopies would be assembled for the chauffeur to collect, resplendent in peaked cap, epaulettes and knee-high polished boots.

Occasionally, if Dick was out, she had to make do with me, although I would threaten hours of penal shelving for any library assistant who dare put her through before I'd managed to swallow at least two cups of coffee. She did not always grasp the likely range of material on the shelves of a medium-sized public library and would frequently confuse our resources with those of the London Library.

I came to expect to have to scour the shelves in response to somewhat esoteric requests:

> *Me:* 'Good morning, Miss Cartland. I'm afraid Mr Busby
> is not here this morning. May I help you?'
> *Miss C: (Faintest of sighs)* 'Well dear, I am sending my
> young people to Nice for the gaming. One is so bored
> with Monte Carlo, don't you think?'
> *Me: (bracing myself)* 'Yes indeed, Miss Cartland.'
> *Miss C:* 'Now, how much have you got on gambling in
> Nice at the end of the eighteenth century?'
> *Me: (exaggerating wildly. True answer 'Nothing')* 'Not a great deal,
> Miss Cartland. Might I suggest the London Library?'

She was always punctilious in sending the chauffeur in with thank-you presents, although the sight of this magnificent specimen of manhood, jodhpurs immaculate and gauntlets gleaming, a brace of pheasants gripped in one hand, knee-deep in tiny tots arriving for storytime, did cause a certain stir among both staff and readers.

Early days and the Great Walk Out

The RNA started with the same aims it has today, those of providing mutual help for members and raising the prestige of the genre. Many of the original members were well-known, respected novelists—Lucilla Andrews, Elizabeth Beresford, Hermina Black, Iris Bromige, Catherine Cookson, Elizabeth Goudge and many others. The early days, however, were not without their traumas and difficulties.

The original membership was divided into three types of authors: so-called founder members, who had had more than 12 books published (and who paid a premium for membership on the grounds that they could afford it), full (or ordinary) who had had at least one full-length novel published, and probationary who were not yet published as novelists. Associate membership was designed primarily for publishers, editors and agents, although other book professionals were admitted under this category, such as Helen McGregor, an experienced publishers' reader, as well as librarians and booksellers.

The committee was drawn from founder members, plus a representative of the associate members. Chaired energetically by Alex Stuart, by the end of the first year it had organised an inaugural party, four meetings, the New Writers' Scheme for Probationers, the Romantic Novel of the Year, a glittering first awards dinner and a regular *RNA News*, all without any back office support.

One of the first causes of tension was the RNA's strong focus on London. There was a concession on membership fees for country members, rather like a gentlemen's club, but that did not really meet the problem. On the one hand, publishing was almost exclusively based in the capital, so the committee had to hold meetings in London in order to attract good speakers from the industry. On the other hand, that meant that a lot of members could not get to meetings and back home in the same day. The *RNA News* tried to mitigate the effects of this by carrying detailed reports of all meetings. But pretty soon regional groups were getting together—in June 1963 Northern members organised their own meeting, which was followed by a writers' weekend the next year; and in 1965 an East Anglian group had their first meeting.

By April 1966, the Membership Secretary was reporting that the RNA had 78 Full members, 35 Founder, 50 Associates, which meant an increase of just over 40 per cent from original membership numbers. Good in one way but stresses emerged as members started to grasp how widely diversified romantic novels and novelists were. By no means all of them shared the glamour of Robins and Cartland.

From RNA News Sept-Oct 1965

NEWS FROM MEMBERS
Butlins buys ...

MARGARET A. COLE stayed for a week at Ayr Camp as the guest of the Butlin Co. while she was writing her tenth Butlin background book. Her largest ever order from Butlin's was for 175,000 copies of 'Holiday Camp Mystery'.

Margaret A Cole was published by Robert Hale and seems to have found product placement before anyone else, with the possible exception of Ian Fleming. She wrote doctor-nurse romances, such as *Love for a Doctor*, published 1960. Her Butlins-based stories are described as 'for older children', which presumably equates to

Young Adult today. We have found *Romance at Butlins* (1958), *Holiday Camp Mystery* (1960); *Thrilling Holiday* (1962) and *Another Holiday Camp Mystery* (1967). The blurb for *Thrilling Holiday* says, 'Judy, Sid, Valerie and the twins Tessie and Ken get involved in dangerous adventures at Skegness holiday camp ...'

Above all, raising the profile of romantic fiction and gathering a bit of respect for the genre was not proving anything like as easy as the founders expected. The awards dinner might be glittering but tickets were beyond the means of many members, especially the out-of-towners who had to stay overnight in a hotel. And the awards did not achieve the desired effect in the media. Individual members might report friendly coverage from their local press but the national media were largely unimpressed.

Anne Worboys

The late Anne Worboys was a just-about-founder member in 1960. She went on to write 24 novels, served on the committee and won the Romantic Novel of the Year in 1975 with her romantic suspense *Every Man a King*. But in the early sixties she was rank and file. She recalled for us what it was like and the importance of our hats in the early days.

Anne Worboys wrote:
It really is a long time since the inauguration of the RNA so there is a great deal that I have forgotten. I was told by my agent about this organisation that had already had one meeting. I went to the second. I was informed that only published authors were to be allowed in. I had had short stories published and one three-parter in a glossy called *Woman and Beauty*, long defunct. Anyway, they were anxious for recruits and I was allowed in.

We met in a hotel on the corner of Bond Street and Conduit Street. I was bowled over by Barbara Cartland who was immense and magnificent in a bright pink dress and out-of-this-world hat decorated with so many plumes that she looked like a Lifeguard, dyed pink. And her eyelashes were the longest in the world. Denise Robins looked elegant. Alex Stuart wore cropped hair and no hat. But hats were the order of the day. We were requested to wear them. Barbara Cartland saw hats as our trademark. We were mainly obedient. I remember Anne Britton, short story writer and Fiction Editor of *Mother and Home*, saying she would not be seen dead in a hat. I wanted to wear one but feared the competition.

Filling in time on the morning of the third meeting, I wandered into the millinery department of Selfridges. I was gazing entranced at a little hat in a wonderful shade of red that was exhibited in a glass case on the wall when a very, very handsome man approached and suggested I try it on. I said I couldn't really afford it. He said, 'Come on.' He opened the case and put the hat on my head. I looked in the mirror and was defeated. The gorgeous man said: 'I am Aage Thaarup, and that colour is the red of the Danish flag.' (You may know that Aage Thaarup, in the early fifties, was the Queen's milliner.)

'Charge it,' I whispered to a hovering sales girl.

He told me that a hat parade was due to start, adding, 'You shall sit in the middle of the front row,' and led me past curious patrons to the centre chair. Afterwards I went off down Bond Street in a daze. I would like to say that Barbara Cartland admired the hat but I don't think she noticed.

Sir Alan Herbert was the guest of honour at the dinner that year. I remember standing in the foyer while the press were busy photographing him with Miss Cartland and possibly Denise. (You didn't see other people when Miss Cartland was there.) Sir Alan got bored and said: 'I want to be photographed with one of the young ones.' Quick as a flash he pulled me out of the crowd. As I took my place beside him Miss Cartland trod on my toes. I am quite sure it was an accident.

The accent at the time was on respectability. Romance was a jokey word. Everyone apologised for writing it. Fleet Street sneered. We said they were jealous because we made more money than they did. (How would we know?) Some husbands felt threatened. One wife, I remember, had to give up writing altogether. Another shoved her papers into a drawer as her husband came through the front gate. Yet another's husband, who had an important editorial position, insisted his wife sit down with him in the evenings, which was the only time she could write, and listen at length to what he had done during the day.

We overcame all this but it took a long time. And we did it ourselves, without changing our name or letting in writers of other genres. I think we have good reason to be proud of our achievement.

Trying a more low key approach to public relations, the committee organised an At Home, on which Margaret Maddocks (winner of more Romantic Novels of the Year than anyone else, even now) reported.

From the RNA News Sept–Oct 1965
At Home to Readers and Librarians

At Home at the Overseas League on the afternoon of Sept 22nd, it was an exhilarating experience to meet so many readers and librarians who knew our names and recognised us so kindly. Am I alone in feeling that one writes in an empty world and then drops the result in a deep well? It was indeed pleasant to know that this is not so. Incredibly, it seemed one had readers. There they were, from Hampstead and Folkestone and Guildford; librarians too and owners of private libraries, some of the people on whom our future depends.

Around the room an impressive display of RNA masterpieces had been arranged with the help of our publishers, and against this decorative background our Chairman, Sylvia Thorpe, made a speech of welcome. Denise Robins, our President, appealed to us to patronise the smaller libraries which are our lifeblood, so that they should not be squeezed out of existence by the public libraries.

There were about a hundred people for tea and amongst these over thirty authors circulated, under slight pressure from Marcia Webb who, with smiling charm, broke up groups of members who persisted in talking to each other. Authors who had carelessly left their name badges at home, ran the additional hazard of being mistaken for

```
readers, but Marcia unobtrusively sorted out any
confusion. One faithful reader, obviously far-gone in
starry-eyed excitement, or maybe overcome by the hats,
was heard to say that it was just like Fairyland. Gay
and enjoyable as it was, I would not myself have gone
to those lengths to describe it; but it was certainly a
most stimulating afternoon, and we must be grateful to
those who were responsible for this brilliant idea and
to the co-operation of the librarians and the committee
for its smooth organisation.
     The press gave us lengthy coverage, poking their
usual mild fun at romantic novels. Their gentle mockery
we have come to understand and to forgive, for it is
quite obvious that they can never have read our books.
```

The Great Walk Out

Mike Legat writes:

When the Association was first formed, it came in for a lot of mickey-taking. The press and the BBC sent it up something rotten, as they say, doing their utmost to make the members look ridiculous. In those early days, it was de rigueur for ladies to wear hats when appearing in public, and the romantic novelists' hats were an unfailing source of hilarity to the mickey-takers. Denise Robins, who with Vivian Stuart had founded the RNA, was so upset by the constant refusal to take the Association seriously that she called an Extraordinary General Meeting at which she proposed the motion that the name should be changed to English Novelists Association. I thought that was a stupid idea, and I don't think Denise ever forgave me for getting up and saying so. I suggested that the best way of earning respect was by making the Association of real use to the members, by doing everything possible to raise standards, by making the public aware not only that the craft demanded considerable skill, but that many romantic writers were enviably successful (and therefore deserving of a material society's respect), and by ignoring the funnies.

Fortunately, Denise's motion was defeated. I think the Association had indeed gained a great deal of respect, and it is certainly much appreciated by its members. Quite recently the

Association again considered changing its title, mainly because over the years the scope of the members' writing has broadened, but wisely, in my opinion, opted in the end to leave it alone.

It always seems to me a great pity that anyone who lives by the use of words should want to poke fun at other writers, or indeed should decide, usually without having read it, that a particular genre of writing is worthy only of contempt. I am aggrieved every time someone talks or writes slightingly of Mills & Boon. They would do better to admire the ability of the authors, because, believe me, not everyone can write a successful Mills & Boon romance—it takes dedication, a considerable understanding of what is required, and a writing ability far beyond the average. Above all it demands sincerity—you can't write a successful Mills & Boon with your tongue in your cheek.

In the same way, I think that Dame Barbara is to be defended. She may have chosen to make herself look like a clown, by refusing to grow old gracefully, but as a writer she is a true professional, knowing her market exactly, producing precisely what is needed for it, and doing it with a skill which her detractors should envy.

It was a meeting to discuss the renewed proposal to change the name which caused The Great Walk Out. Denise Robins explained her resignation in a 1966 *RNA News*:

'With the full consent of my co-founder Alex Stuart, and the Vice Presidents, Barbara Cartland and Dorothy Black, we decided as the committee to change our title to "Novelists" or "British Novelists' Association". It was because we wanted all young writers, particularly those who did not write pure romance, to have a chance to join us and win the various awards. We hoped the rules and regulations could be made more flexible on account of the fact that so many of these new authors object to the label "romantic".

'I, personally, have long felt that something should be done to widen the literary field under a new name for our Association.

'Unfortunately I met with nothing but opposition, difficulties and chilling disapproval from the present committee which could only end in my offering my resignation.'

Barbara Cartland—who was anyway about to embark on a three-year international PR campaign and increase her output to 20 books a year and more—went too. So did Alex Stuart and Dorothy Black. But the rank and file stayed firm.

The general feeling was that they wrote romantic fiction and weren't going to let mockery stop them saying so. They regretted that their two biggest names had quit but, already, the RNA had an identity which was wider than that of a few authors, however starry. Among members who remained were Evadne Price, a TV playwright as well as novelist, and who, as a journalist, was the first woman into Belsen; veteran Berta Ruck, a big name in the twenties, who survived a spat with Virginia Woolf, and Mills & Boon star-in-the-making Anne Weale.

Causes of the rift

Nevertheless, it was a shock to everyone that feeling had got so bad that the three people who first put the organisation together had walked away from it. How had matters come to such a pass? There were probably three reasons.

The first is illustrated by a spat in mid-1961, when there was not enough tea for everyone at the AGM and members wrote to complain. At the subsequent committee meeting a couple of members went on the war path after the unfortunate party responsible. It was a simple failure of communication, as the committee as a whole recognised. But resentments clearly simmered.

It was not surprising. They had set themselves an enormous task and fulfilled it. Within a year, they had set up a series of awards, run the celebratory dinner, set up the New Writers' Scheme, run several meetings and produced a bi-monthly *RNA News*, all without an office or any administrative help, except for the professional typist who prepared the *RNA News*. The committee was made up of people used to working alone on their own creations—teamwork was a new skill for most of them. Besides, all that work must have been eating into their writing time in a way they never envisaged when they signed up. And then members wrote to complain! No wonder they were scratchy.

There was a spate of resignations in the New Year, including the two most indignant committee members, Mary Howard and Rona Randall. (They both rejoined later.) By summer 1963 the President was worried that some of her author friends were being told by their publishers not to join the new Association because it would make their sales drop. (This seems like paranoia on the part of either the publishers or the President.) And by December that year the minutes record, 'It was suggested that the name of the Association should be changed next year as the word romantic seemed to be detrimental to the Association.'

Proposed: The British Women's Fiction Writers' Association— sub-committee set up of Anne Britton, Stella March, Sylvia Thorpe, Stella Johns, and the President and Vice Presidents to be consulted.

So there was the second and probably more important reason: the word 'romantic' and its effect on the media. Denise Robins and Alex Stuart had set up the RNA because they wanted more recognition for their genre, by which they largely meant thoughtful reviews. Writing to *The Woman Journalist* in spring 1960, Alex Stuart had said that delving into the past she had found enthusiastic reviews for romantic authors like Maud Diver in *The Times Literary Supplement, The Sunday Times* and *The Scotsman* as recently as 1938. Today reviews were patronising or none at all; she wanted that to change. Barbara Cartland, a woman who knew the value of column inches, said she wanted the awards to be like the Oscars. Not one of them seems to have considered that if the RNA succeeded in attracting press attention, it might not prove the kind they wanted. Basically, they were a gift to a male-dominated press who laughed at them unmercifully.

Barbara Cartland, an adept publicity seeker all her life, with an embarrassment threshold as high as a house, might well have written it off as the price you pay. But Denise Robins was the severely elegant Queen of Romance. Normally the press treated her with the respect due to a mega seller. Mockery must have been a great shock to her and truly painful. The associate member on the committee (Roger Duff of Collins) said that he took a serious view of the adverse publicity received by the RNA from certain sections of the Press, 'in which it was depicted as strife-torn, constantly quarrelling and generally ridiculous.' The committee issued a press notice and the gossip died down. But in December 1963 Associate Vice President Alan Boon was writing to the committee expressing support for a change from dinner to luncheon and saying 'the type of publicity we received did more harm than good, and it was important to interest librarians in romantic novels.' He suggested members should be urged to bring their own librarians as guests.

So there you have the problem in a nutshell: Robins and Stuart wanted reviews; Cartland wanted the Oscars; Boon wanted librarians.

The President and Vice Presidents were now convinced that 'romantic' had to go, although the sub-committee, after consulting publishers, only proposed a name change to the Romantic and Historical Novelists' Association. And this was when the third cause began to emerge—the committee started to assert itself. Robins and Cartland brought the name issue back to the table in October 1966, proposing to change the name 'in order to attract young writers and top novelists into the Association in its new form.'

'The Chairman [Sylvia Thorpe], on behalf of the committee, pointed out that this extension of aims, objects and scope of membership, was not in accordance with the present constitution, and it would therefore be easier for a new association with these new aims to be formed.' She suggested the President call an EGM if she wanted to pursue the matter and, after a sharp exchange about the President's public statements, the President resigned.

Clearly this was a classic boardroom battle. In June that year, Thorpe (and the Hon Sec), not yet half way through their term of office, had said they would complete the year but not do another one. After the President's resignation, Thorpe (and the Hon Sec) agreed to continue for their full term.

One feels for both sides. From our perspective it seems so

unnecessary. It lost the RNA valuable members like Paula Allardyce and gave rise to a good deal of cattiness, both inside and out. Yet in another way, as a coda to the hierarchical fifties, it was perhaps inevitable. Every member's voice counted and numbers of votes, in the end, trumped high-profile non-execs. So it was a victory for democracy in a way.

Nevertheless, it is good to know that, eventually, Denise Robins came back as an honoured guest to the tenth awards dinner and Alex Stuart, though she never again held office, remained a lifelong friend and supporter.

Our dear Mary Burchell

It was pure chance that Mary Burchell was in the hot seat when the President and Vice Presidents resigned. In spring 1964 she had joined Cartland, Stuart and the prolific Dorothy Black as one of the RNA's Vice Presidents. Now she was the only one left. No one could doubt her standing but her name was largely unknown in the wider world.

As it turned out, the RNA was amazingly lucky that the baton passed to Burchell. She was a hard-working professional author. She had decided views and firm principles but she was also a natural diplomat, charming, generous, just sufficiently loopy to be interesting, and above all sensible. She set about staunching the wounds at once, and was gracious to her predecessor. She regretted that Robins had resigned, saying, 'I can only promise that I will do my best to emulate her example of devoted work during her six years of office.' In the years to come, she never failed to give Alex Stuart and Denise Robins proper credit for their work in setting up the RNA.

Mary Burchell—the life

When Mary Burchell took on the Presidency, she told the *RNA News* that she had published more than 100 books and produced four annually. She said frankly, 'I passionately enjoy writing romantic novels but I am not a compulsive writer. I adore my work, but I do it for a living and have made a good one out of it for more than 30 years.

I understand and hope I've given a lot of pleasure to many nice people and find no necessity to apologise to anybody about it. The fact is, I have other interests of equal intensity: refugee work, opera and raising funds for leukaemia research and I am quite absorbed in these too.'

Her first full-length work was a serial, *Wife to Christopher,* published in 1935 and put out as a book by Mills & Boon the year after. That was when she adopted her pen name (her own name was Ida Cook). She remained loyal to the publisher throughout her life. In 1966 she told the *RNA News* that her sales were 'estimated at between two and three million in the English language and half a million in German'. At that time she was published in eight other languages, had large Canadian paperback sales and was just about to enter the US paperback market. She had also, though she may not have realised it at the time, just published the first two novels in what would turn out to be her fans' favourite, the Warrender series, set in the world of classical music.

Opera

When she said she was as interested in opera and refugees as she was in her writing, she did not overstate the case. Musically untrained, she and her sister Louise fell in love with opera through the medium of records on a wind-up gramophone, in particular the coloratura soprano Amelita Galli-Curci. Buying the cheapest seats in the gods, they went to Covent Garden and when Galli-Curci first performed in London, they heard her recital in the Albert Hall. They would regularly wait at the stage door for a word or an autograph and Galli-Curci must have chatted to them for some time, because she told them that she only sang opera in New York. The sisters determined to get there to hear her. At that stage they were both typists on modest salaries but in 1926 they each saved £100 (and made their own clothes, including opera cloaks) and wrote to tell Galli-Curci that they were coming.

Perhaps she had some fellow feeling, being a self-taught singer herself. Or perhaps she saw some publicity advantage in the fact that two typists should come all the way from England to hear her. (Mary Burchell would afterwards say that the New York press had a field day.) Whatever the reason, Galli-Curci made them very welcome and became the first of their many friends in the opera world. Mary said that it was an article on Galli-Curci which got her out of a Civil Service typing pool and won her a job on the London magazine, *Mabs Fashion.*

Essentially, she and Louise were groupies, waiting at the stage door to take photographs of their favourite performers and collect their autographs. The musical world was surprisingly responsive. For instance, during the ten months' drought between one Covent Garden Grand Season and the next, the gallery-goers held gramophone parties, to get them through. Incorrigibly friendly—she was always the chatty one, she said—Mary Burchell invited Ezio Pinza, the bass baritone they had met in New York to come to one of the parties. He asked if he could also bring Elizabeth Rothberg, then the most famous soprano in the world, making her first appearance at Covent Garden for ten years. He did and it sounds as if a rollicking party took place at the Cooks' suburban family home. The sisters also became friends with their favourite soprano, American Rosa Ponselle. Burchell began writing short stories to augment their income. First they could afford to go to Edinburgh, then into Europe to hear opera—Verona (where Pinza had great fun pretending to be their chauffeur), Munich, Salzburg, Amsterdam.

Refugees
They met Clemens Krauss, then chief conductor of the Vienna Staatsoper, at Covent Garden in 1934, when he was conducting *Arabella*, starring his wife, the soprano Viorica Ursuleac. It was Ursuleac who set them on the road to helping refugees escape from the Nazis. Would they, the soprano asked when she met them on one of their opera trips, look after her friend Mitia Mayer-Lismann, official lecturer at Salzburg, who was coming to lecture in London. Puzzled but gratified, they said of course they would. 'In my mind's eye,' Burchell wrote later, 'I still see the scene on the platform of Amsterdam Station as Ursuleac turned to her companion and said, in a tone of sombre satisfaction, "Now you will be all right."'

The visit was an education. The Cook sisters showed their guest the London cathedrals and were taken aback when she said she was not Protestant or Catholic but Jewish, and told them something of what the Nuremberg Laws meant. 'We didn't know—imagine! In those days we didn't know that to be Jewish and to come from Frankfurt-am-Main in Germany already had the seeds of tragedy in it,' Burchell wrote. When they did know, they had to do something to help. Neither of them saw it as anything extraordinary: 'We just happened to be lucky enough to see the problem in terms we could understand. In terms of personal friends, in fact.'

Louise learned German, to help with the correspondence. Burchell herself, having sold her first book, was working full time as a writer. She would often say that she started writing to feed her opera habit but the truth was that she spent most of those early earnings on refugees. 'Our guardian angels must have been looking over our shoulders at that time,' she wrote. 'Before we had any chance to alter our way of living or get into the habit of spending what seemed to us then great sums, the full horror of what was happening in Europe finally, and for all time, came home to us.' The British authorities required financial guarantees before they would accept adult refugees. When the Cook family ran out of their own resources, Burchell embarked on fund raising, collecting small amounts and aggregating them with what she called the same naïve technique which had helped them save for their great expedition to New York. Every few months—or as often as was needed—they went to Germany to meet the people they were trying to help.

Typically they would fly out of Croydon Airport on the last plane on Friday night to Cologne, and take the overnight train to Munich. Going or coming they would usually stop in Frankfurt, where most of their cases came from. Then they would leave by train, through Holland, taking the overnight boat to Harwich. Louise would walk into her office on Monday morning just in time. When officials at Cologne asked awkward and unfriendly questions, Clemens Krauss, by then at the Munich Opera, arranged for the sisters to have seats on the dates they needed to be in Germany and they became known as dotty opera fans. Even so, it was safer to leave the country by a different route, as they were often smuggling the possessions of refugees, to be held in England awaiting their arrival. The sisters would wear the furs and jewellery and leave looking seriously over-dressed. They used to take labels from London furriers, which they would sew into the furs—and always went first to the refugee's apartment, so that they arrived at their hotel wearing the furs.

On one occasion, Burchell was asked to bring out a very expensive brooch, which represented someone's entire capital. She was appalled to discover it was a great oblong of blazing diamonds. So she pinned it onto her six-and-elevenpenny Marks & Spencer jumper (jacquard satin with glass buttons down the front) and trusted that everyone would assume the brooch came from Woolworths. It worked.

She dealt with visas and tussled with bureaucrats, saying wryly, 'You never know what you can do until you refuse to take no for an answer.' Her autobiography (re-published by Mira Books in 2008 as *Safe Passage* under her real name of Ida Cook) does not disguise the heartbreak. One day she came back to the family home and simply burst into tears in the kitchen out of accumulated tension. Her mother went on making pastry—which Burchell said was exactly what she should have done—and she calmed down.

There were people who disappeared, even while she was striving to get them sponsors. Professor Cossmann, 'who refused to have any strenuous efforts made on his behalf,' went on to die in Theresienstadt, 'an example of moral courage and great fortitude'. In a Frankfurt flat one night, remembering the golden 1920s, she thinks, 'Now I am sitting here in the semi-darkness, hoping that no one will guess that someone lives here, wondering if we shall be able to save this wonderful old man from the concentration camp.' He was Mitia Mayer-Lisman's father. He was one she *did* get to England.

In March 1956, she was the subject of an early *This is Your Life* with Eamonn Andrews. In it she was reunited with refugees she had not seen for years, including a worker from their displaced persons' camp in Bavaria. Rosa Ponselle spoke on the telephone from New York. Most important of all to Burchell, Viorica Ursuleac came from her place in the Tyrol where she lived in retirement, after the death of Clemens Krauss in May 1954. Afterwards several people asked Burchell who was the tall, very good looking foreigner who didn't speak—and identified Krauss from her description. She always had an interest in spiritualism and was delighted to think that he might have been there in spirit.

In 1965 she and Louise were named Righteous Gentiles by the Israeli Yad Vashem Martyrs and Heroes Remembrance Authority, who said they had helped 29 people to escape. They had also been 'feted in the United States where they were awarded decorations as Women of the Year', the *RNA News* reported. And in 2010 she was made a British Hero of the Holocaust.

President and reconciler
Mary Burchell never made a song and dance about her refugee work, but it had clearly given her a sense of perspective which, allied to her great sense of fun, was what the RNA desperately needed. At the seventh Awards Dinner in May 1967, the *RNA News* reported 'The President recalled how the late Nancy Spain had once said—Cherish romance! Any fool can be a realist. "Of course any fool can also be a romantic," Miss Burchell added dryly. Nevertheless it was fortunate for this country, she went on, that we were not led by a realist in 1940. "If a realist had told us that we were going to have a miserable time, and asked if we could survive it, we might not have done so. Luckily, Churchill was one of the great romantics."'

It was only just over 20 years since the end of the War, which all her audience would remember vividly. One of the guests of honour that year was Russell Braddon, a survivor of Changi. When Mary Burchell spoke of survival, she was not being metaphorical.

Right from the start, Mary Burchell told RNA members that she thought it pointless to 'battle madly for an unrealistic degree of prestige in the writing world'. Again and again, in her 20-year

Presidency, she urged moderation: romantic novelists needed 'to have a sense of humour, a sense of proportion and, above all, a true understanding of the importance and unimportance of their work. We should never be apologetic, but nor should we be aggressive.'

Aggressive, she clearly wasn't, but Mary Burchell was not self-effacing either. One of the other guests at that 1967 dinner was Ginette Spanier, the (English) directrice of the House of Balmain. They obviously got on like mad and we find Burchell offering to organise an RNA trip to Paris to see the spring collection in 1971, saying 'no doubt Miss Spanier would provide a splendid welcome'. Miss Spanier came up trumps and a group went to Balmain, saw the collection, were hugely impressed by the crystal chandeliers and gossamer drapes—and also by Madame Spanier's dishy husband who helped entertain them in the Spaniers' Paris apartment afterwards. And when they got back to the hotel, clearly a party girl at heart, 'Mary Burchell entertained us with fascinating sidelights on her experiences lasting until midnight.'

The RNA's finances were struggling by the mid-seventies and, privately, Mary Burchell gave the organisation £200 a year (probably worth seven or eight times that in today's money) to keep going. In 1975, she hosted the RNA summer party at her own expense in the Churchill Room at Dolphin Square, the prestige apartment complex opposite the Thames in Pimlico, where she kept a *pied-à-terre*, originally used by those poor anxious refugees. Thereafter, the President's party became a feature of the summer, spilling out into Dolphin Square's three and a half acres of tranquil gardens when the evenings were sunny. The food could have come straight out of a Mary Stewart novel—'the wine when 'twas rosé, smoked salmon, caviare and prawn canapés'—but even more memorable was the welcome from Mary Burchell and her family, particularly her sister Louise with whom she shared her home and her travels. Dorothy Mackie Low, another RNA Chairman, wrote after Mary's death, 'None of us who enjoyed her hospitality at a Mary Burchell party will ever forget her beaming smile after being thanked, as she flung her arms wide and said, "Darling, I enjoy it too. I love talking and I love you all!'"

In the seventies, Mary Burchell slowed down her rate of four novels a year for Mills & Boon so that she could work with her friend Tito Gobbi, on his autobiography, *My Life*. Later in 1982 an ambitious, handsome baritone on the make slipped out of her imagination into *Masquerade with Music*, but in her friend she saw only the best, both as an artist and as a man.

She wrote, as she remained RNA President, up to the last. When she died, the affection in the tributes to her was unmistakable. She had steered the organisation through choppy waters, but people spoke also of her kindness, her wit, her good sense— and the legendary parties. When she first became President an interviewer for the *RNA News* asked: did the new President have any unfulfilled writing ambitions? 'No, none at all,' she said. 'I am a born romantic and I am sure I will never change.' She didn't.

Mary Burchell—the work

Mary Burchell had already written around 100 books for Mills & Boon before she wrote the first Oscar Warrender novel. At once her readers recognised that this was something special and she went on to write a whole series around him, set in the world of classical music. Whether or not he was deliberately based on the conductor Clemens Krauss, who was movie-star handsome and dead fifteen years before the books were started, Burchell must certainly have drawn on her many conversations with him about his work and the rehearsals she attended.

RNA member, Marjorie Goodridge, writes:
The Oscar Warrender Novels of Mary Burchell.
Among her prolific output of romantic novels for Mills & Boon was a series of twelve books, the subject matter of which was dear to her heart—that of music and more especially opera.

Published in 1965, *A Song Begins* introduces readers to Oscar Warrender, a charismatic, brilliant, handsome, arrogant orchestral and operatic conductor. At no time in this—or any other of the books—is his age mentioned, and it is probably fair to assume that he is between 35 and 40. There is no indication of the passage of real time in any of the books, and as the last one, *On Wings of Song*, was published in 1985, it is not to be automatically presumed that Warrender was by then in his mid to late fifties—although he could be. In this first book he guides unknown singer Anthea Benton towards a career as a leading operatic soprano, as he falls in love with, and marries her.

Thereafter he and Anthea appear in all the other books, as the *eminences grises*, behind the lives and loves of the subsequent heroes and heroines. As a couple they make perfect foils for one another. He, ruthless in his constant drive for perfection, and unsympathetic towards human weakness, physical or emotional. She, although also always aware of the need for the highest endeavour in all things musical and professional, can temper this with the understanding of human emotional need. But Warrender does not always put work first. In *A Song Begins*, on the day before her debut, he drives Anthea 200 miles to visit her seriously ill mother, returning alone to Covent Garden the same night. In each of the books Mary Burchell allows his veil of professional implacability to be lifted—but usually just once. It is what makes Anthea love him and endears him to the readers.

The other 11 books all have to have different heroes and heroines, although by necessity the themes remain the same. In eight the heroines are would-be singers, mostly sopranos, in five they are secretaries and in two they are both (*Damaged Angel*, also published as *The Broken Wing*, and *Masquerade with Music*). The heroes vary more widely. Two are tenors, two composers, three operatic or musical directors, one pianist, one critic, one teacher, one journalist.

There is a rich cast of recurring characters: Dermot Deane, the artists' manager; Max Arrowsmith, the impresario, and various high-powered divas, usually angry with Warrender for one reason or another, and whom he puts in their place with a few well-chosen words. Between *Unbidden Melody* (1973) and *Remembered Serenade* (1975) Oscar received a knighthood.

The plots are classic romantic girl meets boy; girl loses boy; girl finds boy again, with the added twist of the Warrenders being on hand to help mend broken fences and hearts. The books are alive with Mary Burchell's love and knowledge of music, and of opera in particular. She conveys the problems and difficulties faced by singers, in their techniques and in the roles they are to play, usually through the monumentally severe requirements set for them by Warrender, who, as supreme Maestro, spares no one, least of all himself.

The sexual aspects of the romances go no further than kissing and in this they were of their time, but that by no means undermines the strength of emotion and passionate feelings. Opera was not a natural background for a Mills & Boon, then or now, but the character of Oscar Warrender caught the popular imagination and kept the readers coming back for 20 years.

So let the last word be Sir Oscar's—it usually is. Quoted from *A Song Begins*: 'I may not be a generous or an easy giver. But what I give I never take back. Not my word, not my friendship, not my love.'

Quick Guide to the Oscar Warrender Novels:

A Song Begins, 1965	Oscar falls in love with and marries young singer Anthea.
Damaged Angel, 1966	Lame singer falls for festival director.
When Love is Blind, 1967	Blind pianist (recovers) falls unwittingly for girl who blinded him.
The Curtain Rises, 1969	Secretary eventually falls in love with music director she believes responsible for her fiancé's death.
Music of the Heart, 1972	Ambitious singer falls for disillusioned composer.
Unbidden Melody, 1973	Secretary falls for widowed tenor.
Song Cycle, 1975	Family troubles force singer to turn down chance of a lifetime, angering musical director, then Warrender steps in.
Remembered Serenade, 1975	Singer gets financial help from admirer, which annoys his nephew, a music critic.
Elusive Harmony, 1976	Daughter of aging opera star is torn between her father and love for rising new tenor.
Nightingales, 1980	Teacher of young singer is dismayed when she chooses musical stage instead of opera, but love prevails.
Masquerade with Music, 1982	Unknown to Oscar his niece becomes his secretary. Then journalist discovers deceit.
On Wings of Song, 1982	Sister of would-be opera singer is 'discovered' by Oscar. Then financially supported by unknown admirer.

The new regime

The new regime had a different profile from the founding cadre and its members did not know each other very well. There was a slight feeling of travelling into the unknown. Anne Worboys remembered Mary Burchell telling her that she only accepted the Presidency as a temporary measure until they could find someone else, but then found she so enjoyed it she agreed to stay on. Sylvia Thorpe, who had intended to resign after a year, also agreed to continue and there was a new Editor of the *RNA News* in Anne Weale (see pages 226-232) and a new and very distinguished Vice President.

Elizabeth Goudge, Vice President

If Mary Burchell was gregarious, down-to-earth and nearly unknown, the new Vice President, Elizabeth Goudge, was painfully shy, deeply spiritual and rather famous in a ladylike, literary way. She was not well enough to come to meetings, but in her quiet fashion she was as much a reconciler as Mary Burchell and contributed thoughtful pieces to the *RNA News*. She had won the Carnegie medal in 1948 for her children's novel *The Little White Horse* and achieved bestseller status with *Green Dolphin Country* (1944) which was made into a film. Both still have passionate fans—JK Rowling says *The Little White Horse* was her favourite book as a child.

Born in 1900, an only child of a career clergyman and a semipermanent invalid, Elizabeth Goudge was one of the generation of women whose possible husbands died in the Great War—though there is the hint of an unhappy love affair when the family lived in Ely—and there is an elegiac quality to the love stories in her books. She clearly had a happy (if old-fashioned) childhood, educated at home by a beloved governess, until she went to an equally sedate Hampshire boarding school where, she said, Jane Austen would have been happy. But life got darker as her father became more successful in the church and her mother's health gave way.

Goudge herself suffered from depression and was hospitalised for it several times. Maybe it is that which gives the curiously old-fashioned, potentially sentimental work, that snap of truth which keeps it fresh. When her characters are tormented, as many of them are, she knows how deep the darkness can go.

She had a painter's eye and was enormously sensitive to place—Guernsey, where her mother's family came from; Wells, Ely and Oxford where her father's career took the family; and Devon, where she and her mother moved in straitened circumstances after her father's death and she said that she did not so much put down roots as find roots that were already there.

By the time she accepted the Vice Presidency of the RNA, however, she was sharing an old Oxford cottage (where she set *The White Witch*) with a friend/housekeeper Jessie Monroe and her beloved dog, and writing pretty steadily at the rate of a book every two years. Still shy, her capacity to socialise was further limited by increasing arthritis. In her autobiography she claimed to be not very hospitable but that her cottage was the reverse and that, when she entertained 30 writers to tea, she imagined the old house purring contentedly like a cat. She concluded that the wise old house knew how much human beings need each other. The writers were RNA members.

RNA News New Year 1970

THE WRITING VIRUS
by VICE PRESIDENT ELIZABETH GOUDGE

I have already discovered that getting old, though it has its drawbacks, has its compensations too, and how pleasant it is to be an old writer on the going-out fringe. Not the going-in end, which is all very well in youth, when it can be as invigorating as fighting your way through the waves to bathe, but is not so enjoyable later on when you have less breath.

If you have been lucky, and I write from the point of view of a writer who has been undeservedly lucky, there is a wonderful feeling of relaxation on the going-out fringe. By the time you reach your sixties you will, of course, have developed certain occupational diseases. You will have arthritis in the back of your neck, cramp in your writing hand, stooped shoulders and bleary eyes. But what does it matter? You need no longer spend hours and hours pounding on a typewriter, for you will be able to afford a tape-recorder and a typist to help you.

Nor need you burn the midnight oil writing endless short stories and/or articles when you would much rather be writing books that don't sell and plays that fail on the first night. 'Build your reputation with your novels while you earn you living with short stories,' was the advice given me by a literary agent when I was at the plunging-in end. I took the advice, writing dozens of short stories that were all dreadfully alike, all the same steamed cod but with different sauces — parsley, mayonnaise, chopped egg and onion — disguising the sameness.

And often there was a deadline for them. Oh, the nightmare of deadlines! Even now the very thought of a fixed date for anything whatever makes me tremble with the absolute conviction that I'll never be there, do it, be it or have it on the dotted line. But when you are through the thicket you can relax, take your time over your work and not be hounded or prodded, or even reminded unless your dilatoriness passes all reason.

Of course, the work is not necessarily better for not being hurried, frequently it is worse, but it is nice not to be hurried. I notice that the majority of

writers, especially the old hands, love to grouse about
their work. It's an exhausting business they will tell
you. People think it just flows like a tap turned on.
How little do they know! To hear them, you would think
they were longing for the day when they could lay down
their pens for ever. But do they, when they could?
Practically never. For those with the writing virus in
the blood a pen, once taken in hand, becomes a sort of
unremovable wart. Even on their death-beds they are
clinging to the thing. The fact is they love their pen
as much as a violinist loves his violin or a painter
his brush, and they are only hypocrites if they pretend
anything else.

Someone (and it is a sign of old age that I can't
remember who) once said that writers can be divided into
three categories:

1. Highbrows
2. Authors
3. Bestsellers (the lowest form of life)

Bestsellers, faced with this moment of truth, can
at least comfort themselves that we are all writers.
Anyone who has a pen growing on him/her like a wart is
a writer. We are a great fraternity and why shouldn't
we say so? We never give up. We always think that one
day, if we hold on long enough, we shall write something
that is really good, something that satisfies us as
being the best we can do. Of course, we shall never be
satisfied because the only good poem, book, play, script,
or article is the one that's in our head and isn't
written yet, but we never give up hope. And it is a
comfort that there is no criterion in art. If a thing
really is the best we can do, even though we think it
isn't, it's good.

Sylvia Thorpe, Chairman

Sylvia Thorpe, the strong-minded Chairman whose term of office,
1965-67, spanned the two Presidents and the Great Walk Out, was
a popular historical novelist. Since she started in 1950, she had
written 15 novels, and was a one-book-a-year woman. The RNA
upheavals meant that there was a three-year gap, though, and she
did not publish her next, *Dark Heritage*, until 1968. It is good to report,

therefore, that she got back into her stride after she stepped down and was eventually, and quite rightly, named an Honorary Life Member.

Her novels covered a range of periods, Civil War, Georgian and Regency, and had a good deal more action than most 'historical romances' as Corgi labelled them. (She was mainly published by Hurst & Blackett in hardback, Corgi in paperback.) Her heroines were practical self-motivating women who dealt well with smugglers, pirates, spies and duellists in the course of the love story. There was often a strong swashbuckling subplot—she was clearly influenced as much by Rafael Sabatini as Georgette Heyer —in which her books were unusual for the time. Her publishers promoted her as 'one of England's most exciting romantic writers'.

Proops, passion and PR

It was clear, however, that the RNA needed to think seriously about its public image and the public perception of the genre.

The committee let the dust settle for the rest of Sylvia Thorpe's period of office and then the incoming Chairman, Stella March, invited in the big guns. These came in the brisk (and frighteningly spectacled) form of Marje Proops, *Daily Mirror* journalist, campaigner, social commentator and agony aunt.

It is difficult to grasp from this distance of time quite how influential Marje Proops was at the time. Hugh Cudlipp had hired her as a columnist on the *Daily Mirror* in 1954, only two years after he took over as Editorial Director. Later he was to say that she was the first British journalist to attain the Instant Recognition status previously enjoyed by film stars. In some ways Marje Proops became the woman's voice of the sixties, charting changing social habits and expectations in a practical, non-judgemental way, at the same time as she mined her readers' letters for new problems on which to hang serious articles about previously taboo topics: pre-marital sex, the Pill, drug addiction, the abortion law, the rate of illegitimate births, calling for better sex education in schools and a more tolerant attitude to homosexuality.

Only the year after she addressed the RNA, she was made an OBE and, in the seventies, she was called on to join two government committees. Woman of the Year in 1984, she continued to write her column for the *Mirror* until she died, at the age of 85, in 1996.

The RNA had asked her along specifically to talk to them about publicity. She gave them a sparkling talk and some good advice and seems, typically, to have charmed her audience.

The talk

From RNA News Sept-Oct 1968

MARJORIE PROOPS ON PUBLICITY
London, 23rd October 1968

There was no real need for Anne Betteridge's able introduction. There she stood, Marjorie Proops, in the flesh, looking at us over the table just as she looks out of her pages in the 'Mirror' and 'Woman', dark eyes behind dark-framed glasses as telling as ever, slenderness enhanced by a slick, high-necked navy dress with horizontal bands in which flame colour predominated.

Mrs Proops greeted us with a friendly 'Hello' and said it was cosy to be among a company of women, since males in an audience were apt to tag her with the name of feminist — she preferred to describe herself as a humanist. She said that publicity rarely entered her conscious mind, in witness whereof she contrasted two current London shows.

'Hair' at the Shaftesbury Theatre, a jolly romp, had been written up in such a way that the audience was in expectation that the cast would eventually emerge with no clothes on, and it didn't happen — this was a let-down, a disappointment and therefore poor publicity. 'Fortune and Men's Eyes' at the Comedy Theatre opened with a display of masculine nudity which neither shocked nor startled her. It was the play's presentation of prisoners' life in gaol that really did impress her and, in writing about its brutality and cruelty, she used the words, 'This makes "Hair" look like "Alice in Wonderland",' and was astonished to find herself billed and quoted in large type outside the theatre, entirely without context. It was undeniable that she had written it and it taught her to watch every word as she put it down.

On inviting questions she was asked if she considered bad publicity better than no publicity. 'No,' she

replied. 'No story is worth printing if it undermines
integrity for the sake of titillation.' She sympathised
with authors whose books were badly reviewed. 'It's as
bad as telling a mother that her first-born is an ugly
little devil,' she said, and added that her own office
was crowded with books received for mentions — mostly
about sex!

Dear Marje, as her readers address her, gave us
generous information on the answering of the two
thousand letters she receives in a month. She has six
secretaries and one personal assistant, who thinks as
she thinks. The secretaries supply factual replies
to enquiries on travel, careers and general women's
want-to-know. The PA mainly tackles personal problems,
usually matrimonial or from unmarried mums-to-be.
Really dodgy conundrums are answered by Marje herself
— occasionally she rings up a psychiatrist who may or
may not be able to advise her — a few problems have no
solution. 'I carry the can,' she remarked.

Published readers' letters evolve from a combination
of several letters on similar problems. She is careful
to preserve anonymity.

She writes by hand, not by typewriter, and she writes
spontaneously, producing her copy within two hours. She
said she would never be capable of the mental discipline
required to produce a sixty thousand word novel. She
warned against the danger of ideas beyond one's station
— a writer must remain humble and never over-pleased
with her own performances.

BETHEA CREESE

The article

But a week later there was a sting in the tail. Mrs Proops used the
experience in her *Daily Mirror* column, published on Wednesday
30th October. The *RNA News* reprinted it, with the permission of the
Daily Mirror (as we do, now) and Mrs Proops herself. She had liked the
RNA—and her paragraph headings were brilliant—but basically she
thought romantic fiction was dead as a dodo. As the *RNA News* Editor
said wryly, 'This will arouse tremendous interest—and controversy.'

From RNA News Sept-Oct 1968

HAVE WE READ THE LAST ROMANTIC CHAPTER?

The Romantic Novelists are a very nice group of ladies.
Some, greyhaired and getting on a bit; some in well-
preserved, smart-hatted middle age.

All of them are deeply dedicated to the preservation
of idealised love and the tender side of the
relationship between men and women.

They think of the girls in their books as heroines.

The other afternoon I had tea with some of the group.
One said, sadly: 'It's very difficult for us, in this
permissive age, to understand our heroines. They are so
different,' she sighed, 'from the way we were when we
were young.'

The word heroine struck a curiously old-fashioned
note. What, in fact, is a heroine? Does such a creature
exist beyond fiction and the imagination of Romantic
Novelists?

LOVE

Have the vicissitudes of the fictitious heroine,
anguishing over her love for the equally fictitious hero
in chapter after chapter until the final happy ending,
anything to do with flesh and blood girls of today?

Clearly, unless Romantic Novelists can update their
heroines they are clinging to a dying market for their
products.

The big deal about novel-writing, I imagine, is to
produce books which have characters with whom the reader
can identify.

LADY

They may go overboard for a distinguished married man,
but they settle in the last chapter for the honest
fellow they knew in their hearts they loved all the
time.

They may have little revolts against their parents
and sometimes even leave home to take a flat In Town, but
mummy and daddy are always at the inevitable wedding on
the last page with forgiving hugs and kisses all round.

The Romantic Novelists are beginning to realise with

alarm that real-life girls are apt to be very different. Real-life girls, if they are tempted by a bold, rich man consider themselves very lucky indeed and the bolder and richer the better.

A real-life girl who goes overboard for the distinguished married man hops into bed with him at the first available opportunity.

Real-life girls who leave home to live In Town frequently set themselves up in a seedy establishment with a scruffy non-hero, and they don't bother about anything so bourgeois as a wedding.

LUST

'We'll see,' they say to the alarmed parents, 'how we get on before we get married if we ever do get married, that is. We might, if we have any children.' I daresay that the most parents can hope for is that if they have any grandchildren they'll be legitimate ones.

Certainly, the Romantic Novelists have a big problem. Should they reflect life as it really is? Or should they carry on pretending that nothing has changed?

Should their heroines go overboard for freaky pop-singers, take pot, lust around, join protest marches, sit-in at college (with babies in their arms), proclaim themselves to be anarchists, anti-establishment, anti-church, anti-social, just anti?

It's useless for novelists to pretend that the innocent dewy-eyed heroine of twenty or thirty years ago has anything to do with the far-from-innocent, jaundiced-eyed non-heroine of now.

I suppose there are still a few isolated pockets of society where old-fashioned heroines seeking happy-ever-after endings still exist. There must still be girls who believe in love and romance.

LIKE

There are still plenty of young married couples setting up home and following the pattern set by their parents, taking out mortgages, pushing prams with legitimate infants inside them.

I think there's a big enough residue of the old-fashioned heroine to keep the Romantic Novelists going for quite a time yet.

I wouldn't, however, like to put any bets on how much

```
longer there'll be a steady, ready market for sweet
romance.
   To most of today's non-heroines, romance is a corny
joke. I have every sympathy with the Group — struggling
to understand them, trying to model heroines on them,
heroines who are both romantic and contemporary at the
same time.
   It must be a pretty daunting task.
```

The fallout

That article must have been a severe disappointment to the Chairman and her committee, not only for its dismissive tone and faintly patronising sympathy, but also for what it was going to bring forth from the membership. Was this where the spats all started again?

The Editor of the *RNA News* had invited comments and this seems to have let out most of the hot air. The Editor wrote, 'As was to be expected, Claire Ritchie disagreed violently with Mrs Proops,' before giving her the best part of a page to sound off. Ritchie, whose first novel, *The Sheltered Flame*, had been published in 1949 by Hodder & Stoughton, was a regular impassioned correspondent in the *RNA News*. She was not a moderate arguer but underneath the fiery phrases there ran a genuine concern to reflect what she thought was decent behaviour and good writing.

It's probably worth a word here on what the 1960s members thought was their responsibility to the reader. Alex Stuart undoubtedly had what we think of as patronising concern for what she called 'the impressionable reader' and she was not alone. Anne Weale recalled in 2007, 'when the RNA started, there was considered to be a "factory girl/shop assistant market"—it was a v snobbish era.' Of course there were other writers, like Mary Stewart, who told *Argosy* magazine that she thought it contaminated the writing process to think about the people who would eventually read her books. But there was certainly a school of romantic novelists at the inception of the RNA who worried about the unsophisticated section of their readership and conscientiously worked hard not to lead them astray. That was not Claire Ritchie's position at all. She fulminated against any suggestion that 'intelligent, educated women should write down to morons for the sake of (doubtful) extra sales and—perhaps—popularity with the modern teenager.'

However much she disliked Marje Proops's article though, she did not seem to blame the committee for inviting her in the first place, unlike Hilda Nickson (Mills & Boon, doctor-nurse romances), whose protest carried more than a hint of the bad old offence-taking days. Fortunately other RNA correspondents, while disagreeing with Proops, seemed tolerant and even amused. Nobody demanded a public apology and there was only one whiff of a threat to resign. The committee could stop holding its breath and the Editor made a selection of comments—editors of this book have followed suit and selected even harder.

From RNA News Nov-Dec 1968

SOME COME-BACKS TO PROOPS ON DAILY MIRROR ARTICLE

BARBARA PERKINS in her 'hatless early thirties' was amused by the description of the Romantic Novelists and said it seemed to her that Proops's 'description of modern mores was almost entirely geared to so-called swinging London. We aren't only read in London — or only even in England!' And added, 'She underestimates us if she thinks we can't invent believable reasons for keeping our heroines out of bed. For example, in an increasingly feminist world, a modern young woman might well have too much of a mind of her own to want to shack up with the nearest chance-acquainted male! A view which says female aims and interest are always sexual seems to me to be outdated. Lastly — is romance a dying market? If so, why are so many pop-songs toe-curlingly sentimental?'

    CLAIRE RITCHIE said that Proops was either behind the times or did not read modern romances. 'The fictitious heroine anguishing over her love in chapter after chapter, has long departed from our novels.' But she really let rip on sex: 'Some girls in real life may behave with as little regard for themselves as Mrs Proops suggests, but thank heaven, there are still many who find promiscuous "bed-hopping" a fit pastime only for fleas, and recoil in distaste from scruffy non-heroes.'

'Are dirty-minded females in the majority?' asked Claire. She challenged, too, the sweeping statement that 'life as it really is consists chiefly of immoral anti-social activities and ideas. Does Mrs Proops favour encouraging muck, lust, marital infidelity and drug taking? Have these any place in our fiction?'

HILDA NICKSON wrote: 'Speaking as a Vice President, I feel this is just the sort of publicity we DON'T want. If I thought for one moment that this is how we really were or appeared, I would not remain a member of the RNA. (How many members do we lose as result of this sort of thing and how many are put off joining?)' She went on, 'Many of us don't write about teenagers. We write about mature women who have other problems, besides their sex life, women who have seen the horrifying results of venereal disease and drug-taking. The world does not consist wholly of students and bobby-soxers.' She concluded caustically, 'The task is not all that daunting. Some of our members are already achieving it as an increase in sales shows, both on the Continent, at home and in America.'

GLADYS FULBROOK answered Proops's question 'should the romantic novelists reflect life as it really is or carry on pretending that nothing has changed?' with: 'We reflect quite a big slice of life as it really is. Not all young girls are the ultra-modern swinging London type of this permissive age.' But she admitted, 'We are inclined to wrap things up in tinsel and floss. Youngsters of today call a spade a spade — and we should do the same.'

MARY DUNN: 'I thought the article was very amusing but disagree with most of it. The "isolated pockets" where girls seek happy-ever-after marriages are more widespread than she thinks; in fact they are universal.

She is also wrong about the girls of twenty or thirty years ago being innocent and dewy-eyed. Even fifty years ago, girls knew a thing or two! It was much more fun then, when everything was unpermissive. You really got a thrill out of life.'

The follow up

An unexpected coda to this encounter was an invitation to the RNA to appear on BBC TV with Marje Proops to discuss Is Romance Dead? The RNA fielded the current chairman, Stella March; her immediate predecessor, historical writer Sylvia Thorpe; Anne Betteridge, who wrote foreign-setting romance with a hint of mystery; Juliet Armstrong, a long-term Mills & Boon author; Nancy Sawyer, then on her first pseudonym (Nancy Buckingham) in what was to be a distinguished career; and romantic suspense author Anne Worboys, who was using her pseudonym, Annette Eyre.

It all sounds a bit of a shambles. They recorded in a bedroom at the Mount Royal Hotel. The bed had been dismantled and they had to send out for flowers from Selfridges to hide it when the bedstead, propped up against a wall, was clearly in shot. The film kept running out—and before they started again Continuity insisted that Marje smoke her new cigarette down to the length it had been when the film ran out.

The RNA awaited the outcome with trepidation. 'Remembering back to the "out of context" interviews some of our prizewinning members have suffered in the past,' wrote Worboys, 'I somewhat apprehensively allowed various friends who have no BBC2 to come to my home to view.' But she found she need not have worried.

From RNA News Spring 1969

RNA ON TV

Dear Marje played it completely straight. She began by reading from 'The Sheikh'. 'Scorching lips, close union with his warm, strong body' etc. She commented that she couldn't imagine Rudolf Valentino seducing a modern girl in tights. Romance, in her view, stopped being romantic when they started calling it sex.

Teenagers were shown in a discotheque looking rather bored with their lot; an old couple who had a long, warm relationship commented on the modern picture. Marje's hairdresser gave his view that it was okay to be unfaithful as long as his girl did not find out, but if he found she was being promiscuous, that would be the end. A young couple living together, hiding behind a wedding ring so that people would not talk, said there was too much 'possession' in marriage. A pop writer saying he thought old songs were very formal and not applicable now. Some rather sad young married women in a Manchester laundrette who had too many children and too little money. All very disillusioned.

Anne came on the screen saying her piece about Rules. She told how she was summoned to her publisher in the early days of writing [Betteridge's first novel, 'The Foreign Girl', was published in 1960] and told what she was allowed to do to her heroine. That the girl might, for instance, enter into a bigamous marriage as long as she did not know that the man was married. She said she was now able to have a divorced heroine.

Juliet appeared talking of markets, explaining how there could be no divorce in her books because of the Irish (Catholic) markets. Also that the overseas romance markets, including Canada, Australia and the U.S. tended to be more puritanical.

Nancy gave her view that it was sometimes difficult to be sympathetic with a girl who had casual relationships. That a promiscuous heroine was not really a popular one.

The programme as a whole came out strongly on the side of romance. Marje interviewed her hairdresser, the owner of a man's boutique, children listening to a fairy story, Sacha Distel, looking to my mind like a genuine twenties hero. He thought Frenchmen were brought up to say 'I love you', to not allow their eyes to wander when talking to a girl, to make them feel very special. And I must say my lady guests positively melted during his interview.

A Cinderella wedding made the Grand Finale. A working girl [*Eds:* We don't think it meant that then!] in Manchester marrying a rich American boy whose father owned the hotel she worked in. I think this tied the whole thing up. Crowds of women of all ages, all starry eyed, the street packed with them, all voluble on the subject of the Cinderella romance.

To me, there were three patches of warmth in the programme that highlighted the question, or rather the

answer to Is Romance Dead? The couple married for 60
years, Sacha Distel and his Frenchman's view that girls
want to feel very special. And the Cinderella wedding. I
don't think any of us ought to give another thought to
romance packing up. Anyone who saw that programme must
have been persuaded that it's here to stay.
ANNETTE EYRE

The end of the sixties

By the end of the sixties it was clear that the world of publishing was changing very fast. The private commercial libraries were closing and they had always been great purchasers of books for recreational reading, an area in which public libraries were very patchy. Many publishers tended to be cautious about authors trying out new plot lines or more characters who embraced the Swinging Sixties, especially in the area of sexual mores. This especially frustrated metropolitan authors who could see the changes all around them.

The end of the commercial libraries

Almost unnoticed by the RNA, amid the simmering discontent of 1966, Boots had closed the last of their Booklovers' Lending Libraries in February of that year. Jesse Boot had first opened them in 1896, at the instigation of his wife Florence, charging the borrowers 2d a book for a week's loan. It became a profit centre in its own right, but in the beginning the object was partly philanthropic—for people who could not afford to buy books—and partly to lure customers into the shop, since customers had to walk past all the merchandise to get to the library.

They became hugely successful and by 1938 were clocking up 35m borrowings a year. During the War, when paper shortages kept books expensive and comparatively scarce, the number of subscribers rose to over 1m and Boots ordered 1.25m books a year. Their purchasing power made them a serious player and, as a result, they influenced publishers. They were aimed at women of all classes—doctor's wife Celia Johnson goes to Boots Library every week in *Brief Encounter*.

So important was Boots to the RNA that Mr ES Moore, Head of Boots Libraries, was one of our first guests and led a discussion on commercial libraries at a meeting in 1961. Boots were in the process of acquiring the subscribers of WH Smith lending library, which had closed, and he was relatively optimistic. But the truth was that, with the proliferation of paperbacks, the cost of books to the consumer was falling, and such libraries were no longer a commercial proposition, except as an incentive to customers to visit the store and buy other things. Even Boots were soon to start a closure programme —for instance, the Booklovers' Library in their Westbourne shop closed in 1964—and by 1966, the whole operation had wound up.

With the sector giant gone, a few commercial libraries remained— Mrs Ladenburg, Head Librarian at the Army & Navy Stores, was asked to be a final judge of the Romantic Novel of the Year in 1966— but they could not last long. The days when you didn't have to take your holiday reading with you because every seaside town had newsagents with a small commercial library were over.

Romance lists close

Publishing, however was in the melting pot with hardback sales, the core of the business, giving way more and more to paperbacks, produced by new, and to some extent, rival, publishers. This had a particular impact on popular fiction. Publishers and lines which relied mainly on library sales struggled, unless they could forge a link with one of the paperback houses.

The first blow was the closure of Ward Lock's fiction list altogether, ending a distinguished tradition of publishing popular fiction, including Dornford Yates, Harrison Ainsworth and the first *Poldark* novel. In December 1967, Colonel Shipton told the RNA committee of Ward Lock's decision and resigned as Associate Vice President. Editor Monica Bax asked to remain an associate member, presumably while she looked for another job. Ironically, Ward Lock's title *Comfort and Keep* by Doris E Smith won the main award the following year.

The next year the *RNA News* published an affectionate farewell to senior editor Tom Eagle, retiring from Herbert Jenkins. Marjorie McEvoy, who sold him her first romantic novel in 1960, wrote an appreciation of TW Eagle. She wrote, 'Never extravagantly over-enthusiastic in praise of manuscripts, a word of congratulation from him was all the more to be treasured when it did materialise.' (How true that was. He was head judge the year that Constance Heaven's *House of Kuragin* won the RNA Award and his adjudication was calculated to depress pretension: the historical background was 'lightly but adequately sketched' and the novel had 'a not too contrived happy ending'.) With his departure, however, the publisher wrote to the RNA to say, 'In Mr Eagle's absence we cannot devote the special care and attention to romantic novels which was so much his forte. We have elected, therefore, no longer to compete in this field.' When one of their books shared the Romantic Novel of the Year Award the following year, it received minimal support from the publisher. Indeed one wonders how big the print run was, as it is the only novel, out of 50 years of prize winners, that the RNA has completely failed to find, after three years of searching using all the resources of the internet. It was *Cat on a Broomstick* by Joanne Marshall (the pen name of active RNA member Anne Rundle). Any information gratefully received.

Publishers remaining …

In the light of all this bad news, it was timely that the committee had invited a panel of publishers to the September meeting in 1969, in the smart new venue at the Royal Overseas League. There was, not surprisingly, 'a splendid attendance.'

From the RNA News Autumn 1969

PANEL OF PUBLISHERS

In a meeting on 17th September 1969, a panel of
publishers explained what they were looking for in MSS
submitted to them. All agreed that essentially they
wanted books that were well-written and interesting from
start to finish. So much ground was covered that this
report must be given in note form.

DOROTHY TOMLINSON (Hurst & Blackett) said a book
should have a good plot, interesting characters and
exciting dramatic situations. Characters could be single,
married, divorced, pregnant, and could have slept
together before marriage. Some love interest necessary,
but need not be of prime importance. She advised reading
widely to discover what made a good book.

JOHN GITTENS (Robert Hale) said he could take MSS of
45,000—60,000 words. Almost any subject acceptable if
well plotted, feasible and having wide appeal. For the
romance list Hale preferred books with a modern setting
and these should be up to date in, for instance, medical
techniques. Crime now acceptable with romance.

IAN HARRAP (Harrap) stressed that the publisher had
to be able to sell a book in a market that was highly
competitive. He warned against plots being too topical
so that they quickly became outdated. He aimed at
books that were distinctive enough to get reviewed as
that always helped sales. Word of mouth was still the
best recommendation for a book, but anything an author
could do to get name better known helped — serials,
appearances on television and radio, lecture tours, and
contact with local libraries.

MICHAEL LEGAT (Corgi) gave his rule of the three
As. 1) Action - a book should progress, with minor ups
and downs, towards an ultimate climax. This sense of
'shape' is required by the reader, albeit unconsciously.
2) Authenticity — the demand for this has grown
recently (Cf 'Z Cars'). 3) Authorship (a professional
approach) clean, clear typescripts, attention to grammar
and syntax, keeping to promises on time. Paperback
publishing was highly commercial. Corgi's romance sales
were 'steady' and they liked to build up an author's
name. Unfortunately for us, the list was very full
and they could only take on an author whose work was
outstandingly good.

NANCY SAWYER

New blood

One bright spot for the RNA in the growing gloom, however, was the fact that younger authors, like Anne Worboys, Anne Weale and Lucilla Andrews, were now happy to come onto the committee. Additionally, many of the members who had quit during the bickering years, returned. Mary Irvine, Fiction Editor of *Woman's Realm*, was one of them:

Early years

The beginning of the RNA will always be, for me, linked to the birth of *Woman's Realm*.

In 1957 I was working in the Fiction Department of *Woman* when we heard that a new magazine was to be launched in 1958—and it would be called *Woman's Realm*. The rumour went around they were paying lavish salaries. Although *Woman* was immensely successful, Mary Grieve, the great editor and a canny Scot, did not throw her money around. She had also let it be known that anyone considering applying to the new magazine would have to 'consider her position'. I had been on *Woman* since 1949, there was no prospect of advancement, as the Fiction Editor was a fixture, so the temptation of fresh fields was very great, even if it meant losing my present job.

When I write my autobiography—and that is highly unlikely—I shall devote three chapters to the dramatic events that surrounded my application for and eventual acceptance of the Fiction Editorship of beloved *Woman's Realm*.

We move forward. John Gammie, Editor in Chief of Odhams Press who had masterminded the birth of *Woman's Realm*, had bought about six romantic novels which he handed to me to be cut and edited for the new mag. And one of his first directives—join the RNA, which had just been formed. There, said he, you will find rich plums, romantic novelists dying to write for you and agents who will help that happen. And he was right.

I joined the Association—I was not a founder member—and certainly I attended meetings and the very first RNA dinner. Although the war had been over some twelve years, the early fifties were still pretty austere and we had been starved of glamorous occasions. And that first dinner stays in my mind to this day. I just wish I could remember where it was held. The ladies really shone, beautiful evening dresses and naughty furs. Alan Boon had asked me to join his table, but in fact I went with John Smith of the Christy & Moore agency. John was Catherine Cookson's close friend and original agent. He was also a poet and wrote under a pseudonym for *Woman's Realm*. A lovely man and if anyone knows where he is now, please let me know.

But I wander. After three/four years I left the RNA. I was busy producing three short stories and two serials a week—and I didn't like the in-fighting that went on. I seem to remember that the founding members of the RNA wanted to raise the profile of the romantic writer, but nothing very much happened for a little while. It was still very much a London Association, it felt inferior to its Big Brother counterpart, the Crime Writers' Association and it was looking inward. It was Lois Low (aka Dorothy Mackie Low) who persuaded me to rejoin. She said bitchiness was a thing of the past—and the Old Guard had dropped off the bough. And she was absolutely right. All the legendary romantic names had departed and the Association was on a very firm footing with the steady guidance of Mary Burchell, wonderful President of the RNA.

Looking back, I remember four guest speakers who really grabbed their audience—Maurice Edelman, an MP and a writer himself, the beautiful Evelyn Anthony, darling Maeve Binchy and John Rae, incredibly handsome Headmaster of Westminster School. Members will have other memories. I also remember the disasters! We had expected a lot from Dennis Wheatley—and we got it. He droned on for hours and the audience really became restive.

Agents

It is fun to remember the agents of the day who will have represented so many of the early members. Love them or loathe them, literary agents played an important part in the early days of the RNA. In the late fifties and the early sixties, the editors of women's magazines had come round to accepting that there were some good romantic writers in this country and it would be easier to encourage them instead of buying American fiction and having to anglicise it. The agents of the day had seen crime writers' profiles look up through their association, the Crime Writers' Association, and perhaps the same could happen to romantic writers through the RNA. So ... not only did agents urge their romance writers to join the RNA, they dipped into their own pockets—some of them—to help the Association.

I think of the great agents of those days. Many readers will remember Dorothy Daly of Curtis Brown. She loved her writers dearly, became part of their families, but later trotted off to Perugia University to study and eventually settle in Italy. Then there was Jean LeRoy of David Higham, a much respected figure—if slightly terrifying. She represented a string of 'literary' writers but worked diligently for her romance writers, even though they didn't rate reviews in the Sundays. Her stable included Victoria Holt, who had, at one time, written under five pseudonyms, but settled for two, Victoria Holt and Jean Plaidy in her latter years.

Across the years, I remember Pauline Rose, the most elegant lady with all the latest gossip, who had been married to Leslie Charteris (author of *The Saint* suspense novels) before marrying Neil Innes. I think of her fondly for many things, including introducing me to Bloody Marys. Eileen Lewin of the Lewin Agency, whose husband had had a distinguished war career, particularly in the Italian campaigns. Nora Blackborrow of the Hughes Massie Agency. Nora's firm looked after Agatha Christie. Before Christmas Nora would receive a list of presents to be bought for Agatha's relatives and friends. I thought this was certainly going that extra mile in the duties of an agent, rather like an editor I knew who brought in her blouses for her secretary to iron. I asked Nora if Agatha gave her a present. 'No,' she said, 'but she sends me a Christmas card.'

There was the Heath agency with Hettie Nutbrown and later Jennifer Hassell. With an extra beat of the heart, I recall the charming

Peter Watt and his younger colleague, Michael Horniman of the oldest agency in existence, AP Watt. They were not terribly sure of 'romance', but nevertheless were ready to support the new Association. Mary Crew, who lived in the coldest part of Kent through the week, ran her agency with the devoted help of Shirley Russell and Doreen Montgomery. Rupert, her husband, had launched many newspaper journalists, including Beverly Nichols and Godfrey Winn. Mary looked after Barbara Cartland and her own sister, Sonia Deane. She was a delightful lunch companion, but could drive a hard bargain.

The Pollingers, Gina and Murray, will be remembered by RNA members, and Rosemary Gould. I have already mentioned John Smith of the Christy & Moore Agency, who started life as a hairdresser, became a poet (published slim volumes) then an agent and was Catherine Cookson's good friend and adviser. And I do not forget dear John Gibson who had been James Agate's secretary—Agate was possibly *the* drama critic of the twentieth century—and gave our ten-day-old son his first teddy bear.

This was the golden age of the expense account lunches. Publishers, editors and agents met regularly and after two/ three hours of good food and wine, chat and some gentle bargaining, each party would go away well satisfied. Happy days...

We salute the agents who helped the Romantic Novelists' Association in the early days.

Magazine stories

One also remembers the great editors of the day. Women's magazines provided a very valuable source of income for writers of the day. NJ Crisp, a contributor to *John Bull*, reckoned that a story sold to a magazine here and in the US, perhaps to the *Saturday Evening Post*, would pay the school fees for a year.

It's been fun tripping down Memory Lane. It only remains to wish the RNA a happy birthday and all good wishes for the next fifty years.

The seventies

In 1970 the Awards Ceremony returned to the Park Lane Hotel, where it had started. The Banqueting Manager presented the RNA with a special cake in the form of a book inscribed Success Story by the Romantic Novelists' Association, while crime writer John Creasey proposed a toast to the next ten years.

A film was made by the *Man Alive* team as part of the dinner, followed by visits to the homes of romantic novelists. Again, when it was shown, members were taken aback by the sneering tone. The Chairman wrote to the BBC to remonstrate.

Above all, 1970 was a year of reconciliation. Denise Robins was an honoured guest at the awards ceremony and was gracious. Alex Stuart, who had retained her Life Membership, was profiled in the *RNA News* as co-founder of the Association. 'Without Alex Stuart's tremendous drive and enthusiasm during the three years of her chairmanship, it is doubtful whether the Association would have got off the ground. Between them, she and Denise Robins were able to interest a splendid number of people: some sceptical, others willing to help,' said the Spring 1970 *RNA News*, with some justice. Miss Cartland had already had a couple of friendly mentions in various newsletters. The RNA went into the new decade with wounds healed.

This was a period of consolidation. The ground rules had been set and the President and committee were united in wanting no further big initiatives. They would concentrate on the regular programme of meetings, while regional meetings increased and became more popular, driven by local members rather than the committee. As far as public image was concerned, they would respond when asked and protest against gross denigration of the genre. But mainly they would rely on individual members' efforts to publicise their own books to add lustre to the RNA and concentrate on the Romantic Novel of the Year as the RNA's one big outing onto the PR stage.

You can see the beginning of the self-help culture, too. Talks, which had previously focused mainly on industry gurus, came more and more from members. Prophetically, one of the first such talks, on 28th January 1970, was from Catherine Cookson, about a genre which she was to make peculiarly her own and which was, as it turned out, on the brink of major resurgence. (See chapter on 'Changing fashions' for the contemporaneous report in the *RNA News*.)

The quarterly *RNA News* remained a major focus, with country members very much in mind. It contained a mix of RNA matters, such as announcements, full reports of meetings and local events. Dorothy Mackie Low (then Chairman) wrote in the New Year 1970 *RNA News*, 'If there were no RNA it would leave a great gap in my life. I would be lonely, and would long for the news of other writers. Receiving the *News* is like having a bumper mail from a host of old friends.'

Public image

After the furore over the *Man Alive* programme following the tenth anniversary award, the RNA became even more cautious about the public image of the genre.

Committee minutes, January 1971
Woman's Hour
Elizabeth Beresford reported that 'Antony Derville's office at the BBC [*Woman's Hour*] told me this morning that they'd had a very good response from listeners about the "Romantic Novelists" item. People said (a) how much they enjoyed reading Romance and (b) that they *did* have difficulty in ordering them or borrowing them from

their local libraries. Antony is considering taking up this point in *Answers and comment.*'

RNA News   Autumn 1973

Sex Appeal on Radio 4

The Chairman [Leila MacKinlay] was invited to take part in one of five programmes (Radio 4, 11pm 9th August) on this subject. The speaker was David Harsent, who reviews books for one of the quality papers. He was supposed to be 'exploring the magical fascination of the romantic novel' and his talk was interspersed with heavily edited extracts from taped conversations with Leila MacKinlay and Barbara Cartland. Like others before him, he couldn't resist this golden opportunity to mock à la 'Oh God Nigel..!' Why, one can't help wondering, are men driven to sarcastic fury over the worldwide popularity of romantic fiction? Could it be uncomfortable awareness of how far they fall short of what women would like them to be?

But sometimes the media attention was just fun, pure and simple. Country member Berta Ruck, a regular contributor and the Association's oldest member, was also one of the raciest—and living history into the bargain.

The *RNA News* reported her appearance in the BBC2 series *Yesterday's Witness*:

In a delightful duet with a contemporary of the Gay Nineties, Miss Frances E Jones, they recalled what it was like to be working girls in the horse-and-buggy days of Victorian London—'Effie' Jones as one of the pioneer typists, Berta as a student at the Slade. From her sitting room in her home in Wales, Berta conjured up memories of the Bohemian set who were her friends when it was the thing among the young to be 'decadent'. We shall long remember her wonderful rendering of the drunks' bawdy songs when the pubs shut, and her description of writer friends like E Nesbitt and HG Wells. As she said, Queen Victoria's passing closed an era—an era when it was believed implicitly that 'of course' nothing would ever change.

Berta Ruck

The oldest founder member of the RNA had to be Berta Ruck. At 82 in 1960, she lived in Wales, still writing, though the period of her biggest success was between the wars. In fact, she had just published a volume of autobiography, *A Smile for the Past* (Hutchinson, 1959). She kept up a lively correspondence with the *RNA News*.

Born in India, when her father was a serving officer, she was mostly brought up in Wales, where Colonel Ruck was Chief Constable of Caernarvonshire from 1888. Berta (actually Roberta) went to boarding school in Bangor, North Wales, and thence launched herself into the world, working briefly in Germany, before studying at the Slade in London. She clearly had a whale of a time, making friends with E Nesbitt (who called the heroine of *The Railway Children* after her) and HG Wells, who was formulating his ideas of the New Woman, emancipated and financially self supporting. She paid the bills by doing illustrations for magazines like *The Idler* and eventually wrote a short story and, thereafter, serials. She published her first novel in 1914, *His Official Fiancée*, a new version of her 1912 serial in *Home Chat*. In 1909, aged 31, she had married writer Oliver Onions and he helped with the revisions. *His Official Fiancée* was an instant success in the UK and the States and eventually made into a movie.

Like many romantic authors, she was prolific, sometimes writing three novels a year, a major achievement when you had to write them by hand or bang them out on a heavy old typewriter. She was also very successful, with her books advertised on the tops of London buses, as her outraged husband pointed out to the Woolfs in their well documented spat. In October 1922 the Hogarth Press had published *Jacob's Room* by Virginia Woolf, in which she speaks of tombstones which say 'I am Bertha Ruck' and 'I am Tom Gage'. Onions wrote to Leonard Woolf, apparently threatening legal action, on the grounds that this was a deliberate slight, since it was impossible that Virginia could be unaware of the famous novelist Berta Ruck. The two women made peace, however. In his biography of Virginia Woolf, Quentin Bell records that some years later Berta Ruck went to a Bloomsbury party where she entertained the company with a performance of 'Never Allow a Sailor an Inch Above Your Knee', all differences over tombstones long forgotten. Could the lively Berta Ruck have thought the Bloomsburyites needed a bit of pep in their party?

For the truly enquiring mind, RNA member and authority on pantomime, Lesley Cookman, after persuading her music hall contacts to mine their memories and archives, suggests that the song in question is a folk song, 'Home Boys Home', whose lyrics vary from singer to singer, but one version of which ends:

> Come all of you fair maidens, a warning take by me
> And never let a sailor lad an inch above your knee
> For I trusted one and he beguiled me
> He left me with a pair of twins to dangle on my knee.

By 1928, Virginia was writing to Berta on Christmas Day, 'I am more pleased than I can say that you have survived my burial. Never will I attempt such a thing again. To think that you have bought my book!' They were never intimate though the two authors corresponded intermittently but with perfect friendliness for some years.

Berta's novels have been described as jazz age romance. For the most part they are upbeat and lively, about young girls in suburban villas of London flats who venture out into the daring world and find love. Sometimes they are perky shop girls, sometimes their families have come down in the world. At some point they all play tennis, go to parties, survive the daily commute to work, and are (or aren't) asked to Go Away For The Weekend. Often her books had a leavening of social comment. (In her journals she was noticing the rise of anti-Semitism and increasing support for the Nazis during her travels in Austria in the late twenties.) She was not hidebound by genres, though, and happily introduced a touch of the paranormal in, for instance, *The Immortal Girl* (1925) where an elderly village spinster drinks the Elixir of Life and becomes a flapper.

Her last novel was *Ancestral Voices*, published in May 1972, autobiographically based and celebrating her beloved Wales. She reported in Summer 1974 that Hurst & Blackett were bringing out two very early books of hers. One of them, *His Official Fiancée*, was her very first. They were having to advertise to try to get hold of a secondhand copy of the other book when Berta came across her own copy, bought years ago for sixpence from a Welsh bookshop. 'The jacket was more than ragamuffin,' she said.

In 1978, Chairman Elizabeth Harrison, contemplating what to send Berta to celebrate her hundredth birthday, decided against flowers, which Berta didn't like, and proposed to send her champagne, which she did. The *Evening Standard* noted on 2nd August that Berta had received the RNA's four bottles of fizz, along with telegrams from the Queen, Social Services Secretary David Ennals and the Welsh Office, and enough flowers to fill her retirement home. Sadly Berta died a week later, game to the end.

Barbara Pym

If Berta Ruck's news was always cheering, one of the most heart-breaking entries we have found in the Archive is in the Summer 1974 *RNA News*, announcing the preliminary judges for the next year's main award. There were to be four again, and one retiring judge was to be replaced by 'former novelist, Miss Barbara Pym'. It had to be the description she had given them herself. Enough to strike ice into any author's heart.

She was much valued by the RNA and the affection seems to have been reciprocated. In order to remain a preliminary judge, she was unable to join the Association, since the judges had to be disinterested, which at that time was taken to mean non-members. However, she came to events and in 1978, we find her giving one of the regular London talks.

RNA News Summer 1978

Report of meeting 8th March 1978
By Jo Germany

Once again, the Ulster Room at the Overseas Club was
filled to capacity with members who this time had the
pleasure of listening to the charming Barbara Pym talk
of her writing experiences.

Her first novel was written when she was a schoolgirl
of sixteen. 267 pages, all handwritten, and it took
for its subject, not the country life in Shropshire
which she knew so well, but was set instead in Chelsea.
She now feels that her subsequent study of English
literature later influenced the choice of subjects for
her novels and became more concerned with older people
and the comedy and irony of life rather than romance.
Even so, she thinks of her first published novel, 'Some
Tame Gazelle', as being a juvenile novel because it was
written much earlier than her others and later revised
for publication in 1950. 'Excellent Women' appeared two
years later, with others following at intervals.

It was not until 1974 that she was able to follow
what she considered an ideal way of writing, for she
retired in that year and was at last free to start work
on her novels after breakfast on a weekday. Her earlier
ones were mostly written in her spare time, either at
weekends or before going to work. However, when she had
that time to write at leisure, she was faced with the
ironic situation that no one wanted her books.

In 1963 Cape rejected her seventh book and she was
unable to find either an agent or a publisher willing
to take that or her subsequent ones. One went so far
as to say that the 'climate of fiction writing was not
right for her kind of book'. She herself thinks that the
closure of Boots etc libraries were also partly to blame
for her difficulties. Fortunately rejections did not stop
her from writing.

Later she went into hospital where she enjoyed
reading romantic fiction and began to wonder if she could
write it. She even started one, but an entry in her
diary for March 1972 reads, 'I have thought of an idea
for a new novel, all old, crabby characters, petty,

obsessive and bad tempered.' The ideas grew until they
eventually became the novel 'Quartet in Autumn'. When
she sent it to Cape they returned it saying, 'it would
not sit happily on our lists'. The second publisher
criticised it as being too short.

Then in January 1977 the tide suddenly turned in
her favour and she was rediscovered, for she was twice
named in 'The Times Literary Supplement' [by Philip
Larkin and academic and biographer of Jane Austen, Lord
David Cecil] as being the most underrated author in the
last seventy-five years. At this time her novel 'Quartet
in Autumn' was being considered by Macmillan and they
decided to publish it. She received the glad tidings on
Valentine's Day of last year.

Ironically enough, this novel, which two publishers
had previously turned down, went on to be shortlisted
for the Booker Prize.

Barbara Pym's interesting talk was encouraging proof
that it is worthwhile continuing to write regardless of
adversity. One can never tell when luck will change for
the better, for another novel of hers, 'A Sweet Dove
Died', is due out soon.

Hurst & Blackett closes

A real blow for many RNA members was the closure of the Hurst
& Blackett list, by whom many had been published from the start of
their careers, including Chairman Elizabeth Harrison. The end of
Hurst & Blackett was a worse blow than the closure of any of the
others. Their authors had won the Main Award more times than any
other publisher—nine winners in 18 years. (Hodder & Stoughton,
their nearest rival, had four. Collins, the other casualty of the
seventies had had two, including the very first, *More than Friendship*
by Mary Howard.) Many of the RNA's most active members,
including a high proportion of the committees over the years and
innovators like Maynah Lewis, were on Hurst & Blackett's list.

RNA News Winter 1978

Hurst & Blackett Closure — a Note from the Chairman

Sad news with which to open our New Year, I'm afraid. After months of rumour, just before Christmas our forebodings were confirmed, and we were told that the Hutchinson Publishing Group are to close the Hurst & Blackett list during the course of 1979. This is a bitter decision for many RNA writers and for me personally.

It seems, to say the least, ironic that at the present time, when we are assured on all sides that the genre is flourishing as never before, two of the best-known romance lists, first Collins and now Hurst & Blackett, should cease publication. In the past many Award winners — indeed, in one year the entire shortlist — came from this one imprint, presided over in those days by our indomitable Dorothy Tomlinson.

However, I do myself firmly believe that when one door closes another opens, and my New Year message is simply this. Keep on writing. The future for romantic fiction, I am sure, remains bright.

Keep up your spirits

Elizabeth Harrison, as will be illustrated elsewhere in this book, was a great problem solver and, like the illustrious President, knew the value of a good party. By the time author Susan Sallis joined, the social aspect of the RNA had become a major selling point.

Sue Sallis recalls:

Such happy memories of the RNA beginning in the late seventies when Nancy Sawyer suggested I would enjoy the whole thing. Oh, she was right.

She shepherded me into the Overseas League Club and there, in the foyer, Mary Burchell waited to welcome everyone. She called me darling—later I discovered this was because she could not remember names—and immediately invited me to her summer party at Dolphin Square, which was taking place in the very near future.

Nancy took me in and made several introductions. She was retiring Chairman and Elizabeth Harrison was taking over. The room was full of a sense of things happening here and now; excellent atmosphere for writers who before were solitary people. The RNA gave us a chance to see each other, our agents, publishers ... to breathe in the whole literary 'thing'!

Someone else will be writing about Dolphin Square of course. It was there that I first heard Mary Burchell's amazing story culminating in Eamonn Andrews and *This is Your Life*. It is still a constant reminder that truth is inevitably stranger than fiction. I don't think I missed one summer party, starting with a swim in the basement pool, a 'sit' in the garden where people like Raymond Huntley strolled and then the party itself. Alice Chetwynd Ley, Leila MacKinlay, Helen McGregor, Anne Weale, Charlotte Lamb, Alan Boon (did he arrive once in a top hat straight from the races?), Sheila Walsh, Marie Joseph, Anne Maybury, Constance Heaven ... wonderful people, very special friends. Wonderful food!

To meet them again and again at Nutford House, the Café Royal and the Savoy has been a privilege and such a pleasure. Our speakers are always enthralling—Molly Kaye, Barbara Pym, Monica Dickens (who regaled us with a wonderful recipe for Hollandaise sauce!), Harry Bowling ... never a dull moment!

Thank you to everyone who has made the RNA what it is today. Let's keep it up!

The women's magazines and
their editors

As Mary Irvine (former Fiction Editor of *Woman's Realm*, who began her career on *Woman*) reminds us, a huge outlet for romantic writers were the women's magazines—an outlet which, alas, has more or less died. Every magazine (and there were many) published in every issue a serial and at least two, sometimes three short stories, each up to 5,000 words long.

Standards were high. Short stories and serials had to have depth, characterisation, convincing plots and also be well written. Authors of the calibre of Alec Waugh, Brian Glanville, NJ Crisp and Christiana Brand frequently appeared in the fiction pages, as well as up-and-coming new writers. With regard to serials, once it had been published, the author could do a bit of linking work and then get a book publishing deal.

The magazine editors regarded themselves as infinitely superior to book publishers and, indeed, in terms of money and publishing opportunities, they were. Unless you were Georgette Heyer or Norah Lofts or Mary Stewart and could command a big advance from a book publisher, most romantic writers did far better from magazine publication than from book publication. As Mary points out, for a serial of six to eight instalments you could earn £1,500. Diane Pearson's first novel in the sixties received an advance of £500 for both hardcover and paperback rights. And the short stories, which were excellent training grounds for novelists, paid handsomely too—anything up to 80 guineas in the 1970s.

Mary Irvine recalls those days:
We must never underestimate the power of women's magazines in the fifties, sixties and seventies. Mary Grieve, the great editor of *Woman*, was asked why they had become a feature in so many households. She gave a thoughtful answer: Families have split up, she said. Mothers and daughters no longer live side by side. When a daughter needs a mother's advice on cooking, knitting, sewing, fashion, beauty, health problems—and being a good wife and mother —she can turn to her favourite magazine for help. And alongside this good practical advice, most magazines, certainly the weeklies, ran a serial lasting for perhaps eight instalments, and two short stories, sometimes three. And this was all for the price of 4d to 6d.

For first-time writers of romance, the magazines of the day provided a marvellous training ground. For the established writers it gave them extra cash and brought them to a new audience of readers. A serial sale in the fifties and onwards was worth anything from £1,500, a great deal of money in those days. Any writer invited to contribute was delighted even if it meant an instalment of a serial being returned for revision, two, three times. Editors were very exacting. And after the serial, there could be book publication. That wasn't the end of the good times. A story appearing in *Woman* would sell again in Norway, Sweden, Denmark, Holland and Italy and, if you were very professional, the United States.

The leading magazines of the day for romantic fiction were *Woman* (Editor, Mary Grieve), *Woman's Own* (Jimmy Drawbell, later Joanna Chase and Lesley Saxby), *Woman's Weekly* (Winnie Johnson, later Brenda McDougall). These magazines were joined by *Woman's Mirror* and *Woman's Realm* in the late fifties. The DC Thomson group in Dundee was also a tremendously good outlet for romantic writers, even if the monetary rewards were less. Possibly the grandest editor of them all was Peggy Sutherland at *Woman's Journal* who serialised Norah Lofts, Mary Stewart and Georgette Heyer.

In the early fifties I was a junior working in the Fiction Department of *Woman* under Camilla Shaw, the Fiction Editor. *Woman* was just about to break through the three million copies-per-week sound barrier. The rivalry between magazines (particularly *Woman* and *Woman's Own*) was intense and all eyes were on circulation. These great lady editors were giant stars and terribly famous, almost akin to footballers of today.

Why did most editors keep their hands on the fiction, even though they had fiction editors? (Joyce Ward of *Woman's Realm* was the exception and she allowed me an absolutely free hand to buy and suggest ideas to writers. This was very unusual because we must remember the fiction budget was possibly the highest in the magazine, certainly the amount of space made it so.)

Magazine editors were god-like. To be called in for an interview with the Great One was an awesome experience; to meet her in the corridor meant one flattened oneself against the wall, head down. We, 'her girls' as she called us, regarded her with enormous respect and devotion. Many years later we met at a *Woman* reunion. The girls had all become middle-aged ladies but their feelings and attitude towards her remained the same. Of course, we were never asked to iron her blouse before she lunched, which would not have been unusual for the staff of Anna Wibberley, editor of the monthly magazine, *Everywoman.*

The editors of the day were a breed apart. Discreet, hard-working, immaculately dressed and wonderfully inspiring to the people who worked for them. And then the wonderful illustrations —artists like Walter Wyles and Eric Earnshaw, Len Thurston —illustrations that were collectors' items of the day and still are. But going back to the editors—they all thought they knew more about fiction than their staff—it became personal choice, of course.

And the parties—and the lunches—and the idiosyncrasies of the various editors ... We, on *Woman*, at the time, were involved with one of the key characters in the Ruth Ellis shooting case. You remember she was the last woman hanged in this country. We had reporters besieging Odhams Press and we all had to leave by the back door ...

The RNA regularly invited the powerful magazine editors to talk to the London meetings and authors shared tips that they picked up from hearing them speak in other fora. Stella March heard Jean Twiddy speak at the Swanwick Summer School in 1970 and reported in the New Year *RNA News* that Twiddy said the secret was knowing your reader. The *Woman's Weekly* reader had well-polished shoes and handbag, allowed drink but not drunkenness, the occasional cigarette but not heavy smoking and believed in conventional marriage—and not enough people were trying to write for her. 'Puzzle: why are publishers closing their romance lists while a magazine catering for the same readership enjoys sales figures that continue to go up and up?'

A friendship forged between an author and magazine editor was touchingly displayed when Lucilla Andrews wrote a tribute to that same Jean Twiddy on her death in 1972.

RNA News Winter 1972

JEAN TWIDDY

We first met her in 1955. I remember a computer fast mind, spilling pencils and notebooks from a bulging holdall. We spoke — she spoke — in rapid telephone calls, about everything.
   A very breathless call, 'I don't believe this — but they've made me publishing director of IPC.' Over the years, sometimes at midnight, sometimes at eight am, sometimes in the small hours of Sunday morning. 'Jean, you're not STILL working?' 'Darling, I've had this idea I think they'll like.'
   THEY, the readers she so loved. Yes loved. THEY were those millions of her fellow women whose lives she entered, cheered, comforted, though most never even knew her name. Jean Diana Twiddy, born 1926, died 1972.

She had been lauded by her peers in several respectful obituaries but, said Lucilla,

> ... One accolade, to the best of my knowledge, has yet to be added.
> Romantic fiction today is booming. Romance has a new status which the RNA has vastly helped. Jean Twiddy printed us; believed in us; shared our views. And with her terrific strength of character and editorial genius, boosted her magazines' circulation, proved to those who required proof, the public's hunger for romantic fiction — and turned it into big business.
> Seldom if ever was she on time for anything but a deadline. Gentle manner, untidy, hilarious, at the end of the day would burst into 'All things bright and beautiful' at her desk or her great favourite, 'We plough the fields and scatter'.
> 'When they buy the magazine,' she said, 'they want to buy a bit of themselves. They're my friends. I must give them the best I can.'
> She gave them her life.

The committee invited almost as many magazine editors as publishers to talk to the membership and they generally came up with a crisp list of things which they were looking for. No nonsense about being author-led here.

RNA News   Spring 1973

From an informal talk on 'Woman' magazine

Miss Patricia Brougham, Associate Editor of 'Woman', told an RNA meeting on 30th January 1973, '"Woman" needs tougher fiction these days.' Stories did not have to end happily — if the feeling was right, this was the main essential — and one could safely leave it to the couple in the story to decide what they were going to do, not tie everything up neatly.

Asked about 'foreign heroes', Miss Brougham said that the magazine was not against them and quoted Mary Howard's serial with its Indian hero, and added that the readers had been furious that the end of this serial had been left in the balance, when the couple had parted; they still received letters about this!

It was impossible to say what taboos existed as regarded type of plot these days; mainly it depended on the way the subject was handled. The hero must never be a rather shadowy figure who was out of the story for a long time, and scarcely present between Chapter One and the end of the story. She had prejudices, Miss Brougham admitted frankly: the first person story, the very sentimental type of story, an old-fashioned background, the type of heroine who meekly accepted everything and never stood up for herself, the heroine who was too naïve to tell the cad from the hero, or was not as sweet and charming as she appeared on the surface. Humour? Yes, though she realised it was difficult to write. Foreign settings were quite acceptable in these days when people travelled widely; reader identification was immensely important; there must be good reasons for the characters behaving as they did.

One realises how tough it is these days for romantic writers to find lucrative and plentiful outlets for their work. The magazines were indeed a golden age for romantic fiction.

Traditional versus modern

In all the comments on the *Daily Mirror* article in 1968, only Hilda Nickson actually suggested a novel that Marje Proops might read to see that the romantic novelists of the day did, indeed, grapple with contemporary issues. It was *Mirror of the Years* by Margaret Maddocks.

But perhaps the best illustration of how romantic fiction was changing was Maynah Lewis, winner in 1968 for *The Future is For Ever*. Lewis—incidentally another RNA committee member—explained that the Happy Ever After ending was no longer universal in romantic fiction. She ascribed this to women's widening horizons. 'In my first novel the heroine didn't get her man, in my second the heroine was 64 years old, my third was a romantic suspense set behind the Iron Curtain, my fourth had no wedding bells, not even in the far distance.' Yet she won the award a second time for *The Pride of Innocence* in 1972. The modern romantic novel was not just about the relaxation of sexual restraints on behaviour and expression, which the new permissive climate allowed. It was now possible to find a publisher for grittier plots altogether and several RNA members were taking advantage of it.

The March meeting in 1973 was tabled to be a discussion between Maynah Lewis, the previous year's winner of the Major Award for *The Pride of Innocence* (Hurst & Blackett), and the President, Mary Burchell, who, of course, was published by Mills & Boon, on modern versus traditional romantic fiction. This was the second time that Lewis had won the award. She had also come through the New Writers' Scheme and her first novel had won the Netta Muskett Award.

Maynah Lewis

Lewis was eminently suited to describe and defend the 'modern' romantic novel. She had not only won the Main Award twice, she had been shortlisted in 1973 as well. Talking about her career after the 1973 AGM, she made it clear how far she was from the generally accepted concept of a romantic novelist. (Diane Pearson feels that Lewis wrote 'relationship novels' and was a generation ahead of her time.) A professional musician (*Lieder* accompanist and teacher), Lewis began writing articles, then short stories, of which she sold about 50 per cent. Then she got an idea which she thought was too big for a short story, and between the Summer School at Swanwick, the New Writers' Scheme, and the new (male) editor at *My Weekly* she worked it up into a full length serial and novel, *No Place for Love* (1963). As she said herself, it did not sound like the right formula for a romantic novel: it was about a 35-year-old tough career woman who did not get her man.

The *RNA News* of summer 1973 records that Maynah freely admitted breaking the rules of romantic fiction, and pointed out that, so far as reader identification was concerned, three of her serials had been written from the man's angle. Hero and heroine, in her serials, could be any age between 29 and 60, and her characters were drawn from every walk of life; among them were the daughter of a millionaire, a bookie, a Russian pianist and a novice from a convent. She enjoyed developing her characters and often found herself looking at things from their point of view, which meant the story did not always develop along a straight course and she often had to make sure that the minor characters did not take over.

Lewis was probably the most extreme of the untraditional

romantic novelists to emerge so far, but she was not alone. There was a long and honourable line of authors who wrote about mating and marital relationships, in terms of the challenges (including pain, disappointment and emotional or sexual frustration), the supremely popular Netta Muskett among them. Nor were strong minor characters unknown, though discouraged by publishers of traditional romance, especially Mills & Boon. Where Lewis was innovative was in subordinating the romantic relationship to the 'happening', as she called it, of her plot.

As it turned out, Maynah Lewis had been unable to come to the March meeting—which may well have been why she was invited to speak after the AGM two months later—and her place as the advocate of modern romance was taken by Mary Howard, in discussion with President Mary Burchell.

Mary Howard

Mary Howard was a founder member of the RNA, having written 38 novels up to then. She was a committee member under Alex Stuart and took responsibility for organising the first year of the New Writers' Scheme. She also won the very first Romantic Novel of the Year Award in 1960 for *More than Friendship*.

Her father had been George Edgar, journalist, novelist and leader writer for many newspapers and she nearly always mentioned him, when talking about her writing, even though he died in 1918 when she was eleven. (She told the *News* in 1980 that he had been very well known in the first decade of the century.) She wrote under two pen names—Mary Howard for contemporary novels and, later, Josephine Edgar for period novels set during the nineteenth century up to the end of World War I. Her first novel to be published was *Windier Skies*, 1930, when she would have been 23. In March 1973, at the time of the big debate on modern versus traditional romantic fiction, she was 66, married to a businessman, with two daughters and at least one grandchild.

The debate

RNA News Summer 1973
MODERN OR TRADITIONAL ROMANCE?

Our President opened the batting by saying that there
was, of course, room for both the modern and traditional
novel. Once, there had been a tendency to be apologetic
about traditional romantic fiction — but as a writer
of this type of fiction for many years, she remained
convinced that romance existed as an integral part of
everyone's life and a tremendous need. To almost every
woman, at some time in her life, she was of supreme
importance to some one, or (at 80 or even 85!) she hoped
she would be; a romantic story reassures her, makes
her remember her own romance. There has never been such
a demand as there is today for the straightforward
romance. Mary Burchell told us that books she had
written in the late 1930s and early 1940s still brought
her fan mail from all over the world, and quoted the
writer of one letter, received that morning, saying
that 'writers have no idea of the happiness they give
to people.' Youngsters today are still eager for the
traditional romantic story that has a beginning, a
middle and an end, and a right sense of values. She
declared that a bad romantic novel was just about as
great an embarrassment as any book could be.

    Escapism, she continued, 'is considered a dirty word
today, but people escaped in many ways, even into the
country, away from town. Illusion, provided that it was
not total, was an important part of anyone's life; life,
after all,' she pointed out, 'is a mixture of illusions
and reality, and provided that the mixture is in the
right proportions, that is fine.' She concluded by saying
that romance gave an air of probability to our dearest
dreams.

    Mary Howard replied by reminding us that she was the
RNA's first Major Award winner; she spoke with disarming
frankness of her early years as an author's daughter,
who found it too easy to write romantic fiction and sell
everything she wrote. In later years, and after winning
the Award, she had found herself becoming more critical
of her work. Romance comforted people and she felt she
did not want to comfort them, nor was she sure it was

right to do so; it was better, she considered, to face reality. She had felt there was no future for romance, though in this she had been proved wrong. She had felt she wanted to write real stories about real people, which has meant she no longer has total serial sales, relies on book royalties, but has had the satisfaction of knowing she is doing her own thing. Escapism, she said, was only good if people realised it was escapism; self-knowledge and courage in facing up to life were the most important things of all. You must, she emphasised, do what you believe in doing, with as few compromises as possible; if you felt that conscious romance – nice, sweet and comforting – was right, then you must write this.

Our President replied that she considered herself to be a craftswoman, turning out a skilled job of work, but that Mary Howard was a compulsive writer, who would have to go on writing no matter what happened. She said she did not compromise but really believed right triumphed and love was the most important thing of all.

Mary Howard said that, where writing was concerned, she hated to do the same thing twice – although she admitted, ruefully, that this was not always commercially viable!

The discussion was then thrown open to all members. Anne Britton suggested that the kind of books Mary [Howard] wrote now might not have sold in the early days, and said that they were not run-of-the-mill, even then. Mary told us that in those days she could write a book in one month flat with little or no correction – now it took her as long as nine months to a year, and often she was not satisfied with her work, at the end of that time. She raised a very interesting point: that women, at the end of the last century and the beginning of this one, needed the consolation of romantic literature in a way they do not need it today, when contraception had made such a difference in their lives. In the old days, much as most women loved their husbands, the result of expressing physical love was usually another baby and – with little or no knowledge of contraception – the only answer was not to have sex; and so they created a romantic world that compensated for this – Ouida, Elinor Glyn, the kissed hands, the roses on the terrace.

Our President replied that there were an enormous number of homes today where there existed unmarried

mothers of twelve to fourteen years who had become
pregnant through having no idea what to do, and she felt
that, in their case, vicarious romance would have been
better than the real thing!
    Mary Howard pointed out that it was a mistake to
regard sex as the only sin. Cruelty and dishonesty were
far greater sins. In her opinion, the most romantic
novel she had read during the last five years was 'Love
Story'.

[1970 novel which originated as a screenplay by American Erich
Segal; it became the bestselling novel of the decade in the USA.]

    In response to a request from Anne Britton, both Mary
and the President gave their definition of a romantic
novel. The President said that a romantic novel was,
she felt, one that relied on feelings and fact rather
than realism. Mary Howard summed up her definition in
the phrase 'the world well lost for love' and quoted
'Wuthering Heights' in its final scenes as being romance
in its truest sense.

Crossed swords

Someone was going to challenge Mary Howard and, in the
Autumn edition of the *RNA News*, it was the always fiery Claire
Ritchie. She made four points:

1. quoting Kipling, 'Is it not possible that romance can
    inspire people with courage to face the boring and
    terrible things in life?'
2. she takes issue with the inference she draws that Howard
    thinks love can only be expressed physically; also takes
    issue with the phrase 'have sex' when Howard means
    'indulging in physical intimacy';
3. *Love Story* is full of blasphemous and disgusting phrases
    like 'bullshit';
4. will Howard agree that her novels—'and I do not dispute
    their excellence'—are far removed from 'romance' as
    understood by the majority of women?

The letter arrived in time for the Editor (Leila MacKinlay) to allow Howard to reply, which she did at length, though with relative good humour and proper gratitude for Mrs Ritchie's compliment. She repeated her support of *Love Story*—'a highly romantic story of young love, sharpened by the cool, off-beat, very authentic campus jargon'; and for 'the world well lost', adding the rider, 'Cathy and Heathcliffe were a pair of emotional Hitlers ready and willing to pull down their own and everyone else's world for their passion. It is Emily Brontë's understanding of their fierce obsession, the mystery of her implications, and the beauty of her prose that make it a great romantic novel. But they were not really very *nice people*!' Her main point, though, was, 'I believe romance has no reality, that is why it is called romance, but paradoxically, this does not mean that it does not exist. Dreams exist. It can inspire all the noble things that Mrs Ritchie mentions, but it can also be silly, boring and destructive, and even downright evil.'

The RNA—how it works

What we do

We operate under a constitution which is not so very different from that originally drafted by the founders. It says: 'The aim of the Association shall be to raise the prestige of romantic authorship and generally to encourage and foster the writing of romantic works.'

Volunteers

The RNA is now, as it always has been, a volunteer organisation. We have no paid staff and no regular office space. All the many tasks it takes to run the organisation are undertaken by busy authors— sometimes very busy, like our current chairman, bestseller Katie Fforde or New Writers' Scheme organiser Louise Allen (five books at 80,000-ish words and a novella coming out for Harlequin Mills & Boon this year)—in what is laughingly called their spare time. The tasks can roughly be grouped into three headings: education, promotion of romantic fiction and services to members.

It will be clear from this book how important the President is, for her counsel, her experience, occasionally her diplomatic assistance, and her continuity (just three in 50 years!), though notionally her term of office lasts for three years, renewable by agreement. She is entitled to attend meetings, and generally does, but she is not a member of the committee and is not expected to undertake an administrative role.

There are five officers: Chairman, whose term of office is limited to two years, after which he or she leaves the committee for at least a year; Vice Chairman, Hon Secretary, Hon Treasurer and Hon Deputy Treasurer. In the days before email, the officers would often run their bit of the organisation without consultation, simply reporting their activities to the committee *post hoc*. Now that consultation is easier, it is usually possible to consult, even when something needs a quick decision. Committee membership is limited to eight consecutive years. Only full members (that is, published authors) and associate members may sit on the committee, which is limited under the constitution to a maximum of 16. We are currently up to that figure.

Education
Our two major education activities are: the New Writers' Scheme and the annual conference, both covered in separate sections. We also arrange regular London meetings, addressed by individual speakers or a panel from the industry, and from time to time we hold one-day workshops, as the need seems to arise, such as a Money Day for Authors in 2005.

Promotion of romantic fiction
The big push on this comes from awarding the Romantic Novel of the Year, to which we are committed by our constitution. With 200 or so titles submitted, running the Award itself is a big job and the committee member responsible may have administrative assistance from among the general membership. Our younger Award, the Love Story of the Year, presented at the same time, is run by another committee member

Since 1960 the RNA has run a lunch or dinner to present the Association's major awards. Organising that event is so time-consuming that another committee member has to undertake it, again with administrative assistance from the wider membership.

And finally, the PR for the awards falls within the remit of a dedicated PR officer, a third committee member. The PR Officer is also responsible for managing the new RNA blog and the website, re-launched in glittering new form for the 50th anniversary at *http://www.romanticnovelistsassociation.org/*

The website contains information about the RNA, a calendar of events and application forms if you have to book, and a dedicated media centre for our press releases. The latest feature to be added is an A to Z of author members, with a photograph and a brief profile. The PR Officer is usually the first port of call for the media and organisations seeking a speaker—now they will be able to browse. She also issues press notices on notable RNA activities, such as the awards or the launch of our 50th anniversary collection of short stories, *Loves Me, Loves Me Not.*

Services to members

The main service to members, of course, is to keep them in touch with each other and with developments in the industry as we hear about them. The main RNA production is the in-house magazine, now called *Romance Matters*. The Hon Editor and Production Editor sit on the Committee. The magazine is almost unrecognisable from the old Gestetnered *RNA News*. These days it is in beautiful colour and full of photographs of our events. But it still contains think pieces and contributions from members. The old Sales talk, however, has been discontinued, as authors announce their books just before publication date on the RNA e-group and on a monthly forthcoming titles list, which appears on the RNA blog.

Libraries continue to be of major importance to us (PLR is an important constituent to the income of many RNA members) and we enormously value the co-operation we receive from them, for instance Jane Mathieson and her team at Manchester Central Library. There is a committee member with responsibility for libraries liaison.

Finally, there are the mainly social events, the central-London summer and winter parties. Building on Mary Burchell's proud tradition, we have achieved a bit of a name for giving a good bash.

These parties have become a regular fixture and are well attended by all sections of the membership. The organiser sits on the committee.

Regional chapters

Chapters and regional meetings, which are some of the liveliest RNA get-togethers, take place at the initiative of local members. The committee is not involved in organising them but a list, together with the contact details of the local organiser, appears in every copy of *Romance Matters*. In addition, the organisers generally remind members of an imminent lunch or meeting on the ROMNA e-group. Some will get together for lunch; some will have speakers on every occasion; some have speakers from time to time. At the last count, RNA chapters are active in: Birmingham, Cambridge, Carmarthen, Chelmsford, Leicester, London-South-East, Maidstone—possibly the newest—Manchester, Marches, Northern (Flying Ducks)—probably the oldest—North Devon, North Wales (Dragon), North West, North-umberland (Border Rievers), Oxford, Reading, Southern.

Who can join

To quote the constitution again:

> **Full members** Those who have published or had accepted for publication at least one full length romantic novel, whether modern or historical, or one romantic serial. Have full voting rights.
>
> **Associate members** Publishers, editors, literary agents, booksellers, book reviewers, publishers' readers, librarians and, by invitation of the Committee, such other persons who can, in the opinion of the Committee, provide specialised services to the Association. Have full voting rights.
>
> **Probationary members** (that is, on New Writers' Scheme). Unpublished writers who shall submit each year for evaluation a suitable manuscript for the New Writers' Scheme. New Writer membership does not carry any voting rights.

Full members

When the RNA first started, the organisers expected that the main problem would come from published writers of unromantic novels wishing to join. (In the earliest days there was a bit of feeling about whether historical novels could be regarded as primarily romantic, for instance, or were another genre entirely.) In practice, unless there are very obvious difficulties, successive committees have tended to take the view that if you think you have written a romantic novel, you probably have. This has meant that the RNA manages to keep up with a rapidly evolving genre without continually amending the constitution.

The concept of what constitutes publishing, however, is altogether more thorny, especially since the growth of e-books and print-on-demand. Both these forms of book production involve a great deal less capital investment than traditional publishing. As a result self-publishing is now an affordable option for many writers who have failed or chosen not to sell their work to a recognised publisher. The committee continues to keep the issues under review but, at the time of going to press, we had evolved the principle of looking for proof of an arm's length relationship between writer and publisher for a writer to be eligible for full membership of the RNA. For that reason, if a book has been published by a press previously unknown to us, or by an e-publisher with a range of different contracts, the Hon Membership Secretary has the discretion to ask for sight of the terms of the contract.

E-published eligibility

The committee's position remains the same as that set out in the March 2005 *RNA News*:

The e-published writer

Increasing numbers of people ask the RNA whether being electronically published counts in the criteria for full membership. At our March meeting the committee discussed the issues in some detail. We acknowledged that we don't want to be Luddite but we strongly suspect that

there are scams out there on the World Wide Web which do professional authors no favours. So in coming to a conclusion we took into account:
- the need to guard our professional standards
- continuing development of electronic media in general
- the need not to appear to endorse fly-by-night operations which exploit authors.

We have come up with a solution that, we hope, deals with these points. For the purposes of eligibility for full membership, publishing in electronic media shall be acceptable provided that:

1. the author has an enforceable commercial contract from the electronic publishing company, which must be properly established as a bona fide business in an appropriate jurisdiction
2. the contract provides for the author to receive an advance and/or royalties
3. the contract stipulates that the author will receive a proper accounting of sales and payment of royalties at agreed dates
4. it is not an essential part of the contract that the author contributes to publishing costs
5. the novel is subject to publisher selection before acceptance
6. the novel receives proper editorial input.

Meanwhile we will keep the whole issue under review. Anyone with experience, pro or con, of an electronic publisher - or other relevant information or experience - is encouraged to let one of the Committee have the details.

Self-publishing

Again, we are looking for clear evidence that the author has not contributed in any way to the publishing venture, either by capital investment, bearing part or all of the costs of printing, distribution or publicity, or by forgoing royalties until the 'publisher' has recouped his costs; or by any other form of influence.

That is not to say that the RNA disapproves of self-publishing *per se*. (Although, having said that, we are aware of many elephant traps, especially unexpected costs, into which hopeful but unwary authors have fallen. We pointed out some of these in an article in the 2010

Spring edition of *Romance Matters* about the information needed and risks to be aware of in self-publishing.) Yet self-publishing has a role in the twenty-first century. Several of our members have self-published books they believe in, both fact and fiction, which could not expect a sufficiently wide sale to interest a commercial publisher.

To be eligible to join as a Full Member of the RNA, however, you must have one book or serial published under an arm's length contract with a third-party publisher.

Information essential for writers

The RNA is not a campaigning organisation; members' interests are generally too disparate for that. But we do seek to share information of use to people who may want to join relevant campaigns or simply to alert members to industry risks and opportunities. This we do through *Romance Matters* or the RNA e-group. A historical example, however, is the RNA's long-term interest in Public Lending Right.

Public Lending Right campaign

Popular romantic fiction took a terrible hit from the closure of commercial lending libraries. Increasingly authors were looking to the public libraries, who had now become a monopoly supplier, to provide authors with some sort of financial recognition of the loans their books achieved. Public Lending Right Schemes existed in Germany and Denmark but there was a lot of resistance to introducing one in the UK.

In New Year 1970, the *RNA News* reported a letter to the *Daily Telegraph* from an Erith Councillor, John Cade, replying to an article of 27th August dealing with the public library boom and pointing out the case for a small charge to form a royalty for authors. How much longer, pleads the *RNA News* Editor, 'will people make sensible suggestions of this kind without the slightest action following from official circles?'

But objections were real. Many people, including some RNA members, wanted to maintain the principle of free borrowing by all. Librarians were worried that the cost of administration, as well as the royalty itself, would absorb too much of their budget for buying books. Others had objections of principle to State payment for what they felt should be a commercial activity. Many authors had lost heart and never believed it would happen.

WAG

Then the Writers' Action Group (WAG) was set up by Maureen Duffy, Brigid Brophy, Lettice Cooper, Michael Levey and Francis King. They had a friendly peer in Lord Ted Willis, the television and screen writer responsible for *Dixon of Dock Green* among other programmes, who sat on the Labour benches. By charging £1 a year to join, they managed to finance a study which concluded that a sample of 10 per cent of library loans would be sufficient to reflect a fair pattern of library borrowings. There were, of course, some squabbles between various interest groups in the early days but some RNA members, conscious of the loss of commercial libraries, signed up immediately and set out to convince others. RNA minutes show that Jane Aiken Hodge, pledged to speak at the RNA on 6th March 1974, asked if, in addition to speaking about her own writing, she might put in a few words on Public Lending Right. The committee welcomed it.

Already, on 31st January 1974, WAG had held an open meeting at Caxton Hall. Vice President Anne Maybury and the Chairman, Leila MacKinlay, attended as did Renée Shann, Anne Worboys and other individual members not part of the RNA's committee. There was a full report in the *RNA News* which emphasised that WAG 'have now made up their differences with the Society of Authors' – that would be important to a number of the Founder members in particular – and urging members to get involved.

From RNA News Spring 1974

Open Meeting on Public Lending Rght

The first speaker was Lord Goodman, introduced by the Chairman, Lord Willis. 25 years have passed since the idea of a Public Lending Right for books was first

```
mooted and Minister for Arts, Mr St John Stevas, thinks
'efforts will be crowned with success'. 'The only thing
you don't pay for in a library is the author,' said Lord
Goodman.
     Maureen Duffy then read letters; some very sad,
from elderly writers on the breadline, and among the
telegrams of good wishes was one from Denise Robins.
     The original AP Herbert scheme included a 10% cut for
publishers, and this idea has now been dropped.
     Phillip Hughes of Logica, a computer firm, said that
taking a random sample of borrowing was 'technically
possible'.
     Footnote: 'Owing to the Election there was no second
reading of the PLR bill in February; however we are
assured that three major parties are in total agreement
that the Bill should go ahead. When? Meanwhile keep on
at your local MP!'
LEILA MACKINLAY
```

Betty Neels, not yet a legend, though she had been a loyal Mills & Boon writer for many years, wrote to congratulate the Editor on the Spring issue of the *RNA News*, 'Most especially the Public Lending Rights article. This seems to be something the general public know almost nothing about and, as I know of no one else who writes in this part of the country'—Westward Ho, Martinstown, near Dorchester—'and find it well nigh impossible to get to meetings, I was delighted to hear something about it.'

Nothing happened under the new Government and in 1975 there was a march through central London by authors protesting in support of PLR. Bills were drafted and rejected. In Winter 1976 one actually got to the floor of the House but the *RNA News* reports, 'Chances for the Public Lending Bill seem nil since, owing to a technical ploy in Parliament, it was "talked out". With a crowded (and controversial) session ahead, what are the hopes that authors will ever get their fair deal with regard to Library borrowings?' Keep up the pressure is the message, then and for the next three years.

Public Lending Right Act

Then in March 1979, the Public Lending Right Act was passed under the Callaghan government. It gave writers a legal right to receive payment for the free lending out of their books by public libraries. The government fell in May and prospects for implementation of PLR did not look very hopeful under the incoming Thatcher administration. But, in the end, the detailed PLR Scheme was put in place in 1982.

Public Lending Right payments

In 1984 they made their first payment. Most borrowed author? Catherine Cookson. She remained in the top bracket for the next 20 years. And Georgette Heyer was the most borrowed author in 2005, 84 years after her first book was published and 31 after she died.

Public Lending Right payments have been of enormous importance to RNA members. As RNA author Liz Fielding said, raising a virtual glass on her blog to the hard working staff on PLR's 30th birthday, 'It provides a vital source of income for all authors, but most especially those whose books are primarily a "library" read. There are in fact some publishers—Severn House, Linford, FA Thorpe, Robert Hale for example—whose books are bought almost wholly by public libraries. The reality of the situation is that while a handful of authors make the headlines with seven figure advances, the majority earn considerably less than the minimum wage.'

As the RNA told the *Guardian* (28th June 2010), 'PLR is important to people who are having hiccups in their career and pretty important for newly published authors as well. The division between bestsellers and everyone else is huge. If you don't produce huge sales in your first couple of books, you're gone. The point about PLR is that it will actually help to feed the author while they're trying to find another voice or genre or pen name, because that's what they have to do.'

We were very glad to welcome the first director, John Sumsion, in 1987 and the present director, Dr Jim Parker, has given talks both in London and at the conference in Leicester in 2005. One of the earliest arguments against the scheme was the cost of administration, but technology and good management was delivering the service to 45,000 authors in 2009 by just the director and the equivalent of nine full time staff. In May 2010, they undertook to find further savings in the running costs of the Scheme to help offset the overall three per cent reduction in PLR funding by the incoming Government.

For the benefit of RNA posterity, as this book goes to press, funding for the next three years (2011-14) will be agreed by Ministers in the autumn after the government completes its spending review. PLR is the only government support offered to an industry which is a big contributor to the Invisibles account. We hope that the next agreement on public funding will recognise that.

Chairmen

2009-	Katie Fforde
2007-09	Catherine Jones
2005-07	Jenny Haddon
2003-05	Anthea Kenyon
2001-03	Jean Chapman
1999-2001	Norma Curtis
1997-99	Angela Arney
1995-97	Elizabeth Buchan
1993-95	Jean Saunders
1991-93	Marina Oliver
1989-91	Margaret Pemberton
1987-89	Tilly Armstrong
1985-87	Sheila Walsh
1983-85	Diana Morgan
1981-83	Constance Heaven
1979-81	Clare Cavendish
1977-79	Elizabeth Harrison
1975-77	Nancy Sawyer
1973-75	Leila MacKinlay
1971-73	Alice Chetwynd Ley
1969-71	Dorothy Mackie Low
1967-69	Stella March
1965-67	Sylvia Thorpe
1963-65	Norrey Ford
1960-63	Alex (Vivian) Stuart

Presidents

1987-	Diane Pearson
1966-86	Mary Burchell
1960-66	Denise Robins

The Major Award

Diane Pearson writes:

The Major Award event is as old as the RNA itself and it is interesting to observe that the same problems and criticisms have beset the occasion since the very beginning. Expenses: endeavouring to keep the cost of the tickets at a level that members could afford and, inevitably, making a loss, have been with us right from the start. Notes by the various committee members are perennially fully of anguished contrivance as to how to balance the budget. Similarly there has always, right from the beginning, been criticism of the way the judging of the entries has been organised. This has resulted, over the years, in the methods of judging being constantly revised, a process that still continues. The more things change, the more they stay the same.

In the early days there were numerous awards, the Major, the Best Historical, the Fleetway, the Elinor Glyn, the President's Award et al which resulted in a criticism from Anne Britton that there were too many awards. Eventually, some were abandoned and others moved to different occasions.

In 1964 some members complained that that year's winner had treated the RNA 'rather casually'. Apparently the winner, Suzanne Ebel, had gone on TV after winning the prize and said—what? Not recorded, but obviously putting the RNA in its place. Later it was reported that she was upset to think her interview had given offence and she subsequently joined the Association.

Another interesting snippet from 1964 stresses that a notice must be put in the *RNA News* that 'the dinner is black tie'. Obviously someone had turned up inappropriately dressed at the previous year's dinner.

The guests in those early years were remarkably distinguished and famous. We obviously concentrated on celebrities rather than, as now, hard core book trade people—that is, publishers, agents, booksellers and journalists. One has a lingering regret for those glamorous names—Dame Sybil Thorndike, Sir Lewis Casson, Dorothy Eden, Ernest and Diana Raymond, Richard Gordon, Ian Fleming, Ginette Spanier. I also remember the dinner when I first joined and they were very glamorous indeed. Every gentleman was in black tie, and ladies wore extravagant long evening dresses, furs, and occasionally the odd tiara. For my first attendance I took an elderly Hungarian gentleman who was knocked out by the glitter! 'So many romantic ladies,' he kept murmuring as one fabulous evening dress after another swept down the stairs.

There was constant discussion over whether the award ceremony should be a dinner (glamorous) or a luncheon (practical). One former chairman complained that the dinners were boring. (This may have been because we had rather too many speakers and some of them went on too long.) It was discovered that more people came to the dinners as they brought their partners, but more RNA members came to the lunch. So infinitely wise Mary Burchell said that was a good reason for keeping both, and so it was for quite a few years until finally the dinners were scrapped altogether.

Prizes

In the early days the prizes varied between a brooch, a small sum of money, a specially bound edition of the prize-winning book, and a small statue/symbol of some kind. Then, in 1985, Rosie de Courcy said that in order to give the award clout and attract more publicity, there must be a large, lavish cash prize and Anthony

Cheetham suggested that publishers should be approached for a contribution. In all, the system worked and some publishers were very generous (others were not) and £2,000 was raised and presented at the next awards luncheon. This, in fact, was not the first time a publisher had been generous to us, as in 1965 Hurst & Blackett had donated ten guineas towards the prizes.

In 1988 we had our first major sponsorship from Boots who gave a prize of £3,000 plus £2,000 in public relations services. Boots, who at that time were a major bookselling chain, were delightful sponsors and each year presented every guest with a small gift. There was one of our members who took her small box of coloured jellies and ate one on the train home only to discover they were soap bubbles. Alas, Boots finally made the decision not to sell books any more and in 1994 we no longer had a sponsor. We were back to relying on the publishers' contributions with a top-up from the RNA's own funds. Then, in 1998, Parker Pens came on board (lovely pens as gifts for all the guests) and stayed with us until 2004. In 2005 and 2006 we had Foster Grant Reading Glasses (a pair of glasses for every guest). During the reign of these last two sponsors the prize went up to a hefty £10,000. Since then we've managed with the help of the publishers' contributions and whatever the RNA could afford. Inevitably the amount of the prize has fluctuated.

The Awards ceremony

The RNA Awards Luncheon involves an enormous amount of planning and preparation—booking the venue, haggling over prices and menus, organising the seating plan and managing the Press Room. There was one occasion when our guest speaker, subsequently a disgraced Tory peer and an avid seeker after publicity, refused to leave the Press Room and its reporters. So we had to start the lunch with his seat at the top table unoccupied. He eventually joined us when the Press Room was empty.

We have used a wide variety of venues over the years—the Connaught Rooms, the Park Lane, the Waldorf, the Café Royal, the Savoy and, at present, the Royal Garden. There is always a team at the venue from quite early on the actual day, organising decorations such as balloons, roses and streamers, and setting out displays of books and the placement cards.

Recollections of the Awards ceremony

Calligrapher Pamela Hudson on the run up to the great day:
It's many years since I opened my copy of the RNA magazine and saw a small paragraph asking if any member could do calligraphy. It caught my eye because I've always enjoyed doing this kind of writing, but as I'm self-taught I was reluctant to volunteer. However, though I don't think I am committee material, I am very happy to do something behind the scenes for the Association from which I receive so much. I tentatively offered a sample of what I could do and it was accepted almost by return of post. I have been writing place cards for the RNA Awards Luncheons ever since, first at the Café Royal, then the Savoy Hotel, and this year the Royal Garden Hotel.

Over the years I've worked with several different people whose job is organising the tickets and place settings, beginning with Sue Sallis. She sent me lists by post, the computer not being so readily used then, and I posted the finished cards back in batches ready to be sorted. Since then I've liaised with Betty O'Rourke, Audrey Willsher, Roger Sanderson, Catherine Jones, and most recently Jane Gordon Cumming. The system of sending lists by email and the cards by post seems to work very well. Usually there are over 300 to write so the process begins in January as soon as enough people have applied for tickets. Near to the date it becomes a little hectic, with phone calls to add extra names, and I always arrive at the venue with a calligraphy pen and spare cards, but it's something I enjoy doing and will be happy to continue with as long as the organisers approve.

Claire Lorrimer's account of the inauguration dinner:
I was at the inauguration dinner, a truly gala romantic affair, at which such celebrities as Ian Fleming were present. With

AP Herbert as Guest of Honour, the new Association got off to an excellent start with the publicity it needed.

For once I was feeling appropriately dressed for the occasion, my mother (Denise Robins) having lent me her beautiful emerald necklace as it matched so perfectly my emerald evening gown. I was seated next to a childhood friend, Michael Pertwee, the playwright, best known perhaps for the Brian Rix comedies.

We were both looking forward to the speeches, unaware that the main speaker, Dennis Wheatley, was one of those authors who are brilliant with the written word but not with the spoken—as Michael muttered to me as the minutes ticked laboriously by. Had the contents of the speech been amusing, witty or informative we, along with the rest of the guests, might not have been so relieved when the author stopped talking and reached for his glass of water. As it was, we all started clapping enthusiastically. The noise of our adulation slowly petered out as Mr Wheatley drew a deep breath and, to our acute embarrassment, proceeded with the second half of his lengthy speech. I do wish Michael was still alive as he often recounted this little irritation in an otherwise wonderful evening, quite hilariously.

Anne Weale on the first Awards dinner:
Who would have guessed, on the glamorous night of the first Awards, when Denise Robins' black velvet dress was trimmed with chinchilla and the cloakroom was full of mink coats bought with royalties, that 30 years on furs would be taboo?

Nancy Sawyer on some of the early Awards dinners:
Sadly (maddeningly) the RNA archives don't have any written records of its first year's activities. No minutes, no *RNA News*—just a solitary photograph of that dinner. Written records only start in 1961 when the Association was already a year old. The dinner in the autumn of 1961 was held at the Connaught Rooms and the price of the tickets then was £11.25. Despite the small membership of the RNA no less than 311 people attended the dinner. The functions were

very grand affairs, thanks to the presence of those two queens of romance, Barbara Cartland and Denise Robins. And in those days of course everyone had to stand waiting in a receiving line to have their names announced by the toastmaster and be greeted by the President and Chairman. This practice went on until at least 1977.

It's great to see the names of all the celebrities who graced the Award functions in earlier days: John Braine, Russell Braddon, Ted Willis, AP Herbert, Beverly Nichols, RF Delderfield, Dorothy Eden, Sybil Thorndyke and Lewis Casson, Michael Dennison and Dulcie Gray, Rupert Davies (Maigret), Michael Gilbert, Victor Canning, Winston Graham, Henry Cecil, Monica Dickens, Ginette Spanier, Claire Rayner, Penelope Lively, Robert Kilroy-Silk, Jilly Cooper, Katherine Whitehorn and Simon Brett, to name but a few.

Another big change in our fortunes came in the mid-eighties when, in an effort to add further prestige to the RNA Award, the committee decided to invite those publishers who had romantic authors on their lists to become sponsors. Several generously agreed. This meant that in 1986 the RNA was able to give its winner a prize of £2,000. Then for several years Boots became our main sponsors.

The late Tilly Armstrong remembered:
When I first joined the RNA, the Awards lunch was very much more formal than it is now—in fact it alternated with an evening dinner which required considerable dressing up. I remember one dire occasion in my early days when the after-dinner speaker was completely incoherent and we had difficulty in understanding a single word he said. Subsequent inspection of the hotel bill revealed that he had ordered himself several double brandies, in addition to the wine on the table, which was an expense we had not budgeted for.

At another lunch we nearly wiped out Mills & Boon when a whole table of editors and authors succumbed to food poisoning caused by duck which had not been properly defrosted or adequately cooked. As Secretary, I got in touch with the RNA solicitors who needed to be supplied with the names of everyone who had been affected, and then it came out that there had been a scattering of people at other tables. The hotel refunded the cost of the lunch and, I believe, some compensation, but Mills & Boon were down to a skeleton staff (almost literally) for several days.

It was while I was Chairman that we negotiated our first sponsorship when Boots responded to one of my hopeful letters. The idea of sponsorship had come from Rosie de Courcy who was also responsible for gingering up our ideas about our newsletter, which was then just a couple of sheets of photocopied A5 paper stapled together. Boots at that time had offices at Putney Bridge and Elizabeth Harrison and I went along to talk to their representatives. Of course that was in the days when Boots had a book department and they planned to promote the shortlist in store. My memory is a little hazy on the figures, but I seem to remember that, with a dry throat and aghast at my daring, I suggested that the Award should be no less than £3,000, only to find that was exactly the figure they had in mind.

They also offered to do the publicity in-house, which seemed a good idea.

What I should have done was to ask Boots to pay for the journalists' lunches as well. They turned out to be quite an expense for the Association. One coup Boots managed to pull off was to get Katherine Whitehorn to write an article about the lunch. I went to meet her at the Arts Club in Chelsea, which was a bit of a disaster because I was early, she was late, and no one thought to tell her that I was waiting for her. However, when we did get together we had lunch and I filled her in with all the details about the RNA, trying to put across that we were an organisation worthy of respect. The resulting article was very funny—if you were not on the receiving end. The Boots representatives loved it and I smiled with the best of them, but in private I sat down and cried. It was so exactly what we did not want written about us and the description of me was a far cry from the way I saw myself.

Recollections of Award winners

Early days

The very first winner in 1960 was Mary Howard with *More than Friendship*, published by Collins. (A profile of Howard and her work appears in our chapter 'Traditional versus modern'.)

Mike Legat recalls:

There was an early arrangement that Corgi bought the paperback rights in whichever book won the RNA prize. That was when I first met Vivien (Alex) Stuart who was one of the joint founders of the RNA. The presentation was at a dinner when all the top people were present, including Barbara Cartland. She was wearing a crinoline and looked like a life-sized version of the thing that some people used to have to put over their telephones. Rosetta [Mike Legat's wife] thought it was part of the decoration especially for the RNA. She was quite startled when it turned out to be Barbara.

I know that Margaret Maddocks was a subsequent winner and we published her book. Of course it was in the days before Mills & Boon and Hurst & Blackett were producing their own paperbacks, but when trade conditions changed it was no longer possible for Corgi to have the exclusive, so the arrangement fizzled out.

Margaret Maddocks

One of the curiosities about the Main Award is that the person who holds the record for winning it most often was neither a bestseller nor hugely prolific. Margaret Maddocks won first in 1962 for *Larksbrook*, in 1965 for *The Silver Answer*; in 1970 she tied with Rona Randall and Joanne Marshall (Anne Rundle) with her novel *Thea*; and in 1976, the first year in which the RNA selected two winners, one historical, one contemporary, she took the Modern Award with *The Moon is Square*.

Nancy Sawyer recalls Margaret Maddocks loving to tell the story that her husband said to her, 'For God's sake don't win the RNA Award again—we can't afford it.' In those early days the winner was informed in advance and was expected to attend the dinner or luncheon—but she had to buy her own ticket and pay all the expenses involved. On one of those occasions Margaret was obliged to return from a holiday in Portugal for the event. And what was the prize? A brooch and a leather-bound copy of her book. As for publicity, almost none. 'The RNA Award at that time did little to further a writer's career,' says Nancy wryly.

Reviewers spoke of Margaret Maddocks's books having a quiet charm of style. Winston Graham (of *Poldark* fame), adjudicating in 1976, said *The Moon is Square* was a novel whose characters thought and talked convincingly and who were manipulated with a detachment that never became patronising. He wondered whether her portrait of a romantic novelist was a self study. ('Not entirely,' said Margaret, 'perhaps partly.') She herself described the book as being about misunderstandings between two generations.

She was a much valued RNA member, who used to host 'delightful RNA Fork Luncheons' in her Kent house—but in those days all Award Judges were held rigorously at arm's length from the RNA and could not even be members. So her Fork Suppers cannot have influenced their judgement. Besides, there were always many other valued RNA members on the shortlist too.

She had been educated at St Helen's Northwood, and Dresden, and travelled in Central Europe as her father's interpreter, becoming, at twenty, secretary to the manager of an oil company in Bucharest. But by the time she joined the RNA she was married, wrote poetry, short stories and articles, as well as novels, liked gardening, cooking and sewing and was an active member of the Women's Institute.

She wrote 17 books in total, mostly for Hurst & Blackett until it folded.

Constance Heaven. Diane Pearson writes:
I can recall the shock when Constance Heaven won the RNA Award in 1973 with *The House of Kuragin*. It proved to be a watershed in the prize's history. Until that time, the winners had all been shorter books with more concise plots and smaller cast lists. Suddenly an epic-sized, huge-canvassed book had won, romantic in the grandest sense. I

remember the publishers being gobsmacked as they realised they could have put in *big* books that, while still coming generally under the heading romantic, were also vast in content and ambitions. From that time on, the books submitted for the award expanded to include an enormous range of subjects, treatments, size and interpretations.

Constance Heaven, a convent girl and former actress, told the *RNA News* that she grew up on a diet of *Don Quixote*, ancient Egyptian history, Homer, archaeology and *The Three Musketeers*. History was her passion and, under the name Constance Fecher, she had already published a novel about Raleigh. It was written at a time of great personal distress, she said. Widowed and in debt, she was working as an understudy to Cecily Courtneidge and a friend challenged her to make Raleigh live as a person. Writing that book saved her from floundering into self-pity. Later, in a talk to the RNA in January 1975, she confessed that *The House of Kuragin* had a less emotional genesis; 'it had been written in a fit of rage because Heinemann's turned down my book *The Night of the Wolf*. So I decided to write what they wanted me to write, and the result was so good and so successful that my views have changed as a result'.

Her win certainly got a good deal of media attention, including a television interview. And in February 1974 she went on a breathless Pan Promotion Day in Birmingham with a whole day full of interviews, several book shop signings, and a cocktail party for 75 press, publishers and booksellers. She and her 'Pan boys' eventually sat down to dinner at 10pm!

She became a bestseller and a great supporter of the RNA. She was Chairman 1981-83.

Jay Allerton

The winner of the 1975 Award was *Vote for a Silk Gown* by Jay Allerton, otherwise known as RNA member May Martin. She recalls:

Like all women I remember what I wore, a two-piece dress

consisting of shirt-waist top and accordion-pleated skirt. Clothes have always meant a great deal to me.

Nancy Sawyer was appointed as my guide, philosopher and friend, and we have kept in touch since then, if possible. My family were thrilled, and I know Helen, my daughter, was there. I have no recollection of my husband or son. If they weren't there, they would have had a good reason, but I do remember masses of flowers, and being presented with a specially embossed copy of my book.

I remember being impressed by the comments of Maurice Edelman MP, because truth to tell I felt a bit of an impostor, as I thought *Vote for a Silk Gown* was scarcely a romantic novel. At this stage I should explain the title; there is a Scottish saying which was frequently used by my mother, 'Vote for a silk gown and you'll get the sleeve of it', in other words, 'Aim high'.

However, I cheer myself up by telling myself that perhaps my book helped to break the popular conception that the romantic novel was stereotyped.

Certainly it was the butt of many journalists. I do remember the words of one publisher or commentator that in the writing of them the bedroom door should be firmly shut. You can't say that of many novels of today. The best example of a romantic novel in my opinion would be *Wuthering Heights*.

Subsequently I wrote for many publishers, including Harper Collins, and under different pseudonyms, Jane Wallace, Jay Allerton and Frances Paige. I always wrote full steam ahead, and my Olivetti went with me everywhere.

When publishers began to want tapes or discs, at the age of 80 I bought my first computer, and I couldn't be replying to you today were it not for my familiarity with the keyboard, despite having lost my sight.

Latterly, I've been writing for Severn House. I have written two books for them since the age of 90, and it's been a great blow to me to have to give up. My advice to all writers is to keep on writing as long as you can. You'll miss it!

From the RNA News Summer 1975

Romantic Novel of the Year 1975

Winning Author of 'Vote for a Silk Gown' (Troubador),
Jay Allerton says:'The work ethic of my war-time Glasgow
did not permit a young wife and mother to take time
off to write novels. Consequently I was in my forties
and happily settled in Lancaster before I had a rush of
words to the head.' Forgetting Calvinistic forebears she
confesses to a pretty ragged life style. Only 'essential
chores' are done. She and her husband travel 'at the
drop of a hat . . . anybody's.' He is a psychiatrist. In
between they have frequent visits from their daughter
'on the Guardian staff' and even 'more infrequent taped
messages from our son who is working as a radiologist
under the aegis of Harvard University.'
    She ends by recounting a dream in which she imagines
herself being interviewed by the national press and asked
to 'define a romantic novel'. She replies: 'A novel first
and foremost. The prefix romantic does not indicate that
a changeling has been born. It must have imagination and
sympathy.' Happy ending? 'Not necessarily. It should
follow life more closely than that.' Ignore what goes on
behind the bedroom door? 'Where have you been all these
years? Haven't you heard of open planning?'
    Adjudicating, Maurice Edelman MP described
'Vote for a Silk Gown', as having lucidity, shape,
elusiveness. He said the award was going to an
outstanding author of an outstanding book. Hearty
congratulations to Jay. And also to Miss Leslie Saxby
of the new Troubador company who published the book.

Madeleine Brent:

Merlin's Keep won in 1978. It was by Madeleine Brent who had been
previously shortlisted in 1974 for *Moonraker's Bride*. She was said to
be in Mexico on the date of the dinner, so her publisher picked up
the award for her. The mystery deepened when her biographical
details claimed that she had written for newspapers, magazines, films
and TV and that *Merlin's Keep* was inspired by tales of a great uncle

who served with Younghusband in Tibet. Members were invited to guess Brent's identity—apparently without success. Many years later she turned out to be Peter O'Donnell, author of *Modesty Blaise*.

Valerie Fitzgerald and Susan Kay:
Zemindar by Valerie Fitzgerald, which won the prize in 1982, was another huge epic-scaled book with a distinguished provenance. It had already won the hugely coveted Historical Novel Competition set up by Bodley Head and Corgi Paperbacks in memory of Georgette Heyer. And in 1991 Susan Kay, another winner of the Heyer prize, won the RNA Award with her second novel *Phantom*.

Joanna Trollope:
For three years, a separate prize was given for the best historical and the best modern romantic novel. On the last occasion, 1980, the best of the best was judged to be the historical novel *Parson Harding's Daughter* by Joanna Trollope. She had rather mixed reactions when the prize was actually presented, however. She recalls:

William Douglas-Home was giving the prizes and I was, at that time, and under my then married name of Joanna Potter, teaching at a mixed prep school in Hampshire. Among my pupils was WD-H's sweet daughter, Dinah, and—for reasons I won't go into!—WD-H and I had just had what my grandmother used to call words, at a recent parents' evening. So, as I approached the stage to receive the prize, WD-H was reading out his polite praise of *Parson Harding's Daughter* by Joanna Trollope, without looking up... And then, when I was practically standing on his feet, he glanced up and his expression completely changed and he exploded. 'You're not Joanna Trollope!' he almost bellowed. 'You're wretched Mrs Potter!!' Except that he didn't say wretched...!

Marie Joseph:
Marie Joseph was already a major bestseller when *A Better World than This* won the RNA Award in 1987. Set in the 1930s, it vividly recounts

the hard life of a young girl in a family business and the bullying and petty cruelties of one generation of strong, grudge-bearing women against another. Then a man who looks like Clark Gable walks into spinster Daisy Bell's shop and she is lost ... Her publisher called it 'undoubtedly the finest novel that Marie Joseph has ever written.'

Her daughter writes:
Marie Joseph was born in May 1920, in Blackburn Lancashire, to a cotton weaver mother and a father who had been nearly blinded by mustard gas in the Great War. Her mother died a day after Marie's birth and her father, broken-hearted, walked out of the hospital and left the premature baby in the arms of a shell-shocked soldier, who kept her under his blankets for two weeks, saving her life and giving him a renewed sense of purpose. (Fourteen years later an embarrassed Marie was introduced to him on a bus by her aunt and she fled in horror at the thought of this still attractive middle-aged man having held her to his bosom in bed.)

Having spent her first seven years of life with her maternal grandmother, who encouraged her quick brain and quietly adored her, she was then brought up by Aunt Lizzie, one of her mother's sisters, after little Marie had woken one morning to find her grandma dead in bed next to her.

Marie always loved words and read her first short story aloud to the school at the age of seven. It was about a snowdrop pushing its way through the cold earth one bitter January morning. There was no praise from Aunt Lizzie, who told her she was 'a show-off, just like your father', whom Marie had never met.

Marie went on to win a free scholarship to Blackburn High School for Girls and excelled at English, French, history and drama, failing miserably at maths, which she could never understand the point of! She won the English Prize three years running and her intense love of words encouraged her to start writing fiction after she had developed rheumatoid arthritis at the age of 25, at the end of World War II, when her first child was only four months old. Her devoted husband Frank returned from Canada, where he had been an officer in the RAF, to find his wife crippled with pain but struggling bravely to look after their baby daughter.

After many years of painful and largely unsuccessful treatments, Marie stoically accepted that she would never be able to climb mountains or ever cope with a journey into London for a job! She bought a cheap typewriter and started to write all the stories she had carried in her head for years. To her great delight, her very first story was accepted for publication by *The Lady*. It was called *A Rose by Any Other Colour,* a lighthearted, warm little story, with a twist in the tail, for which she received the grand sum of £10! Her two daughters were by now awkward teenagers, and more lighthearted stories followed, published by both weekly and monthly magazines.

From the age of forty for the next fourteen years, Marie wrote hundreds of short stories and serials for major women's magazines. In 1974, however, the Fiction Editor of *Woman's Own* persuaded her to expand one of her short stories into a novel, and her first book *The Guilty Party*, was published in 1975. In the same year a fellow writer, Jean Bowden, encouraged her to write an account of her struggle to come to terms with rheumatoid arthritis. Her autobiography, *One Step at a Time*, became a bestseller in its own right, was serialised on *Woman's Hour*, and was translated into many languages.

In the next 13 years of intense activity, she published another 13 novels, all of them set in her native Lancashire, principally in the inter-war years. Her last six novels all made the bestseller lists and seven of her books were shortlisted for the Romantic Novel of the Year, which she eventually won in 1987 with her penultimate novel, *A Better World Than This*. Her books have sold to more than twenty countries world-wide and sales of her paperbacks have topped two million.

Following the death of her eldest grandchild, Alison, in 1988, however, Marie never returned to her writing, other than to edit collections of her short stories from the 1960s and 1970s.

During the busiest part of her writing career, Marie underwent three knee replacements. (One wore out!) From the outset of her disease she was determined not to give in to arthritis, and to live as full and complete a life as possible. However great the pain was, she never let it show and never complained. She normally worked at her writing for three hours a day, but could type for only short periods because her hands would not hold up—she had to wear splints. (Those were the days before the miracle of word processors.) A lot of her working time was spent in careful research for her books, including long hours at the newspaper library in Colindale, so that every detail of the lives of her characters was accurate. But the most striking feature of her writing was her meticulous observation of the scenes of her youth and of the people among whom she grew up. She possessed a remarkable ability, in particular, to capture the warmth, wit, stoicism and determined optimism of working-class Lancashire.

Marie Joseph's novels are still to be seen, mainly on library shelves. Her hallmarks of humour, insight and compassion tinged with irony, have ensured that she is still one of the most heavily borrowed writers.

She was a member of the RNA and of the Society of Women Writers and Journalists until her death, and served on the Council of the latter body during the time of Joyce Grenfell's Presidency in the 1970s.

Marie died on 28th December 1996, her husband Frank dying four years later. She is still greatly missed by her two daughters, Marilyn and Kate, and by her seven grandchildren.

And finally a small tribute from an agent who completed the hat trick of having three authors winning the prize in consecutive years:

Jonathan Lloyd of Curtis Brown writes:
Agents don't win prizes and nor should they. The closest we come is when one of our clients achieves recognition. Even then we take no credit, but do feel pride in the same way as a parent when their child goes up on the stage to receive some accolade.

So I am proud to be the 'father' to three clients who have won the Romantic Novel of the Year Award, namely Erica James in 2006,

Rosie Thomas in 2007 and Freya North in 2008.

There is always a flutter of excitement arriving at the grand hotel for the drink before lunch, especially when one has a client on the short list. There is no point, I have discovered, singling out the judges. They give nothing away. Too friendly—they are feeling guilty about giving the prize to another. A bit cold—they are feeling guilty about giving the prize to another.

Of course the best source should be the client. If they know, they don't tell. And if they don't know, they don't tell! I now know the publisher may work it out from PR enquiries, and I realised when Erica James won that I was the only person on the table not to have been in the know.

The dining room is always packed. Rival agents pretend to be friendly but we know we are in competition. The shortlisted authors wish their fellows well and seem genuinely to mean it.

Drink is taken before and during the lunch and one of the great traditions is that the bar stays open for the afternoon and it is not uncommon for many of us not to make it back to the office.

It is a great day for the agent of a winning author. You don't have to make a speech, you bask in the reflected glory, and the bill for the champagne is not painful until the following morning.

Major Award winners

1960   *More than Friendship* by Mary Howard (Collins)
1961   *The Witches Sabbath* by Paula Allardyce (Hodder & Stoughton)
1962   *Larksbrook* by Margaret Maddocks (Hurst & Blackett)
1963   *House Divided* by Dorothy M Gray (Hurst & Blackett)
1964   *Journey from Yesterday* by Suzanne Ebel (Collins)
1965   *The Silver Answer* by Margaret Maddocks (Hurst & Blackett)
1966   No Award made as ceremony moved from December to following spring.
1967   *The Truth Game* by Anne Betteridge (Hurst & Blackett)
1968   *The Future is Forever* by Maynah Lewis (Hurst & Blackett)
1969   *Comfort and Keep* by Doris E Smith (Ward Lock)

1970   *Broken Tapestry* by Rona Randall (Hurst & Blackett) [joint winner]
1970   *Thea* by Margaret Maddocks (Hurst & Blackett) [joint winner]
1970   *Cat on a Broomstick* by Joanne Marshall (Herbert Jenkins) [joint winner]
1971   *Flower of Silence* by Joanne Marshall (Harlequin Mills & Boon)
1972   *The Pride of Innocence* by Maynah Lewis (Hurst & Blackett)
1973   *The House of Kuragin* by Constance Heaven (Heinemann)
1974   *The Burning Lamp* by Frances Murray (Hodder & Stoughton)
1975   *Vote for a Silk Gown* by Jay Allerton (Troubadour)
1976   *The Look of Innocence* by Anna Gilbert (Hodder & Stoughton)
1976   —Best Modern Award *The Moon is Square* by Margaret Maddocks (Hurst & Blackett)
1977   *Every Man A King* by Anne Worboys (Hodder & Stoughton)
1978   *Merlin's Keep* by Madeleine Brent (Souvenir)
1978   —Best Modern Award *It was the Lark* by Catherine Macarthur (Macdonald & Jane)
1979   *Countess* by Josephine Edgar (Macdonald & Jane)
1979   —Award of Special Merit *The Emerald Peacock* by Katharine Gordon (Hodder & Stoughton)

1980   *Parson Harding's Daughter* by Joanna Trollope (Hutchinson)
1980   —Best Modern Award: *Mr Rodriguez* by Mary Howard (Collins)
1981   *The Red Staircase* by Gwendoline Butler (Collins)
1982   *Zemindar* by Valerie Fitzgerald (Bodley Head)
1983   *Magic Flutes* by Eva Ibbotson (Century)
1984   *A Highly Respectable Marriage* by Sheila Walsh (Hurst & Blackett)
1985   *Sunrise* by Rosie Thomas (Piatkus)
1986   *A Song Twice Over* by Brenda Jagger (Collins)
1987   *A Better World Than This* by Marie Joseph (Century)
1988   *The Juniper Bush* by Audrey Howard (Century)
1989   *The Peacock's Feather* by Sarah Woodhouse (Century)

1990   *Passing Glory* by Reay Tannahill (Century)
1991   *Phantom* by Susan Kay (Transworld)
1992   *Sandstorm* by June Knox-Mawer (Weidenfeld)
1993   *Emily* by Cynthia Harrod-Eagles (Sidgwick & Jackson)
1994   *Consider the Lily* by Elizabeth Buchan (Macmilllan)
1995   *Change of Heart* by Charlotte Bingham (Doubleday)
1996   *Coming Home* by Rosamunde Pilcher (Hodder & Stoughton)
1997   *The Hours of the Night* by Sue Gee (Century)
1998   *Kiss and Kin* by Angela Lambert (Bantam)
1999   *Learning to Swim* by Clare Chambers (Arrow)

2000   *Dancing in the Dark* by Maureen Lee (Orion)
2001   *Someone Like You* by Cathy Kelly (Harper Collins)
2002   *The Other Boleyn Girl* by Philippa Gregory (Harper Collins)
2003   *Playing James* by Sarah Mason (Times Warner)
2004   *Foreign Fruit* by JoJo Moyes (Hodder & Stoughton)
2005   *A Good Voyage* by Katharine Davies (Chatto & Windus)
2006   *Gardens of Delight* by Erica James (Orion)
2007   *Iris and Ruby* by Rosie Thomas (Harper Collins
2008   *Pillow Talk* by Freya North (Harper Collins)
2009   *East of the Sun* by Julia Gregson (Orion)
2010   *Lost Dogs and Lonely Hearts* by Lucy Dillon (Hodder & Stoughton)

Love Story of the Year

As we came over the cusp of the twenty-first century, the RNA reviewed the Main Award and realised that the shortlists no longer represented the broad scope of romantic fiction. Shorter books, specifically those known as romance or category romance in the publishing trade and primarily produced by Harlequin Mills & Boon, just never made it onto the final shortlist. Yet a high proportion of our full members were published by HMB and an even higher proportion of the New Writers were targeting them. We knew that there was some first-class writing in these popular books. If we were to recognise excellence across the whole genre, we could not continue to ignore this large and profitable area of romantic fiction.

In 2003 we instituted our first award specifically for such novels, then called the Romance Prize. It was generously funded for the first five years of its life by our President, Diane Pearson, who also chaired the final judges. To mark the award, Harlequin Mills & Boon presented a silver rose bowl trophy in memory of Betty Neels, an RNA member and one of the readership's favourite authors, even after her death. The winner's name is engraved on the trophy, which is held for one year.

The award is now called the Love Story of the Year, which is perhaps an easier concept for non-publishing professionals. It recognises the best in novels that centre on the developing love affair between the hero and heroine. These stories are usually published in an easily recognisable format, with several books of similar type and length being released on a regular schedule. Serials in magazines are also eligible.

Judging is similar to that of the Romantic Novel of the Year. A panel of readers, who are members of the public, not aspiring or published novelists, read the books and rank them, based on such criteria as most enjoyable, good plot and characters etc. They are looking for books which touch their hearts. The final judges are professional writers, sometimes working in other creative fields such as film making. They select the overall winner from a shortlist of six.

Winners to date have been:

2003	*Illusion* by Julia Wild (Heartline)
2004	*A Damnable Rogue* by Anne Herries (Harlequin Mills & Boon)
2005	*A Family of His Own* by Liz Fielding (Harlequin Mills & Boon)
2006	*Contracted: Corporate Wife* by Jessica Hart (Harlequin Mills & Boon)
2007	*Marrying Max* by Nell Dixon (DC Thomson)
2008	*Breakfast at Giovanni's* by Kate Hardy (Harlequin Mills & Boon)
2009	*Mistress: Hired for the Billionaire's Pleasure* by India Grey (Harlequin Mills & Boon)
2010	*Animal Instincts* by Nell Dixon (Little Black Dress)

The conference

Unlike the New Writers' Scheme and the Major Award, which have been part of the RNA since the very beginning, the conference is a more recent innovation, beginning in 1998. By then many people were happily travelling to writing conferences and writing about them in the *RNA News* and many RNA members, like Elizabeth Harrison, Jean Saunders and others, were lecturing at them.

RNA conferences have proved popular. Indeed, they attract the largest numbers of purely RNA members of any event we organise. (The Main Awards Lunch attracts more people but many of them are non-member guests.) Over the last 13 years, a template for the ideal programme has evolved—and one or two venues have gone on the Never Again list.

Publishers are largely based in London and only willing to send speakers if a) they can get out from or back to the office within the day and b) they don't have to do it at weekends. (One Editorial Director said that her husband would leave her if she spent one more Saturday working away.) It must be said that Harlequin Mills & Boon is an honourable exception to this and, no matter where the conference takes place, regularly sends two of its editors, who will give a talk and also do ten-minute one-to-one interviews with authors targeting an HMB line. So, although we take the conference to venues round the country, every three years or so we return to London, where we add on a preliminary Friday, to invite speakers from the industry. In our anniversary year we were back in the capital, at the historic Royal Naval College in Greenwich.

Programmes vary, depending on the hot topics of the moment and, of course, who is available to speak. But we have found that an author panel at some point early in the conference is a good way to kick off discussion. This year, we aimed for a panel comprised of one member who joined the RNA in every decade of its existence. For the rest, we aim for a mix of the business of being an author (we've had sessions from the Registrar of PLR, the Society of Authors, accountants, PR professionals), the activity of writing fiction (workshops on plotting, character, saggy middles, beating writers' block etc) and pure inspiration.

But the programme is only part of the appeal of a conference. Over three days people can get to know each other in an entirely different way from a party, even an RNA party. Get to know each other and swap problems, advice and experience. The formal programme is only the start—so the conference organisers search for venues with, as a priority, a well-stocked, friendly bar and comfortable kitchens in the residential blocks for midnight networking.

Diane Pearson remembers:
The first one I recall was a one-day conference at Castle Howard in the north, and Joanna Trollope generously agreed to be one of the guest speakers. At the time Joanna was living in Gloucestershire so this required some logistical planning. She came up to town the night before and stayed with me and we set off next day at crack of dawn to travel north. The whole of southern England was baking in the midst of a heatwave (I seem to remember us having drinks in the garden the night before) and investigations revealed the north was also incredibly hot. What none of us knew was that Castle Howard was famous for nestling in a frost pocket, so we were all bitterly cold in our lightweight summer clothes. Nonetheless the conference was an outstanding success, and the following year another one-day was organised in Bath—in a beautiful hotel in the Royal Crescent.

The *RNA News* of October 1995 records the Castle Howard speakers: Diane Pearson on her career both as editor and novelist, saying that romantic fiction was taken seriously by the trade because it makes money; now the next aim must be to improve its literary standing … and we must write better books; agent Mark Lucas, then of PFD, on the author/agent relationship saying, 'An agent needs to be least sensitive to the things the writer most fears'; and Joanna Trollope, 'catwalk elegant', on her worst and best moments. 'The worst, not so much a moment as a long grey period of writing with nothing happening.' Best? Getting back from super-market with a load of shopping to be greeted by husband with the news that she had knocked Jeffrey Archer off the top slot. Referring to what her ancestor Anthony called 'the little daily lacerations of the spirit', Joanna said that she had found she did her best work when she came out of historical novels and in literary terms 'went to Sainsbury's', reflecting the complexity of women's lives back to her readers, who are mainly women.

Marina Oliver, who originated the whole idea and, with Roger Sanderson, ran the first five conferences, recalls the very first residential conference:
This was 1998. We had no idea how many people would come. But I knew that Stonyhurst College, where my son had been, hosted conferences and they were willing to accept a booking however many people turned up, 20 or 200. So a sub-committee was formed and we began to plan.

The oldest part of the Stonyhurst mansion, near Preston in Lancashire, is Elizabethan, extended in Victorian times. It is approached by a long drive between ornamental lakes, leading to a courtyard. Most of the building stretches behind this, and the corridors are spacious, the stairs elaborate, the classrooms airy. The college had been founded at St Omer in 1593, when English Catholics could not send their sons to English public schools. In 1794, after times spent at Bruges and Liege, the college came to Stonyhurst. Old boys include seven VCs and several members of the

English and Irish rugby teams, plus Sir Arthur Conan Doyle.

Angela Arney, then RNA Chairman, Helene Wiggin and Roger Sanderson, who lived nearby, Elizabeth Gill and I, met to visit the college and plan the weekend. Diane Allen, from Magna Large Print Books, which is not far away at Long Preston, offered to give lunch to 30 people and show them round her offices.

Stonyhurst is nine miles from Preston, so we organised a coach to meet people from the train on Friday. The idea was that everyone would meet at the college, and those who were going to Magna would leave their cars and join the coach. The programme was arranged, speakers confirmed, and 103 people booked to attend. Then, on Wednesday, the coach company blithely informed us they couldn't do the job. Panic.

Roger, who fortunately has a driving licence to drive a minibus, finally located one at the tenth or eleventh try. The rest of us spent Wednesday and Thursday phoning everyone we could and arranging lifts where possible, and directing people how to get to Magna. That left the people coming by train, too many for a minibus and a couple of cars. Fortunately, at the M6 junction on the outskirts of Preston, there is a hotel called The Tickled Trout. We asked everyone driving via the M6 to call in there, and Roger and I ferried the train passengers to the hotel from where they were taken on to Stonyhurst or Magna.

Amazingly, it worked. Diane did us all proud, then everyone settled in and explored the college buildings. The accommodation was in single rooms, those used by the sixth form boys and the few girls who had recently been admitted to the sixth form. There were no en suites, which has been the main reason we have not returned, as most people prefer these. Cold weather stopped any but cursory exploration of the gardens, but this was compensated for by the truly wonderful food, the best, I think, of any venue since. It was, too, what the boarders normally enjoyed. For recreation there was an indoor swimming pool, if anyone had time or energy after a series of lectures and seminars.

The programme was designed to cater for everyone, and where we split into groups we tried to have one topic which would appeal mainly to the unpublished, one for published, and one general.

There was a display 'getting to know you' board where people could pin their photos and details. This led to small groups with common interests meeting. Waterstone's of Preston organised a book fair. There was a drop-in demonstration of computers and the internet by an IBM expert. Sue Curran, editing Scarlet romances, presented two awards, to Maxine Barry and Julie Vince. The keynote speaker on Saturday was Josephine Cox, a Blackburn-born writer who, by great good fortune, was doing a promotion tour in the area and gave us a fascinating and inspiring talk. Derek Parker, editor of *The Author*, spoke about fiction in the new century. There were workshops by Michael Legat (Contracts), Sue Curran (Scarlet), Eileen Nicholl (M&B Medicals), Karen Geary (Publicity Director, Hodder), Shelley Sofier (MD of the PR company which covererd the 1998 Awards, on Doing Your Own Promotion), Karen King (Creating and Developing Ideas), Hugh Rae (Structure), Katie Fforde (Characterisation), Freda Lightfoot (Developing a Sense of Place), and Marina Oliver (Revision).

Residential weekends have been organised every year since, in different parts of the country, in modern University Halls of Residence. None have had the same ambience as Stonyhurst.

Jenny Haddon, who ran two conferences, in Guildford (2003) and Leicester (2004) recalls:
At my first conference I didn't control either the allocation of rooms, which the university office did, or the signposting, so there was mayhem, especially as it was a fairly complicated campus. Mind you, I have a theory that jolly graduating students had turned round half the signposts to celebrate the end of their exams. Roger Sanderson was my rock.

For my second, at Leicester, I had learned and was more relaxed, even getting to a few of the sessions. That was the conference at which attendees exhorted the RNA Committee to return to the fray and try to raise the profile of romantic fiction again, in an animated discussion facilitated by Pam Brooks (who writes as Kate

Hardy) and myself. I also recall the hugely impressive Barbara Taylor Bradford demonstrating that it was possible to be businesslike and inspirational at the same time. And Rachel Summerson (who writes as Elizabeth Hawksley) reading the 'Tiger Skin Incident' from Elinor Glyn's *Three Weeks* with truly incredible steadiness of face and voice. Unlike her audience, who wept with laughter.

Victoria Connelly, then a member of the New Writers' Scheme, whose romantic comedy Molly's Millions *was published by Allison & Busby in 2009 remembers:*
I'll never forget my excitement at the RNA's 2004 conference in Leicester. One of the guest speakers was Barbara Taylor Bradford. I'd been a fan of her work for some time but I must also admit to being a little star-struck by her too. To me, she was literary royalty. So, when Henriette Gyland and I saw her signing a huge pile of her books in the reception area, we opted out of one of the lectures and casually sat down nearby just to watch her, wishing and wondering if that might be us someday.

Finally, I went to get my own book signed by her and, knowing I was a writer, she wrote the following: 'Always remember the Ds: Drive, Dedication, Desire, Discipline and Determination!' It's a moment—and advice—that I'll never forget.

Jan Jones, organiser for the last six years, ponders:
The RNA Conference. How to sum it up in a few words? Fun, that would be one of them. Inspiring? Alcoholic? Yes, those too. Friendly? Necessary? Oh, yes.

When then-NWS member Jan Jones ran away to her first conference in York in 2000 and left her room convinced she'd never find her way back again, she was befriended by another cheerful writer, as bewildered by the campus as she was and just as much in need of a cup of tea. It wasn't until they had crossed two footbridges, side-stepped a multitude of ducks, charmed a university porter into releasing directions (we choose simpler campuses these days) and were finally in the queue for refreshments that Jan caught sight of her companion's name badge and realised that for 15 minutes she'd been chatting unselfconsciously to bestselling author Katie Fforde.

This is the RNA—and particularly the RNA Conference. The friendliest, most supportive bunch of people you could hope to find. It doesn't matter whether you are the rawest novice or have a hundred books to your credit—nobody asks what you do, they ask what you write.

They're resourceful too. In July 2005 the conference was at Royal Holloway College in Egham. That day four bombs went off in central London. Main line stations, the underground and buses into the centre of town, all froze while the Emergency Services took over. Did this stop RNA delegates? It did not. They re-routed, hitched lifts and got there by any means possible.

On another occasion, in Leicester this time (the RNA Conference likes to keep members on their toes by hopping around the country), there were so many accidents on the motorways that a generally law-abiding keynote speaker abandoned the bumper-to-bumper jams and drove her 4x4 across a field in order not to miss her session.

The conferences themselves always contain a tightly-packed mix of talks, seminars, panels and workshops. The programme is designed to appeal to published and unpublished alike, as well as those who simply need a lift, for whatever reason. Speakers come from the publishing industry, subsidiary occupations and from within our own ranks. Current romantic fiction markets and honing our craft have always been popular subjects (Diane Pearson on 'The First Line' and Julie Cohen on 'Writing Good Sex' come particularly to mind here), but 'business' issues have also made an appearance in recent years: PR, public speaking (particularly terrifying for many writers and increasingly important), managing money—these are all things authors need to know about.

And then there are the fun sessions. No one who has ever played with Liz Bailey's feathers in her workshop, 'The Tigers Come at Night', will be in any doubt that Getting Into Character can be enormously valuable.

There is also the social aspect. What is the effect of putting 120 normally solitary romantic novelists all into one campus? Well, for a start there are now a dozen university bars around the country that have been astounded by the amount of wine Romantic Novelists drink. Kitchen parties have been known to last until dawn. Firm friendships have been made while standing in the queues for breakfast and lunch. It's also lovely putting on posh frocks (remember Stephen Bowden's Regency Buck outfit, anyone?) for the Conference Dinner and the Elizabeth Goudge Award (short piece of unpublished work, open to published and unpublished writers alike) even if the food, on occasion, has been less than memorable.

Then there was the time at Cheltenham when the showers set off the fire alarms, the incident at Penrith when the chairman walked into her room to find a naked man in the shower, the jaw-droppingly inspiring Barbara Taylor Bradford, Rachel Summerson reading Elinor Glyn, Roger Sanderson's infamous Sunday Night Quiz ...

But mostly the conference is about us. A weekend for RNA members when we can celebrate our achievements, bask in the me-time, network, relax and party. And return home, rejuvenated, to write that next bestseller.

Dates and Locations of the residential RNA Conferences

- 1998   Stonyhurst College, Lancashire
- 1999   Leicester University
- 2000   University of York
- 2001   Cheltenham and Gloucester College of Further Education
- 2002   St Aidan's College, Durham
- 2003   University of Surrey, Guildford
- 2004   Leicester University (Stamford Hall)
- 2005   Royal Holloway College, Egham, Surrey
- 2006   Newton Rigg campus of University of
         Central Lancashire, Penrith
- 2007   Leicester University (New Hall)
- 2008   University of Chichester
- 2009   Newton Rigg campus of University of Cumbria, Penrith
- 2010   Old Royal Naval College, University of Greenwich, London

New Writers' Scheme

In deliberately setting out to foster new writing in its genre, the Romantic Novelists' Association was unique in 1960. It remains so. Although these days there are other writers' associations open to unpublished authors, and other sources of informed critiques (especially facilitated by the internet, of course), we have still not found anything like the New Writers' Scheme (NWS) run by any other association of professional writers. We are very proud of it.

Indeed, it was so successful that there was a time in the early 2000s, when the RNA was being bombarded with manuscripts which, on examination, turned out to be hard-core thrillers, science fiction, fantasy, modern experimental literary fiction and other exotica without a hint of romantic or women's fiction about them. The organiser of the time did manage to find some reader practitioners from the relevant genres. But eventually there were more than even the most willing of flexible organisers could cope with. So the committee decided that enough was enough: only manuscripts in our own genre, wide as it is, would be eligible for the New Writers' Scheme. This is now spelled out on the entry form and seems to work well.

Nothing is ever perfect, of course. From time to time there are rumblings that the RNA spends too much time on its new writers relative to published members. But most RNA published authors are deeply committed to the New Writers' Scheme, and not just for altruistic purposes. 'Whenever I critique someone else's ms, I learn something about my own,' said one, only this year. After 50 years, many of the RNA's members, though by no means the majority, reached publication through that route themselves. In fact, over the years the NWS has nurtured a number of bestsellers, RNA stalwarts, benefactors and Chairmen. Some, like the late Marie Joseph and Fiftieth Anniversary Chairman, Katie Fforde, manage to tick all four boxes.

Early Days

One of the two objectives of the new Romantic Novelists' Association in 1960 was to encourage good writing in the genre. This was not reforming zeal. Alex Stuart said in her 1961 letter to *The Woman Writer*, 'almost all [romantic novels] are well written.' The RNA founders believed that would continue and, by offering a prize for a first novel in the genre, they wanted to confirm and publicise the quality of such writing.

It would be wrong to think of this first prize as a training scheme. It seems to have been aimed squarely at writers who knew what they were doing and were very close to publication already. The founders expected probationer members, as they were then called, to be professional in approach and probably in experience.

Manuscripts from probationary members had to be submitted in September for reading by experienced published members, who gave a full criticism, with positive suggestions for revision. The best were read by a second reader and some, if considered good enough, were forwarded to publishers. (No mention is made of agents as recipients in these early years.)

The scheme was crowned by the RNA's Prize for New Writers, which was essentially a prize on publication. Once the publishers had accepted a book, it became eligible, and the winner would be announced at the awards dinner. Manuscripts which needed more work would be returned—but not until after the dinner, so that all the people who had entered thought they were in with a chance and bought a ticket!

The expectations of the RNA founders as to quality were not entirely met. Committee minutes record that Mary Howard (the committee member responsible and, as it turned out, winner of the first Romantic Novel of the Year for *More Than Friendship*) reported that 'they had received about twenty entries. Out of these only two were worth reading and these had been sent on to the final judges.'

One, submitted to Hurst & Blackett, had been accepted—*The Generous Vine* by Elizabeth Baker. It was a cracking tale set in the eighteenth century, described on the eventual Arrow paperback as 'The story of Kate Hardham, by day keeper of the dame's village school, by night bold and reckless, she joined the smugglers on the Sussex coast' and is on the keepers' shelf of at least one current RNA member. The author, published as Elizabeth Renier, went on to write 28 successful novels, all historical, and served on the RNA Committee herself in the fullness of time.

That first year the prize was called the Pauline Warwick Award, after a romance writer known to a number of the founders. But President Denise Robins suggested that in the second year it be named after Ruby M Ayres (1883-1955), a bestseller from her first novel *Richard Chatterton VC* (1916) and inspiration, in part, for PG Wodehouse's immortal Rosie M Banks. Approached through her publishers, Hodder & Stoughton, the Ayres family contributed £5 to buy an award for the winner. In the third year, with the approval of Mills & Boon, it was called the Kathryn Blair Award, after the distinguished Mills & Boon author, who also published as Rosalind Brett and Celine Conway. In 1963, however, when bestselling founder member Netta Muskett died, the committee decided to name the award after her, with no further changes. Her son, Peter Muskett, presented a trophy in her memory, which the winner held for a year.

The administration of the award evolved, of course. First, an entrance fee to cover expenses (£1 in 1961) was introduced. In 1962 two external judges were brought in—Nell Kennedy and the fearsome

Miss Biddy Johnson, Fiction Editor of *Woman's Weekly*—who read the entries with Mary Howard. By 1963 the committee were agreeing 'unanimously that the names of the judges for the probationary award should not be revealed when the mss go back to the members'. They clearly marked the novels with a percentage, like a school exercise, because Hilda Nickson proposed that all mss receiving less than 60 per cent should be returned before the dinner, which was a good deal fairer to the hopeful writers who didn't have a chance of winning.

It is also clear that the RNA was receiving more entries for the award than it ever expected—entries ran at between one and two dozen a year and reading them was more than the organiser could cope with, until an associate member, publishers' reader Helen McGregor, offered to help, for a professional fee. (The committee, facing greater numbers and more variable quality than they had envisaged, passed the proposal unanimously.)

Helen McGregor

Helen was a founding associate member of the RNA and, like so many of them, a stalwart of the Society of Women Writers and Journalists. She was not a novelist herself, but a publishers' reader and journalist, with a passion for the genre. She read widely, contributing reviews of classic books, think-pieces and even, once, a quiz to the *RNA News*. She had decided opinions and a phenomenal memory, for works by the published and unpublished alike.

She joined the committee early, representing associate members and, when she retired after her two-year stint, was promptly co-opted back as Awards Organiser. That was all the awards, including the Romantic Novel of the Year and its satellites. She was already, from October 1963, reading all the mss entered for the beginner's award at 10/6d a shot. She was a huge success.

Indeed, in 1973 full member Al Pearce asked if the RNA could give a service of criticism and advice on mss, such as that available to writers entering for the Netta Muskett Award, more generally to members who requested it, for a suitable fee. Committee minutes record that they felt the RNA should try, since it had been asked for, and Helen McGregor said she would be willing to read the mss submitted and report on them. She suggested halving the fee with the Association. What is particularly touching in this offer, though none of the committee would have known it at the time, is that Helen McGregor could almost certainly have done with the money. When she died, it became apparent that for some years she had been living in genteel poverty, though she would never have dreamed of mentioning her straitened circumstances. 'She was,' says Diane Pearson, 'a lady.' Fortunately, Anne Britton thought the entire fee should undoubtedly go the reader and the committee agreed.

In 1975 Helen McGregor was made an Hon Life Member. Chairman Nancy Sawyer, who had started off as a probationer herself, said that no one could imagine the RNA without Helen McGregor who had been responsible for so many vitally important aspects of the Association's work and achievements. As a direct result of her advice sixty Netta Muskett entrants had been published.

She did not discuss her health, either, and it was a huge shock to the committee when they heard in November 1983 that she was in hospital in intensive care. By the next committee meeting, she was dead and they were discussing a memorial to her work.

But her greatest memorial, of course, is those writers she helped. They respected her. They listened to her. Above all, they loved her. Some of their memories are below.

Margaret Pemberton
Margaret wrote as Maggie Hudson and Rebecca Dean. She was RNA Chairman from 1989-91. She writes:

In the dim and distant days of the mid-1960s, when I dreamed of becoming a fully-fledged novelist, Helen McGregor was my first contact with the world I was so eager to enter. I had read in my local paper, the *Bradford Telegraph and Argus,* of how a local woman, Joyce Eaglestone, had had her first novel published via winning the Netta

Muskett Award, an award run by the Romantic Novelists' Association. What was good enough for Joyce Eaglestone was, I determined, good enough for me. Entries for the following year had to be submitted to a Miss Helen McGregor. I submitted. And my life was changed.

It was changed because of Helen's all-consuming passion for everything the RNA stood for and her selfless and tireless commitment to helping aspiring romantic novelists become professional romantic novelists.

My entry didn't win the Netta Muskett and was never published. Any other award organiser would, I think, have merely sent a failed manuscript back with a word of thanks for the submission and left it at that. Not Helen. Back came pages of hard-hitting advice. I couldn't become a novelist if I didn't know how to spell. (I thought I did know, but Helen's list of mis-spellings proved me wrong.) And I would certainly never become a published novelist if I continued with my present style of writing. I couldn't do straight romance (Helen never minced her words) and should leave it for those who could. She did, however, think I had it in me to write romantic suspense. She thought I should get on with it. I got on with it.

A couple of years later, shortly after my first novel was published, I moved from Bradford to London and attended my first RNA meeting. Needless to say, the person I most wanted to meet was Helen, though, aware of how intimidating a person she must be, I was nervous of doing so. I looked around a crowded room for an authoritarian, brisk, no-nonsense-looking figure. There were quite a lot about, but Helen wasn't one of them. In the end I asked someone if Helen was present so that I could introduce myself to her and was duly pointed in Helen's direction. It was memorable moment.

Instead of the intimidating figure I had been expecting to meet, I found myself facing a tiny, sparrow-like woman of intense nervous energy. Her hair was worn in old-fashioned plaits coiled over her ears into 'earphones'. Her clothes were well-worn and forgettable. (Helen always had more important things to think about than clothes and, I was to learn later, had, out of necessity, to live with great frugality.) She was the liveliest, most enthusiastic, kindest, most lovable and most simpatico person you could ever wish to meet. And she knew everything about romantic fiction. She was a walking encyclopaedia; her memory was awe-inspiring. What was most memorable about her, though, was her passion. She was passionate about romantic fiction of all kinds. She was passionate about mentoring both aspiring and established writers. It was a passion she radiated. If there was one person you wanted to spend time with when at an RNA meeting or event, that person was Helen McGregor. Those of us able to do so were fortunate.

Sheila Walsh

The late Sheila Walsh, introducing herself as new RNA Chairman in Summer 1985, wrote:

Any sense of awe I felt [at her first RNA lunch at the Adelphi Hotel in Liverpool] soon melted in the warmth of the welcome I received from members like Maynah Lewis, and Stella Johns—and, of course, dear Helen McGregor who in two minutes could make you feel that you had known her forever, and had that marvellous capacity, which all who knew her will remember, for being able to quote your book back at you almost verbatim, including how many commas there were on page 123—very flattering to a new writer's ego! She had read my manuscript and had sent it off at once to Hurst & Blackett (of happy memory). She was almost as excited as I was, though she warned me not to set my hopes too high. 'Start another book,' she said.

Author Mary Nichols recalls:

I joined the RNA in the early 1960s, as a probationer, when Helen McGregor was judging the entries. I wish I had kept her letters. They were all handwritten and very difficult to read and because she wanted to keep her comments to one page, she used the margins and one had to keep turning them round to read them! Her first sentence on the first one of three I offered was, 'This is not a

Romance!' I later (much later) sold it to Robert Hale who called it a delightful romance. Robert Hale took nine more in the next five years. My second offering was *The Poacher's Daughter*, which was also turned down. I cannot remember what Helen said about it, but it was later published (very much re-written) by Orion as a saga.

Marie Murray
Marie, who wrote as Annabel Murray, writes:

The Romantic Novelists' Association—four words that conjure up a period in my life when, creatively, I was at my peak. The existence of the Association was revealed to me by my good friend, Sheila Walsh, herself an established and accomplished writer. Without my membership of the Association my life would have been very different indeed.

Entry to its hallowed ranks was by means of a scheme, known then as the Netta Muskett Award, named after the writer of that name. It now goes by the name of the New Writers' Scheme. Briefly, one submitted three chapters and a synopsis of one's current oeuvre to be read for suitability for publication. This task in the early days was carried out by Helen McGregor, a wee old-fashioned Scottish lady, who wore her hair in earphones and who had a phenomenal memory for the content of the manuscripts she read. Speaking to a writer, she had no difficulty in remembering the name of their hero and other pertinent details. At my second try, Helen submitted my manuscript to the publishers Mills & Boon and the rest, as they say, is history.

Later on in my career I had the privilege of reading the works of other would-be novelists. When I finally retired from writing I had a satisfying thirty-three books to my name. Thank you RNA.

1984-2010
The 1983 round of manuscripts had already been dealt with when Helen McGregor fell ill. Elizabeth Harrison, author of medical romances and former chairman, stepped in to sort out 1984 and the succession planning. In the process she became the onlie begetter of the New Writers' Scheme as we now know it (and indeed, went right on

loyally reading manuscripts for it until her death in 2008). She proposed to the committee in February 1984 that 'for one trial year, manuscripts [for the Netta Muskett award, as it was still called] should be read by a panel of published writers recruited from amongst RNA members. The names of the readers would be confidential to the committee.'

Elizabeth Harrison
Elizabeth was one of the first New Writers to join the RNA in the early sixties and became a full member on publication of her first novel in May 1965. She was first published by Hurst & Blackett and, latterly, by Mills & Boon.

She started working in a hospital office during the war and, as she told an RNA meeting in November 1978, found the life fascinating. She became a medical secretary and then moved on to the Chest, Heart & Stroke Foundation where she worked as research editor and script adviser on documentary films. Thus, she drew on areas she knew well for her fiction, as she often advised others to do. She freely acknowledged that she might have lost a little background by not working as a nurse, as many other writers of medical romance, like Lucilla Andrews or Hilda Nickson, had done. On the other hand, she felt she was able to see the hospital life as part of a whole and from all angles, and specialised in writing medical romances. Ever practical, she had two pieces of advice for writers aspiring to medical romance: 'If technical research must be included in the novel, it is better to insert it as a discussion between two characters'; and 'publishers do not like hospital books which frighten the patients and writers must be wary about writing of things which go wrong in hospitals.'

As well as reorganising and running the New Writers' Scheme, she served on the RNA committee in a number of roles, including Hon Secretary and, from 1977-79, Chairman. She has also been one of our greatest benefactors, remembering us in her Will and thereby enabling us, among other things, to publish this book.

She was twice shortlisted for the Romantic Novel of the Year, the second time in 1974 for *Surgeon's Call*, published by Hurst

& Blackett. She was also a frequent tutor on writing seminars, much valued for her practical and disciplined advice. Like Helen McGregor, she spoke her mind. (Reporting on 1987's submissions, she said crisply, 'about ten were very poor indeed.') As one of the generation of women who had worked since they left school, she was equally crisp about the unconvincing professional woman in fiction: 'We could do without heroines who the authors informs us are successful and assertive career women, but who demonstrate only unworldliness, tears—if not total collapse—at minor obstacles, and periods of abject submission to an apparently deranged hero.' Her judgement was faultess, as we see in her perceptive *RNA News* review of the autobiography, *No Time for Romance* by Lucilla Andrews:

'It opens, bombs dropping, at St Thomas's Hospital in wartime London. And as all of us who know Lucilla Andrews' novels will expect, this is authentic wartime, and authentic young doctors and nurses working through it.

'After this splendid opening the book backtracks to childhood—Lucilla was sent home (from Suez) at the age of only three to boarding school in Sussex. My heart bled for her. But, as she describes her own daughter a generation later, she herself, gregarious and friendly, apparently thrived in the experience. Or did she? For the book is full of unanswered questions. No time, in a rushed, overworked life, for dwelling on the hard times or even investigating them in much detail. Enough to record them—which she does brilliantly, though in some ways she is stronger on other people—the troops she nursed, the colleagues around her—than she is on herself. … It is a measure of her ability as a writer that, again and again, I had to put the book down, simply to pause and go on feeling it all.

'A book to cherish. … And personally, I would have said a truly romantic book, with a real life heroine. But I'd better not. Lucilla Rules. OK?'

A hard-working colleague, a sound judge, a good writer, a generous friend. The RNA is lucky in its luminaries and Elizabeth Harrison is one of the brightest.

The new look New Writers' Scheme

In a businesslike first report in October 1984, Elizabeth Harrison recorded that 52 manuscripts had been submitted. She received support in reading them from Sheila Walsh, author of Regency romances, and Susan Sallis, who wrote family sagas. One ms had been submitted to Judy Piatkus, one to Sphere and one to Mills & Boon. Two more could be submitted to publishers if they were tightened up and 14 remained to be read. Early submissions had been poor and those coming in later were of a higher standard. Some were from writers who had been submitting for many years with no improvement in standard and she thought 'that a way should be found of discouraging these people'.

Relying on in-house expertise had proved effective and the RNA decided to continue it. Elizabeth made other changes too, to streamline the work and make it more publisher-friendly. She scored a coup by persuading Mills & Boon editors to see the most promising six runners-up every year for an hour long consultation with Elizabeth Johnson or Mary Stannard, at least for contemporary romance. It was hoped to extend this to historical romance in the future, and also to persuade other publishers to follow suit. She thought there was a very hopeful future for the Netta Muskett—she had sent out 70 entry forms and received 41 actual mss by the middle of September 1985.

From 1986 onwards she asked entrants to add a synopsis, between 400 and 1,000 words in length, as some publishers now preferred it. Her notice to entrants said that full reports would be sent only where the ms was considered to be of a high enough standard to be offered to a publisher after further editing, or promising enough to warrant specific advice. Those entries which did not approach a professional standard would be returned with a brief rejection slip.

Interest increased sharply that year, following mention of the RNA in a lively How To book by bestselling HMB author, Mary Wibberley, *To Writers With Love: On Writing Romantic Novels*, published in 1985. Probationary members then, as now, had to join afresh every year and by 5th February 1986 Elizabeth reported that 32 had already signed up; 'sixteen of them had come directly from Mary Wibberley's book'.

RNA News Winter 1987

NETTA MUSKETT AWARD FOR NEW WRITERS
Entries for 1986

First of all, my deepest thanks to our panel of readers, who alone make this scheme possible. They worked hard and long — longer than I'd led them to expect — and were a tremendous support, as well as riveting correspondents. I'm afraid, though, that we weren't able to keep pace with the deluge of entries. This year we received nearly 100, twice as many as usual, and over 60 of them arrived in the final two weeks. This has meant that we were still reading in December, which has been hard on both readers and on writers, who had to wait for their reports, and I'm sorry about it.

Of these 100, perhaps about 20 showed real promise, and about 10 were very poor. The standard this year was undoubtedly higher. Most writers had a fairly clear idea of structure and plot, and knew where they intended to go. They usually got there, too, but far too often at the expense of credibility, allowing the plot to dominate the characters. We had to read about highly improbable behaviour from otherwise likeable characters, made to march stolidly through the plot the author had invented apparently with little relation to the people involved. There was also often misunderstanding of what is meant by conflict, which too many writers interpreted as petty squabbles between hero and heroine, from which neither emerged with credit, the heroine in particular seeming petulant and self-centred. Another major fault was the failure to build up a strong emotional bond between hero and heroine, substituting instead unpredictable sexual encounters, sometimes brutal, and without tenderness or meaning. Certainly there is a place for sex in today's romantic fiction, but only as a part of a growing and meaningful relationship.

All readers complained of poor spelling and careless

```
typing. If you can't spell, remember there are
dictionaries, and look for a friend who can spell to go
through your draft, line by line, page by page. The bad
typing — and probably many of the spelling mistakes —
is often due to the typist rather than the author, and
this does mean that you need to make time to go through
your returned typescript very carefully before sending
it off. It's not a good plan to assume that a publisher
will take a good book no matter what it looks like. It
won't happen unless you're a genius, and I'm bound to
say that among this year's entrants we failed to find any
geniuses. What we did find, though, were a fair number
of borderline stories, which might just make it or just
fail, and in this group presentation is important. An
editor is not going to take a marginally acceptable MS
if it's going to need hours of work in the office before
it's even presentable.
     A great number of entries began well, but faltered
about halfway, and finally fell apart before the end. So
try to leave time to work hard on your second half, and
remember the ending is as vital as the opening.
```

At the same time as the Mills & Boon boost, however, the Romantic Novel of the Year was throwing up some doorstop winners. The hardback of *A Song Twice Over* by Brenda Jagger (1986) weighs in at over a kilo; *Zemindar* by Valerie Fitzgerald (1982) only a little less; each must be nearly a couple of hundred thousand words. So the organisers of the New Writers' Scheme decided to waive the idea of a word limit. The two awards were otherwise uncoupled, however, since Boots, in sponsoring the Romantic Novel of the Year, wished to ensure that only one prize was presented at the Awards Luncheon. The Award for New Writers did not return to the main Award Luncheon until 1993 when the Boots sponsorship ended.

In the 1990s the administration of the New Writers' Scheme, as it had been rechristened in 1988, was taken over by another professional associate member, Dr Hilary Johnson, former editor of *The Writer*, who ran (and runs) her own highly respected Authors' Advisory Service. In 1992, 160 typescripts passed through the scheme and she reported, 'it is one of my greatest frustrations as organiser that the current state of the market is such that people who would have been assured of publication a few years ago must now, sadly, be disappointed.' On the brighter side, however, '1992 has proved to be a marvellous year for the New Writers' Scheme, with a total of nine writers in contention for the award. That there were nine novels accepted for publication during the pit of a recession is remarkable and should act as a spur to those who are still struggling.'

Hilary Johnson remembers:
This was when WH Smith Ltd started their 'Fresh Talent' promotion for first novels. I think it was discontinued after about five years, but we achieved, in chronological order: Marika Cobbold; Norma Curtis and Katie Fforde; Christina Jones; Linda Taylor and, I believe, Liz Young, all selected to be among the six authors chosen each year. These were all novels which had passed through the NWS. It gave me particular pleasure that we didn't simply have authors who were 'just' published, sometimes rather modestly, but those who were published by mainstream houses and who have in several cases established impressive careers.

More tryingly, from the NWS Organiser's point of view, after the end of Boots' sponsorship of the Romantic Novel of the Year, the New Writers' Award went back to the Main Awards lunch. Hilary Johnson again: 'All those years of sitting beside women who couldn't eat a mouthful for nerves!' (The ebullient Margaret Holt, just starting a successful run of medical romances based on her own career as a midwife, was the only exception!) Time constraints meant that there was never much time for the NWS winners to say a few words and sometimes the lunch organisers decided to ban them from uttering at all, as Hilary recalls with regret.

So in the twenty-first century the New Writers' Award got more time in the sun by moving to the summer party, where all the candidates and their books can be acknowledged by name. *Readers'*

Digest sponsored the parties in 2001 and 2002 at the Arts Club and, they were as glamorous as, though different from, the Awards lunch.

And, just to prove that we have all been there, an article by a New Writer in the *RNA News* of Autumn 1991.

When Katie Was Hopeful . . .

I was three pages into a brand new novel when Hilary Johnson phoned; 'How would you like to be on television?'

It seemed that a BBC programme was doing an item on romantic fiction. They were to interview the winner of the Romantic Novel of the Year Award, and wanted two 'hopefuls' there too. Hilary gave me as much information as she could, and left the line free for more phone calls.

When the BBC researcher had finished chatting, my desk was littered with fax numbers, addresses and instructions. By the time I had faxed and posted samples of my work to Heather Godwin in St Albans, and Colette at the BBC, my initial euphoria was fading.

It had been lovely telling them at work that I couldn't do Thursday because I was appearing on television (though it meant 'coming out' about being a writer). And it was lovely seeing the disbelief on the faces of my children. But then the anxiety began.

Supposing the expression 'sick with nerves' wasn't just an expression, but a real possibility? Would I disgrace myself, my family and the RNA on live television? Marina Oliver rang to say she'd managed to squeeze in two extra seats for Sue Bentley and me at the Awards Luncheon.

I enjoyed every moment of the lunch. RNA meetings are always enormous fun, but this was special — the delightfully witty speeches, the joy of meeting friends, old and new — not to mention the food. I got to know Sue Bentley, who was the other 'hopeful', and met Susan Kay, the winner of the Award.

Afterwards, Sue and I swept off to the Kensington Hilton in a taxi, feeling like celebrities as we

announced at reception, 'We're booked in by the BBC.'
    We hardly slept. Even Susan Kay, who had appeared on
television before, was nervous.
    At the studio we were led though a maze of corridors,
spotting celebrities as we went. We finally arrived
at the right green-room and met Heather Godwin the
publisher. After a brief chat with her and other guests,
we trooped into make-up. Sue and I were led onto the
set, wired for sound, and 'warmed up' by the floor
manager. By the time the show began I'd almost stopped
being nervous and just wanted to do a good job.
    Sue did well, managing to mention the title of her
book twice. When my turn came, time was running out.
'How do you cope with rejection?' Gloria asked. 'It's
part of being a writer,' I said, 'coping with rejection
and criticism.'
    When I got home my son said, 'Everyone's famous for
fifteen minutes, Mum.' 'If that's the case,' I said,
exhausted, 'I'll have to do that again twenty-nine
times. Let me have a few weeks to recover.'
    But at least Gloria knows where to get in touch with me.

When asked for her permission to reprint, the Former New Writer replied:

'Golly! That was a blast from the past! But I'm perfectly happy for it to be there. Strangely I haven't changed my mind about anything. How nice that there's a copy somewhere. I'm fairly sure I wrote that on my Amstrad!'

Katie Fforde, you're welcome.

Joan Hessayon Award
From 2003 the award for a first novel which has come through the New Writers' Scheme to publication has been presented by a long- standing friend of the RNA, Dr David Hessayon (writer of the bestselling *Garden Expert* books) in memory of his late wife Joan Hessayon, a very valued member of the RNA for many years. In a moving tribute to her, he told the RNA's Summer Party at the Arts Club in 2003 that Joan had always been a passionate supporter of

the New Writers' Scheme. Presenting this award meant that Joan was now able to continue her help to new writers from beyond the grave.

The award consists of a silver rose bowl, to be held for a year and engraved with the winner's name, plus a generous cheque, and is presented at the RNA's annual summer party, where Dr Hessayon provides champagne for us all to toast the winner. A tradition has arisen that the winner returns to say a few words the following year—when they've got their breath back, seen their book in print and actually got their first royalty cheque!

Diane Pearson writes:

Dr David Hessayon, or 'The Doc' as he is more affectionately known to his friends and working colleagues, has been associated with the RNA for many years, initially through his wife, Joan, an enthusiastic member, but more recently as an Hon Life Member and sponsor of the New Writers' Award.

The son of a Cypriot landowner, he grew up in Manchester where he discovered his love of plants in the family garden. He read botany at Leeds University and received a first class Special Honours BSc in botany and chemistry.

It was round about this time that, on a student trip to Paris, he met Joan, a young American girl on her first trip to Europe. It was to be the beginning of a lifelong partnership and a marriage that lasted 50 years.

After work in America, and teaching at University College in Ghana, he obtained his PhD in soil ecology and eventually in 1955 he accepted a position as chief scientist at Pan Britannica Industries, becoming managing director in 1964 and chairman in 1972. It was at PBI that he had the idea for the 'Be Your Own Gardening Expert' books and offered to pay the company back if the first book was a failure. The rest is history. The *Expert* gardening books made the author the bestselling living author of the 1990s, he continually appears on the *Sunday Times* bestseller lists and there can hardly be a home in gardening Britain that does not continually use his books.

He has received countless awards, and honorary degrees. In the *Times* he was described as 'Salinger meets Streisand via Salford'.

For a man as high-powered and busy as the Doc, it would have been understandable if he had had little time for anything else, but ever since his wife, Joan, a romantic novelist, became a member of the RNA he has been an ardent and generous supporter of our organisation, always attending the Awards Luncheons and, indeed, coming to speak to us on how to market our own books.

When Joan, changing direction with her novels, began a series with a strong gardening background (living with the Doc all those years she had picked up quite a bit of gardening knowledge herself) he was very much to the fore. Indeed, I have often thought that every romantic novelist should have a Doc in their lives. For her publications the Doc would give the most wonderful parties, one at the Chelsea Flower Show, another at the Capel Gardening College where we had a magnificent display of professional tree climbing, and another at a stately home where the courtyard had been turned into a striking pot garden and Elizabethan musicians in costume serenaded the guests. He was also a generous host to the East Anglian Chapter giving the most wonderful summer party to all the members at his home in Essex—champagne, a marquee on the lawn, a three course lunch, and a guided tour of the huge and beautiful garden. I think, on that occasion, quite a few members outside the East Anglian Chapter attended, but all were made welcome.

When Joan died in 2001, the Doc took over the sponsorship of the New Writer's Award, now called the Joan Hessayon Award in her memory, as she had done so much for the New Writers' Scheme. Once again he has proved immensely generous, awarding not only the major prize but also gifts to the runners-up. What would we do without him?

Our thanks to Dr David Hessayon OBE.

Where we are now

The New Writers' Scheme continues to be administered by a volunteer member of the RNA, with the assistance of readers from among the published membership. In 2008 there were 50 of them, when 14 million words of romance passed over the organiser's desk.

Inevitably, there are capacity constraints and for several years the RNA has had to limit numbers on the New Writers' Scheme. Applications open on 2nd January and the scheme fills up earlier and earlier every year. In 2008 it was March. In 2010, the RNA had to close entrance half way through January.

These days, the application form asks which sub-genre the author is aiming at. Current categories, in order of popularity are: contemporary with no further definition; historical novels (excluding Mills & Boon); submissions aimed at various lines at Harlequin Mills & Boon; crime, thriller and adventure; sagas (these days more commonly defined by period than area); romantic comedy; literary; short works aimed at *My Weekly Story Collection, People's Friend Pocket Novels* or intended as novellas; fantasy, with a preponderance of time-slip books; chick-lit and (remember these are self-styled) hen-lit.

Lest we get too self-congratulatory, let us admit that, although a great deal of effort goes into the NWS, inevitably, there are glitches. In 2009, industrial action at Royal Mail interrupted the smooth flow of envelopes. It had some new writers biting their fingernails to the quick in case their ms had not arrived. (*Plus ça change.* In 1988, the period for submissions had to be extended because of a postal strike.) When a book does not go for a second read, writers are always disappointed and sometimes they are unhappy with the report, too. Criticism is often hard to take, especially when it is aimed at the book of your heart. But sometimes reader and writer turn out to be a bad match, for whatever reason. It's hard, but it happens with agents and publishers too. After all, not everyone will like a book, even when it's a bestseller. New Writers rapidly become philosophers. But at its best, the reports hit the spot.

Jan Sprenger, a New Writer (at least, as we go to press!) permits us to quote her post to the RNA e-group, dated Tuesday 8th September, 2009 5.56 pm:

The beauty of the New Writers' Scheme

I've just received my NWS report and am feeling decidedly tickety-boo. I was having a crisis of confidence, exploring other potential outlets for my creativity ... basket-weaving at least has a functional by-product. But I'm so chuffed with the report, I'm grinning.

Rightly, the reader points out weaknesses that I knew were there and highlights things that I'd overlooked. There are also valuable and precious words of encouragement.

The best part, of course, is that it will help me work on and improve (I hope) what's there, and THAT is the beauty of the New Writers' Scheme. Huge thanks!

Jan

Phillipa Ashley won the Joan Hessayon Award in 2006. She writes: *The thrill of a lifetime*

It's fair to say that the RNA NWS has provided me with the greatest thrills of my professional life so far. The first was getting my debut novel, *Decent Exposure*, published by Little Black Dress in 2006. This was my first attempt at writing a novel, and I'll never forget when my NWS reader phoned me to say she loved the book and there was a lot more work needed but not to give up. That was all I needed to hear: that I wasn't wasting my time.

After revising the ms, I sent it to the agent, Broo Doherty, who sold it to Headline. I already thought I'd had more luck than a lottery winner so, as I stood with ten other newly published authors in the IMechE library in May 2007, I was genuinely 'just pleased to be there.' When Jenny Haddon read out my name, I was so shocked I kept apologising to the other writers, exclaiming 'it can't be me!'

The euphoria of winning carried me through a whole book. Of course, you have to come down to earth sometime and four years on, I've learned that a novelist's life has more ups and downs than the Lake District landscape where *Decent Exposure* was set. When times get tough, I still sometimes get out my NWS citation and remind myself that I can do it.

And I've been fortunate enough to have some enormous highs. A few months after winning the NWS, *Decent Exposure* was picked up by a Hollywood producer and optioned by Fox Television for the Lifetime Channel. In 2009, I had the ultimate thrill of taking my family to the Canadian Rockies to visit the set of the movie where we met my 'hero' and 'heroine'. In 2009, all four of my books were bought by the US publisher, Sourcebooks, and *Decent Exposure* is being released as a single title romance, retitled *Dating Mr December,* in November 2010.

Without the NWS, my life would have been considerably less thrilling and that's a thought that sends a shiver up my spine!

The Last 10 Winners

2010   *Bought: Damsel in Distress,* Lucy King, Harlequin Mills & Boon (category romance). Number of published NWS books in contention for the award—3

2009   *Tug of Love,* Allie Spencer, Little Black Dress (romantic comedy). NWS books in contention—7

2008   *Pandora's Box,* Giselle Green, Avon (contemporary). NWS books in contention—5

2007   *Decent Exposure,* Phillipa Ashley, Little Black Dress (romantic comedy) NWS books in contention—11

2006   *Blind Date Marriage,* Fiona Harper, Harlequin Mills & Boon, (category romance) NWS books in contention—8

2005   *Stage by Stage,* Jan Jones, Transita (contemporary). NWS books in contention—9

2004   *Landsker,* Brenda Squires, Starborn Books (historical). NWS books in contention—3

2003   *A Sovereign for Song,* Annie Wilkinson, Simon & Schuster (saga). NWS books in contention—3

2002   *Ring of Clay,* Margaret Kaine, Poolbeg (saga). NWS books in contention—6

2001   *Somebody,* Anita Anderson, Harper Collins (romantic comedy). NWS books in contention—6

Names to remember and celebrate

One of the greatest difficulties for the Editors in producing this memoir has been to identify which moments, careers or anecdotes tell us most about their times or, alternatively, reveal how little things change. But sometimes we find the work has been done for us.

With the approaching 50th Anniversary in mind, the committee introduced the RNA's Lifetime Achievement Awards in 2006. The criteria are very simple. The recipient is someone who, the RNA believes, has served the genre of romantic fiction, either by their own work and inspiration to others and/or by helping the work of the RNA itself. Other than that, the awards are entirely ad hominem—or ad feminam—not a regular thing, but given with respect and appreciation when the time seems right. The first three went to authors whom many generations of RNA members had loved: Lucilla Andrews, Rosamunde Pilcher and Mary Stewart. However, certain publishers have done more than their share to publish and promote Romantic Fiction and in 2009 we presented Judy Piatkus and John Hale with awards for their outstanding contributions to our success and prosperity. And in 2010 we honoured authors Maeve Binchy and Joanna Trollope.

The following pages appreciate not only those who have received the awards, but also important RNA members who somehow have not quite 'fitted' into various earlier sections of the book.

With Lucilla Andrews, Jenny has written a particularly long biography, for which we make no apology. Lucilla was a founder member and a remarkable person who, in some ways, embodied what the writing of romantic novels is all about.

The first Lifetime Achievement Awards

The first we presented went to three of our favourite writers. As they were all based in Scotland, we gratefully accepted an offer from MSP Robin Harper (then co-convenor of the Scottish Green Party and also husband of Jenny Harper, co-editor of *Romance Matters*) to host the celebratory lunch in the fantastic new building of the Scottish Parliament.

As the RNA committee said at that first lunch, whenever three romantic novelists are gathered together, their first talk is of authors who started them writing. The citation said that we wanted to congratulate these first author recipients of the new award on their contribution to the gaiety of nations, the reputation of romantic fiction and the Invisibles Account of the Balance of Payments for more than 50 years.

Lucilla Andrews, Rosamunde Pilcher and Mary Stewart: yours is writing of quality and its appeal lasts. You deliver timeless romance, wonderful characters and cracking good stories. In the best tradition of popular fiction, you also hold up a mirror to your times. Thank you.

Lucilla Andrews—the life

Lucilla Andrews was probably the youngest and certainly the prettiest founder member of the Romantic Novelists' Association in 1960. There is a picture of her at the inaugural dinner, all softly curling dark hair and huge eyes which she had inherited from her Spanish mother. (An ancestor was Cervantes' patron.) She joined because Alex Stuart invited her—'Make that told me,' she said in 2005. 'She was a strong-minded woman, Alex.' Barbara Cartland took her to task for not wearing a hat to meetings. When she produced a hat, though, Miss Cartland (this was pre-Damehood) did not notice. She did, however, tread on Lucilla's smart shoes, just as she did on Anne Worboys'.

Lucilla was born in Egypt, where her father worked for the Eastern Telephone Company but she and her sister were sent back to school in England when she was only three. She adjusted, however, and in the process discovered that she was a writer. From then on she wrote notes every night about things that had happened or caught her interest during the day. This was particularly useful when she came to write her memoir, *No Time For Romance* (1977), which primarily covers her experiences during the War, first as a volunteer nursing auxiliary with the Red Cross after Dunkirk. (Her Spanish grandfather had been a general practitioner and, anyway, in the Red Cross you were allowed to wear silk stockings, not allowed to other women volunteers.)

Later she trained as a nurse at St Thomas's by Westminster Bridge, enduring the blitz, rationing and overwork. Once she assisted at a birth to the accompaniment of ack-ack shells, tracer, aircraft engines and explosives and the small shrill whistle of one falling bomb. Curbing her instinct to dive under the delivery bed, she caught the baby as he catapulted into her hands. A devoted nurse, she never forgot that she was a writer. When a V2 hit her Nurses' Home, in 1945, she grabbed her eyelash curlers and the red foolscap file of notes for the books she intended to write.

In 1947 she married Dr James Crichton but he was hospitalised when their only daughter, Veronica, was five months old. Lucilla became the single parent and sole breadwinner permanently. Determined that her daughter should have a first-class education, Lucilla decided that she must earn enough by writing to work from home by the time Veronica was old enough for school. She took a job working nights as duty nurse in a pie factory and wrote during the day. Her first sale was a romantic short story to *Good Housekeeping* for 25 guineas. She recorded that at the time a part-time Sister earned 2s 9d an hour.

She did not set out to be a romantic novelist, as such, and was often quite surprised to be reminded of the term. In her first book she mined her wartime nursing experience. She recalled in *No Time for Romance*, 'I had not consciously chosen the theme or my characters, but directly I began writing, all were released by my subconscious in such a powerful flood that often I had the impression the novel was some private arrangement between my brain and my hands, over which I had no control.' Her first novel was rejected and while her agent sent it out to other publishers she started on her second. Then her agent sent her one of the rejection letters, dated October 1952. It said that no one could be induced to read the book at that time; it was too graphic a reminder of painful things, especially for anyone who had seen the worst of them. But if she could make the story less harrowing and let the past bury its dead, there was some hope for her writing.

Already professional to her fingertips, she took a long hard look at the book she was then writing and realised that the same objections could apply to that one too. She had been so anxious to be truthful to hospital life as she saw it that she had concentrated on the blood and tears and ignored all the humour, absurdities and temperamental incompatibilities. Above all she had ignored the inter-staff love affairs. Thinking about it now, she realised that they were 'as much part of the normal life of any large teaching hospital as the teaching rounds and bedpans'. She remembered how young were the medical staff she had known, how most of them were unmarried and for ever falling in love or recovering from it. And, 'I thought of the laughter I had heard in so many wards and so many places where it would have seemed the angels must have wept. ... I decided to rewrite the whole novel without falsification, but with a much lighter touch, and the inclusion of at least one love affair.' (*No Time for Romance*, page 235) Her first novel, *The Print Petticoat*, was published in 1954.

Her professional approach hit the spot at once. Publisher Willie Harrap told her that he would take as many of them as she could write. She wrote 34 published novels and many short stories in a career that spanned 40 years. She was published in 11 languages and had a worldwide readership. She sold getting on for 3m books. At the height of her powers she was so important to Harrap that a former editor told me at her memorial service that, when her books came in they went straight to print, without editing. Harraps were just waiting for them. When PLR was introduced, she was among the top 50 authors for ten years.

Her work, with its vivid characters, integrity and lively, amusing style, delighted and inspired readers round the world and she maintained a correspondence with several of them who were nurses themselves. One wrote, 'I became a nurse because of your books and they certainly influenced the way in which I treated my patients.' The *Guardian* called her the brand leader of hospital romance, a label which the rest of the media took up.

The books and short stories ensured that her daughter had a stable, loving and stimulating home—and the sort of education that Lucilla had not had herself. Veronica Crichton read history at Newnham College, Cambridge, and became one of the Labour Party's most successful and respected communications advisers. When she died of cancer in April 2002, a Crichton Fund, to support training events for women, was set up in her memory. Just before she died herself, Lucilla told us, 'You never recover from the loss of a child. But I will always be so proud of her.' Lucilla herself was passionate but never doctrinaire about women's rights. She had a right to be. She had, after all, paid her dues.

The RNA made her a Vice President after she moved to Edinburgh and did not make it to London meetings any more. In 2005 we gave her a Lifetime Achievement Award, to be presented in Edinburgh that August. She was amused and, I think, pleased by the honour. She told a neighbour that she was being 'iconised'. When she had a fall and was hospitalised, she was still considering ways of nipping over the wall of the Edinburgh Royal Infirmary to get down to the Parliament Building for the formal lunch. The fact she couldn't get to the hairdresser and had a black eye may have been the clincher against that one.

Three of us (Diane Pearson, President, Jenny Haddon, then Chairman, Evelyn Ryle, then Treasurer) went to see her in hospital, bearing a diva's dressing room of flowers and the citation she would have got the following day. She was dreadfully frail but brisk, funny and so politically incorrect that we quailed. 'So kind but dreadfully fat, poor dears,' she said of the nurses in ringing tones. 'Of course they have to keep sitting down to write reports. We weren't allowed to sit down in my day.'

We made plans to go up to Edinburgh again to take her out for her birthday, as a substitute celebration. It is still in the diary for the third week of November with a note, 'Not Monday; allow time for hairdresser'. She was intelligent, alert and she had been a nurse. She must have known it wasn't going to happen. But she was too brave and too courteous to tell us. When the Chairman went back to Edinburgh, it was to her memorial service on 4 November.

It was clear from the tributes that she met everything, reverse or success, with courage, intelligence and humour. She was clearly a great friend and a terrific Aunt Lucy. A Spanish cousin, studying in Edinburgh, was plied with chocolate cake and whisky. He learned to schedule recovery time after visiting her.

But for the RNA she was not only one of us, she was a model of what a romantic novelist can be—practical in the face of criticism, respectful both of her own talent and of her readers, full of energy and intelligence, of vision and some moral force. How right we were to give her that Lifetime Achievement Award.

Lucilla Andrews—the work

Lucilla Andrews, described by the *Guardian* as 'the brand leader of hospital romance' had two great subjects: nursing and the War. For both of them she drew on her own experience, consulting the notebooks in which she scribbled down events and odd things which caught her attention or reflections that occurred to her. She burned her first completed novel the night before she got married, deeming it dull, pompous rubbish. But under the necessity of earning a living for herself and her child, she rewrote her second attempt. *The Print Petticoat*, about a staff nurse in the maternity ward of a London teaching hospital and her friends, was an instant success when it was published in 1954.

Medicals

She created an imaginary London Teaching hospital, St Martha's, which was clearly based on St Thomas's in disguise. It even had the statue of Miss Nightingale! Readers loved the continuity, as well as the unmistakeable authenticity of hospital life.

There is no glossing over the nastier side. People vomit, bleed and die—and nurses weep. *The Nursing Times* said her novels were 'faultless in their settings… stoical, spirited, humane.'

She kept her background up to date by conscientious research, long after she had left nursing. She wrote an article for the *RNA News* in New Year 1970 on the subject, 'Keeping up With the Professor'. Treatment for shock and burns, for instance, changed so fast that her solution was to check with the most experienced Casualty Sister she could contact at the time of writing the final draft. When she started there was no penicillin—M&B 639 tablets were the preferred treatment for fever and, allegedly, if people had been eating onions or Epsom salts, it turned them blue. Lucilla said she never saw a patient turn blue but she watched them like a hawk, just in case. And put it in a book, of course.

Characters were her great strength. They were completely of their time, yet utterly recognisable across the years. Above all, she was emotionally truthful. Her protagonists were nurses through and through, caught up in hospital politics and regularly confronted by moral and professional dilemmas. Their love affairs mirrored and informed their professional lives. Even when her heroines were very young, they were never trivial. And sometimes her heroines shared some of Lucilla's own personal experiences of being widowed, a single parent of a small child and the only bread-winner, as in *Silent Song* or *Healing Time*. These are very grown-up books by a woman who had been there.

Lifetime Achievement Award appreciation

When the RNA prepared the citation for her Lifetime Achievement Award, they asked three writers for a personal appreciation of her work. This is what they said.

Author Jessica Hart had won a RITA in the US and the UK's Romance Prize for category romance. She wrote, 'I found a copy of *The First Year* in a tiny Scottish post office in 1971. It was the first romance I ever read, and I have been reading it ever since. I picked it up again today with a cup of tea, intending to flick through it and try and work out why it has stood the test of time so effectively, and was instantly transported back to the world of St Martha's Hospital in the fifties. It doesn't matter that this is a world long vanished; the fluency and intelligence of the writing kept me utterly absorbed and I was halfway through the book before I realised that my tea was cold. In spite of the fact that Rose, the heroine, and the hero, Jack Waring, meet only in the most restrictive of circumstances and barely touch, the attraction between them is completely convincing, so much so that I have often continued the story in my head, imagining what happened after they leave Bert's café.

'Creating characters that engage a reader so utterly is a rare gift, a kind of magic, and it is, I think, what gives Lucilla Andrews' books such timeless appeal.'

Timeless indeed. If you try to buy her books secondhand today, you will find that some of them cost hundreds of pounds. One antiquarian bookseller told us, 'The moment I post them on the online catalogue, they get snapped up.'

Diane Pearson wrote, 'Lucilla Andrews was one of the first writers to combine romance with a convincing and realistic medical background based on her own nursing experience. *A Hospital Summer* is one of the best books ever written about WWII and should be required reading for every student of the period.'

Jenny Haddon said, 'My own favourite Lucilla Andrews is *My Friend the Professor*. I first read it when I was a teenager—and the characters were old-fashioned even then—but it has always stayed with me, somehow. It is a touching and truthful story of a weary older man and a life-enhancing Persephone, who can't keep her nurse's cap straight on her curly hair. Frances encounters the mysterious stranger in a rain storm and, when he seems a disinterested and friendly ear, pours out her difficulties and confusion as a probationary nurse. They meet again and he is amazingly understanding, even offering helpful advice. He never tells her who he is and she is too uneasy in the relationship to ask. Their encounters are important to her but she thinks that, to him, they may be an occasional forgettable chat. Like Cupid and Psyche, the relationship is a secret, in which Frances can explore her deepest concerns, as she cannot with her friends at the hospital. Only then, of course, he turns out not to be a disinterested stranger, after all, but one of the hospital grandees who has deliberately deceived her. Frances is cut to the quick, humiliated and betrayed. And he—well, when the mask is off, knowing that he cannot expect her to forgive him, he tells her the truth about what their talks have meant to him. The bleakness, the intensity, the sheer passion are breathtaking.'

An opportunity missed

In 1955 Lucilla Andrews suggested to her publisher that it would be timely to make a television series based on her imaginary hospital St Martha's. A hospital was, she argued, a microcosm of society; full of drama as well as humour, absurdities, incompatible temperaments and love affairs. Her books were successful. She was being serialised to great acclaim. Her writing skills were proven. Above all, her knowledge of the background was unrivalled. Television needed drama. The time was surely right.

So what happened, when she suggested her hospital series?

Flat rejection. Specifically, from her publisher and then agent, who were both equally horrified. Willie Harrap allegedly said to her, 'Oh no, dear, that may do for women's magazines but it won't do for television.' Television, you see, was watched by men. They would not be interested in little stories for women.

And then came ... the phenomenally successful *Emergency Ward Ten* in 1957. It was hugely popular, ran for ten years and Lew Grade always said that cancelling it, as he did in 1967, was one of the two biggest mistakes of his life. It was followed by the North American *Dr Kildare* in 1961; then *General Hospital, Angels*; ... right up to our own day of *Casualty*; *Holby City* and *Green Wing*; as well as the American imports, *House, Grey's Anatomy* and a dozen others.

Did anyone ever—ever—say to her, 'Sorry Lucilla, you were right?' Not by her account, or any other evidence that we can find.

Moral: sometimes authors know what they're talking about.

Personal reminiscence

In 1977 Lucilla published *No Time for Romance*. It covers her whole life up to the start of her writing career but, in effect, it is mainly about the war and its affect on her, a 19-year-old at the start. You can almost feel her growing up in its pages. Those hasty notes, scribbled down when she must have often been exhausted, seem to infuse the book with the urgency and danger of the times.

For instance, a tall young Scottish Highlander tells her his unit had been camped on the beaches at Dunkirk for days, he cannot remember the exact number, as one day was so like another. 'It was the noise that was being the worst,' he told her. She has to take out 23 shrapnel splinters embedded in his leg from a wound on the beach:

> The deepest and longest was in his right thigh. It looked small until I began to take it out. It measured just under five inches and at its widest, half an inch. When all were out I nearly had to use force to get him to swallow an ounce of stock brandy. 'It is you that should be having this, not me, nurse.'
>
> In a few scribbled notes I made that night, I added, 'I didn't dare tell him I had thrown up in the scullery before getting the brandy from Sister or he would have poured it down me. God, he needed it. When I tugged out that big one he hung onto the bedhead so hard his knuckles were white, but he didn't make a sound till I got it out and then he said, 'I am thanking you very much, nurse'.

No Time for Romance pages 81-82

Reviewing it in the *TLS* at the time of publication, PD James said that she had made a memorable and moving contribution to the memoirs of the last war. Lucilla herself wrote, 'In my personal life, nostalgia appealed to me as little as masochism.' This is not self-indulgent basking in the past; this is painfully reported truth, written 25 years after the event, setting the record straight about how she became the person she was.

The War as a subject

In *No Time For Romance* we see the origin of most of her subject matter—caring, over-worked nurses, idiosyncratic patients, the rigid routines of a major teaching hospital and, above all, we see the War through the eyes of a young woman. (Indeed, the book was also acknowledged as a source by Ian McEwan when he was researching *Atonement*.)

The War forms the background to *Hospital Summer* (1958), is a constant influence from the past on characters in many of her novels and is almost a character in one of her most powerful novels, *Frontline 1940* (1990). In *Frontline 1940* the hero is, exceptionally, not a doctor but an American correspondent. He was in Paris during the fall of France and is convinced that Britain has no chance. Returning from witnessing the bombing of Coventry, he gives the heroine an engagement ring, which he leaves at the hospital for her. Between bombs and their crazily busy lives they don't know when they will meet again. They never ask themselves whether each time they meet is the last, but the possibility of death is there all the time, like a ground bass. The heroine, Ann, recognises not only that this is an important pledge of love and serious intent but also that the ring is small enough to hide and valuable enough to sell—a real insurance against the invasion Jack expects. It must have been something Lucilla, nursing in St Thomas's and seeing the dogfights over the Thames every night, must have thought about herself. After all, throughout the second week of September 1940, General Alan Brooke (as he then was) recorded in his diary every night that he thought the invasion of Britain would begin that week. A footling 1990 reviewer criticised Ann for being 'too good'; and utterly failed to notice how vividly Lucilla gets the feeling that the War has these characters, in her own words, 'by the throat'.

The most striking incident in both *Hospital Summer* and *Frontline*

1940 is of a young airman who has had half his face shot away. He was the first person she saw die, when she sat with him as a VAD in the summer of 1940, and it is interesting to compare the novelist's treatment of that dreadful death with the autobiographer's. The medical details are identical—the big baroque bow on the dressings, to facilitate removing them without causing the patient excessive pain, the appalling wound, the rattling in the throat, the wandering mind. Like Lucilla in real life, both of her protagonists tell the dying boy their names, contrary to hospital regulations. In both novels, the boy has a more lucid, even conversational, time. ('You have to be fearfully careful about sepsis,' the heroine tells him in *Hospital Summer.*) But the fictional nurses know that their patient is dying. In the real life version, the most startling, throat-clutching thing is the young auxiliary's lack of awareness:

> Sometimes, for a few seconds, he was quite coherent. In one lucid spell I asked if he was comfortable.
>
> 'Yes, thanks, except for this bandage thing over my face. Bit sort of tight. Could you sort of loosen it?'
>
> I looked round for advice but all the Sisters in sight were busy with other patients and the senior Sister seemed to have vanished. I could not see a VAD in the ward and the two M.O.s present were dealing with blood transfusions. Then, as I did not think it would do any damage to loosen the gauze bows, I let go of his hand, stood up, undid the first and, as the sterile towel beneath it slid off and jerked aside the towel above, very nearly fainted on his bed. The right half of his face and some of his head was missing. I had consciously to fight down the waves of nausea and swallow bile, wait until my hands stopped shaking and dry them on my back before I could retie the bow. Mercifully, he had slid back into confusion before I flopped back onto my chair.
>
> The confusion increased, his breathing grew louder, more laboured and sometimes rattled, as his voice earlier. But he seemed to know I was holding his hand, as whenever I slightly altered the position of my cramped fingers, his cold, stiff fingers slightly tightened their grip. His eye had been closed for some while when it suddenly opened and he stared at me. Before I realised what he was about to do, with a tremendous effort he flung himself upwards from the waist and towards me. I had to wrench free my hand as I leapt up and caught him in my arms to stop him falling out of bed. He was so heavy that, to keep

my balance, I sat instinctively on the side of his bed. He dropped his head on my shoulder and sighed. I thought he was unconscious and was relieved for his sake, but too frightened to lay him back in case the towels fell off and I had to see his wounds again. I wholly forgot I was committing the unforgiveable nursing crime of sitting on a patient's bed.

As suddenly the senior Sister was beside me. She said nothing about my sitting on the bed, but gently uptilted his head from my shoulder. "Poor boy. Put him down, nurse."

I only understood when she closed his one eye.

In the end there are some things that are too fierce, too much themselves, to be squeezed into fiction, even by a master story teller.

Rosamunde Pilcher

Rosamunde Pilcher OBE, long-time member of the RNA, is one of the few authors whose work spans cultures. First published as Jane Fraser by Mills & Boon in 1949, she told the *RNA News*, 'My first book and my first baby came together. The book was published on the day the baby was born. It was called *Halfway to the Moon*.' In December 1953 the *Evening News* wondered whether she was the prettiest author writing romantic novels of the day and published a charming photograph to prove their point. Even then, she was using the name Rosamunde Pilcher on her play *The Dashing White Sergeant*, which was broadcast on television in 1954. She first used the name to sign a novel in 1955 in *A Secret to Tell* and published under it exclusively from 1965.

Always popular, she achieved worldwide bestsellerdom with *The Shell Seekers* (Hodder & Stoughton, 1987), since when her success has increased with subsequent titles (including *September, Coming Home*, the 1996 Romantic Novel of the Year, and *Winter Solstice*), reprints, translations, audio versions and movies. She has a worldwide following, especially in the US, where *The Shell Seekers* knocked Tom Wolfe's *Bonfire of the Vanities* off the top of the New York Times bestseller list in 1990, and in Germany, where she is the most popular post-war novelist. German television has adapted many (estimates vary between 60 and 80) of her novels and short stories into TV movies.

She has sold over 60m copies of her work worldwide. As RNA President Diane Pearson said at the Lifetime Achievements Award lunch, 'The British Book Trade owes her a tremendous amount.'

The Shell Seekers was based on her own memories of a childhood in Cornwall. She said that everything she loved was in that book: Bohemian people, paintings, Cornwall, the way London used to be. She felt bereft when she finished it. The heroine, Penelope, reviews her life and family while considering what to do with her prized possession, a picture, *The Shell Seekers*, painted by her father. The story is told in flashbacks, Penelope's own and those of her three children, and it has a wonderful feeling for the Cornish landscape, for wartime London and for the contrasting lives of Bohemian artists and established gentry. Above all, it is the characters and their tragedies and joys which enchanted the reading public and continue to do so. It has been adapted for screen (1989 starring Angela Lansbury and Patricia Hodge) and the theatre (by Charlotte Bingham and Terence Brady) and stands up well to both. There is a sense of human endurance, of the ability to hunker down and cope, which in theory should have been out of step with the Me Generation and Reagonomics. But the *New York Times* reviewer said that now he had found Rosamunde Pilcher, he was not going to let her go; and in three weeks, almost entirely by word of mouth, it was a US bestseller. It was the highest selling paperback of the nineties in the US and in the UK was nominated by the general public as fiftieth in the 100 books in the BBC's Big Read, along with Tolkien, du Maurier, Dickens and Austen.

Coming Home, her Romantic Novel of the Year, is recognisably in the same world but Judith Dunbar, the heroine, is even more of an outsider. She is embraced by the family of a friend from boarding school, Loveday Carey-Lewis, and when her parents leave for Singapore, spends holidays with the Carey-Lewises in their magnificent, crumbling Cornish house, Nancherrow. The pull of the house, particularly on Judith, struck a nerve with many readers and Nancherrow became a character in its own right. The social upheaval of the war, which threw into the melting pot all previous assumptions about class and property, adds a dimension to the family's story. Pilcher has said that it is the closest she has ever come to autobiography, not because any of the characters are her, but because such things happened to her and she wanted her grandchildren to know what it was like. She succeeded brilliantly. In 1998 it was made into a TV two-parter, starring Peter O'Toole and Joanna Lumley, with a wonderful sense of wartime tensions and gorgeous Cornish settings including Penzance and Prideaux Place.

Cornwall, however, is not Rosamunde Pilcher's only landscape of the heart. She married a Scotsman and much of her work is set there. *September*, for instance, is about two interlocking families in the Highlands, as they prepare for a 21st birthday party. *Winter Solstice* (2000) is partly about the decline of the great Scottish estates, as well as a late-flowering love affair between two people both recovering from tragedies. In 2010 she received an Honorary Doctorate from Dundee University.

What is the irresistible appeal of a Pilcher novel? There are the characters of course, especially the strong matriarch (and the wonderfully affectionate dogs) and a wonderful sense of place. There is warmth and gentleness, along with a sharp eye and and a poignant sense of time. There is also, as Joanna Trollope said in her fiftieth Anniversary address to the RNA, hope. Dreadful things happen and the characters reel back, almost destroyed. Yet they suffer and then regroup and go on, find solutions, mend bad relationships, endure, find new sources of happiness. An Amazon reviewer writing about reading *September* in the terrible months after 9/11 said that it raised her spirits and broadened her hopes for humanity. No accolade could be higher or more deserved.

Mary Stewart

Mary Stewart is quite simply a classic. She virtually invented the romantic suspense genre with her first novel *Madam, Will You Talk?* (Hodder & Stoughton 1954). She has published 20 adult novels, of which 14 were New York Times Bestsellers, including her respected Merlin trilogy.

She was the first author to combine mystery, action and a love story, giving all elements equal weight. Usually, these novels were told in the first person by the heroine, an independent, principled and practical person, who gets involved in the mysterious action by chance. (In *My Brother Michael* it is because she forgets that 'ne' means 'yes' in Greek.) The heroine will stay in the adventure because her sympathy has been engaged by one of the other characters and she wants to help. The events stretch her to new skills and confidence, while the hero is sometimes a challenging stranger, sometimes someone she thinks she knows and will need to re-assess. In every case, hero and heroine grow in stature and self-understanding as their feelings develop, the villains are defeated and the mystery solved.

Above all, the books are beautifully written. Stewart has a poetic sensibility in her response to place, landscape and history. No one writes about food as well as she does, except perhaps Elizabeth David. How British readers, still rationed under post war austerity, must have loved the glorious meal in *Madam, Will you Talk?* and the midnight feast in *Nine Coaches Waiting.*

The books are very much of their time in manners and mores— everyone smokes, including the heroines, especially when needing to collect their thoughts—but at the same time the truthfulness of the characterisation and the beauty of the writing make them timeless. When the publisher reissued the entire works in 2006, Amazon was full of people welcoming them because their last copies had fallen to pieces, as well as a whole generation of new and grateful readers.

Mary Stewart has inspired generations of novelists, from the sixties RNA membership to today's, from Anne Maybury, herself an inter-national bestseller, to Meg Cabot, bestselling author of *The Princess Diaries*, who says Stewart's books are compulsively readable. Ask RNA members why, and they will tell you about her terrific story-telling, lyrical prose, lightly-handled erudition (one of her characters says that poetry is good material to think with) and wondrously sensual description. We can all quote favourite moments—an egret flying out of a lemon grove, a dusty Greek hillside where the heroine hides in a cave listening to a violent encounter she does not understand until it is too late, racing down a misty zigzag, dawn at Les Baux. From a rare interview in *Argosy* magazine in 1967 it was clear that Stewart was a compulsive redrafter, not because she was thinking about her readers but to satisfy her own standards and her faultless ear. Mary Stewart herself said she didn't know what people saw in her books but perhaps she created a picture, a bright world for them to go into.

Yes. Exactly.

Judy Piatkus

When Judy Piatkus set up her own publishing house in 1979 she decided to champion books and authors she believed in. Her rationale was that if she liked the book then she was sure that there were lots of women out there who would too. And time and again she was proved right.

Furthermore, Judy didn't follow trends—she set them. When mass market paperback originals were the rage, Judy bought the hardback rights for such authors as Nora Roberts and Virginia Andrews to sell their titles into libraries. She then branched out into her own hardback list and, when it became harder to sell on the paperback rights to other publishers, she decided it was time to venture into mass market paperbacks herself. Judy spotted the gap in the market for Mind Body Spirit books way before 'holistic approach' or 'feng shui' had entered the nation's vocabulary. What she thought was forward thinking, others might have called risk-taking but Judy's flair and instinct for the industry proved her right time and again.

Judy has always believed in romantic fiction. There were a number of authors at the 2009 Awards Lunch, when Catherine Jones presented her with her Lifetime Achievement Award, who owe their first publishing deal to Judy. 'I am one of them,' said Catherine. 'Judy published my first book more years ago than I care to think about—and I think I got a glimpse of the risk-taking side of her when I met her for the very first time. I'd been invited to her offices in Windmill Street to sign my contract and I was just about to put pen to paper when Judy said, "And what's your next book going to be about?"

'To which I replied, "Next book! But I've only just finished this one."

'Trust me that's not the response any publisher wants to hear, but instead of whisking the contract away from me and showing me the door, she just smiled sweetly and said she was sure I'd come up with an idea *really soon*. I got the hint.

'Apart from giving very many individual members of the RNA their first break—Trisha Ashley, Kate Harrison, Emma Lee-Potter are just a few that spring to mind—Judy Piatkus also looked out for the organisation as a whole. When she heard that Parker Pens were hoping to sponsor a book award she pointed them in our direction. She has sent her staff to our conferences and she herself has spoken at our meetings and she has always supported the RNA Award both by submitting books and with financial help.

'Judy Piatkus has been a fantastic friend to the RNA and by giving Judy this Lifetime Achievement Award we are just touching on the huge debt that we—as authors and as an organisation—owe her.'

John Hale of Robert Hale, Publishers

In an industry which has more than its share of starry 'showbiz' personalities, it is refreshing to come across someone in publishing as retiring and unobtrusive as John Hale. A quiet, witty man, he is rarely seen at parties or literary functions and eschews all the more flamboyant aspects of the trade. Nonetheless he has been an enormous supporter of the RNA over the years, a great many big names have begun their careers with him, Jean Plaidy and Robert Goddard among them, and when an author, having been given a start with Robert Hale, goes on to bigger and more famous things, there is nothing but goodwill from the 'parent' company.

Robert Hale Ltd was founded in 1936 by Robert Hale who had previously been a director of Hutchinson. On his death in 1956 the firm passed into the hands of his son, John, a publisher with an analytical mind and astuteness about the marketing qualities of publishing which perhaps explains why, in an industry beset by giant takeovers and buy-outs, Hale is still an independent and family-run business—practically a protected species in today's publishing climate. The atmosphere within the company is a happy one—staff tend to remain for many years and it is reassuring to know that the third generation of the family is working within the firm.

Although we at the RNA are grateful to him for giving so many of our members a start on the publishing ladder, the firm is by no means predominantly a publisher of romantic fiction and historicals. Biography, travel, topographical, general non-fiction and a wide spectrum of across-the-board fiction grace Hale's list.

But it is for his generosity and support of the RNA that he is one of our most respected Associate Vice Presidents; generosity not just in giving so many of our members their first publication, but for financial contributions towards the Major Award and general running of the Association. We were delighted to give him an RNA Lifetime Achievement Award in 2009 and we thank him.

Maeve Binchy

At the Awards Lunch on 16th March 2010, the RNA presented Maeve Binchy with a Lifetime Achievement Award in recognition of the joy she has given to millions of readers around the world. Her first novel, *Light a Penny Candle* (1982), was the story of an English evacuee's lifelong friendship with an Irish girl. Her books have sold an estimated 45m copies in 39 countries worldwide.

Chairman Katie Fforde said that Maeve Binchy was not only a household name but a national treasure and one of the best storytellers of the last 50 years. Binchy received her award in Ireland and sent a video message saying, 'Thank you very much for giving me this opportunity to say how delighted I am with my Lifetime Achievement Award, and to have it on its fiftieth anniversary is even better. I've always admired the Association because it's managed to make us believe that stories are important and that we can get lost in the lives of other people.'

Maeve Binchy was born in Ireland and first came to fame as London correspondent of the *Irish Times*. Her first novel was a best-seller in the UK and the US. Quintessentially Irish in inspiration, she sets her novels mostly in Ireland and often contrasts the problems characters encounter in that country with, say, those in the UK or North America. Family is always an intensely important part of the characters and plots in her books and so, often, is the tension between urban and rural life. *Tara Road*, the story of a house swap between Ria, an Irish woman, and Marilyn from New England, was Oprah's Book Club choice in 1999. Maeve was delighted, admiring Oprah for taking too much solemnity out of reading and supporting books that would tell a good story.

That is exactly the sort of book that the RNA has appreciated throughout its fifty years and Binchy provides excellent material for readers who feel the same. Not that her stories are without serious themes. She says herself that *The Scarlet Feather* (her book which she always suggests people start with) deals with the huge importance of family in Ireland but also the irrelevance of class consciousness and the necessity of courage.

She is also philosophical about her work. When Hollywood filmed *Circle of Friends*, starring Chris O'Donnell and Minnie Driver, they changed the ending to make it more upbeat. She agreed, as long as the heroine did not take the hero back too easily, but said honestly that in real life she thought nobody would have given him up. He was just too gorgeous.

Her books have a wonderful vitality, are poignant, humorous, touching and, occasionally, tragic. Above all, her characters are resilient and courageous in the face of adversity. To our delight there is a new Maeve Binchy, *The Return Journey*, published by Orion in 2010.

Joanna Trollope

Joanna Trollope was born in her grandfather's Gloucestershire rectory and, as she once said with considerable politeness when approached by a born-again Christian, 'I was born very quietly into the Church of England and have never had occasion to leave it'.

After university and marriage she worked as a schoolteacher while at the same time researching and writing several historical novels, one of which, *Parson Harding's Daughter* won the Romantic Novel of the Year Award in 1980. She was also the author of a non-fiction study of women in the British Empire, *Britannia's Daughters*.

In the late 1980s she completely re-invented her writing career and began a series of novels dealing with contemporary people and the dilemmas of modern life. Because, after her long run of historicals, she said she was 'addicted to research', the first of her new titles did require detailed background investigation. *The Choir*, set in a cathedral city, explores not only the structure and everyday working of a choir school, but also the problems of those connected with the cathedral—the lonely mother of a chorister, the ex-chorister, now a young man who cannot cope with adult life, and—among her most brilliant characters—the ambitious but tortured Dean and his commanding wife.

The book was published but nothing very much happened to it and with her next title she changed to a hardcover publisher who sold her paperback rights to Black Swan, where her sales and popularity began to grow. It was with the publication of *The Rector's Wife* that she exploded into bestsellerdom—knocking Jeffrey Archer off the number one slot on the paperback bestseller list.

Since then every title has been eagerly awaited by her huge readership. She covers an enormous canvas of today's problems—broken marriages, step-children, adoption, falling in love with the wrong people. Her subject matter is commonplace in today's society, but dealt with in her books with sensitivity, sympathy and an attempt to explain how and why these things happen.

She has been a loyal and keen supporter of the RNA for many years and in 2010, exactly 30 years after winning the Romantic Novel of the Year Award, she was presented with a

Lifetime Achievement Award. In 1996 she was appointed OBE in the Queen's Birthday Honours List for services to literature.

Mike Legat Associate Vice President of the RNA
Diane Pearson writes:
Mike Legat, publisher, author and teacher, is one of the founder members of our organisation and has been an ardent supporter, most particularly in our early years when mainstream publishers were perhaps a little slow to recognise us. Publishers who specialised in romance and romantic fiction were of course actively involved in our beginnings, but Mike Legat, as Editorial Director of a large and successful mainstream paperback house (publishers of James Baldwin, Leon Uris, Frederick Forsyth, Joseph Heller etc) not only launched a thriving romance list but set out to find and encourage new romantic novelists.

His publishing career began at the age of 18 when he went to work at the Bodley Head as Assistant to the Publicity Manager, a rather grand title, which, as he himself relates, turned out to be 'office boy'—that is, sharpening pencils, running errands, and making the tea, (which because of war shortages was, more often than not, Bovril). However, he did receive enormous publishing experience as he moved round the various departments and after his war service in the Navy, he returned to Bodley Head as Production Manager, eventually leaving and joining Transworld Publishers in 1950. Here, under the influence of Ian Ballantine, he developed an all-embracing attitude to every possible type of fiction and non-fiction. He became Editorial Director of Corgi Books in 1952, and eventually was recognised as one of the most popular, ethical, and important figures on the London publishing scene.

Corgi Books, like most paperback publishers at that time, was primarily a reprint house (that is, publishing paperback editions of books already hardcovered) but Mike, as well as buying paperback rights to romantic fiction from firms like Mills & Boon, also went out and encouraged new writers. He took them onto the Corgi list as original paperbacks, sometimes indeed finding them a hardcover publisher so they could have that much coveted hardcover edition (much more important then than it is now). Even authors he acquired through hardcover sources received a hands-on editorial relationship with him: Lucilla Andrews, Kate Norway, Ursula Bloom, Claire Rayner (writing as Sheila Brandon) all worked closely with him and indeed, as has been described elsewhere in this book, he commissioned fresh and new genres from them when he felt the marketplace was changing.

It was at this time that I was taken on at Corgi as a junior editor and copywriter. Although I had been writing—unsuccessfully—for some time it was from Mike that I gleaned much of the craft of writing, and most certainly I learned how to edit and relate to authors. Mike gave exactly the same amount of time and creative energy to the humblest writers of westerns, crime and romance as he did to major bestsellers. He was always available on the telephone and his long editorial letters were masterpieces of critical and encouraging advice. His patience was unlimited and he would spend hours going through a typescript in detail until the author 'got it right'.

He was a regular attendee at RNA meetings, giving sound and sensible advice in our early days, the advice of a mainstream, important publisher who also had the wellbeing of the RNA at heart.

In 1971 Mike wrote the first of his publishing guides, *Dear Author*, sub-titled 'Letters from a working publisher to authors, prospective and published'. It was the first of a highly successful series aimed at helping writers to understand every aspect of a writer's life, from how to plot, write historical novels, how to understand publisher's contracts, choose an agent et al. Perhaps the most successful was *An Author's Guide to Publishing* which is regarded as the standard work on the subject.

In 1973 Mike left Corgi to become the Editorial Director of Cassell, and five years later he left to become a full-time writer, not just of his publishing guides, but of five historical sagas, and two horror novels where he worked in collaboration with another author.

Since then his services to writers have been invaluable. He has been on the Management Committee of the Society of Authors, judged several writing competitions including the Betty Trask, has taught creative writing at local adult education classes and at week-long courses at further education colleges. He served as Chairman of the Swanwick School for Writers for several years and has been actively involved in many other writers' schools and teaching courses.

When one is a member of any writing organisation, there is always the danger of one's viewpoint becoming parochial and over-intense. Mike's value to the RNA has been not just his support of our aims and abilities, but also that he has brought a broad and catholic knowledge of publishing and writing across a wide canvas of genres to our organisation.

Anne Maybury Vice President and bestseller

Anne Maybury was a founder member of the RNA. Indeed, she served on an early entertainments sub-committee which failed to provide enough tea at the 1961 AGM (a communication problem, apparently). In 1968 she became a Vice President and remained so until her death in February 1993, aged over 80 and still regularly coming to meetings. She is remembered with great affection as someone who was always welcoming to new members and a good friend to older ones, always ready with entertaining conversation and support, as well as words of advice, if asked.

By that time many RNA members would have forgotten (or never known) that in her day she was a million seller, and much admired worldwide, particularly in the States where she did several book tours in the sixties and seventies. Indeed, she wrote a piece for the *RNA News* in 1979 called 'What America Really Wants'. She had clearly been working closely with her US editors and paid tribute to the time and patience they were willing to expend if they could see mutual rewards. 'The market,' she wrote, 'is immense, the Americans generous in both praise and payment and tireless if they think they can turn a writer into a top seller.'

Her first published novel was *The Stars Grow Pale*, set in China and published by Mills & Boon in 1936, when she would still have been in her mid-twenties. She also wrote as Katherine Troy. But her greatest success was as Anne Maybury in the romantic suspense (or modern Gothic) genre, which really took off in the sixties.

In the *RNA News* April-May 1967, Alice Chetwynd Ley reported Maybury's talk on the genre:

> The suspense novel, she said, is rather like the fairy
> tale, with the King, the Queen, Prince and Demon King
> all brought up to adult life. It touches melodrama, but
> must be light and have constant movement. The setting is
> important, as it creates the kind of atmosphere which is
> so essential a part of this type of novel; but it must
> be kept in outline and never allowed to overshadow the
> story line and the characters. Keep your heroine in the
> forefront of the story, Anne Maybury advised. She must
> be deeply involved in the action, not simply set down in
> a situation with only a passive part to play.
> Finally, concentrate on the opening of the story,
> which will win or lose your reader.

Accepting her Vice Presidency the next year, though, Maybury confided that she disliked labels: 'Gothic; suspense; romance. I feel that a piece of creative work should be judged entirely on its merits without categorising. But readers ask for these categories and we must comply.'

Her stories featured adventurous, lively, well-educated heroines, who were nearly always alone and in danger, pitted against conspiracy or an overwhelming opponent whom they did not understand. Heroes were enigmatic and sometimes you weren't sure they were heroes for quite a long time into the story. The settings were exotic for the time—the Far East (*Green Fire*); a French chateau (*The Moonlit Door*); Rome (*The Terracotta Palace*)—and undoubtedly were part of the appeal. Contemporary readers said that her sense of place was rivalled only by Mary Stewart's. Her heroines, however, were far less confident than Stewart's clear-headed teachers, vets and actresses, and the menace was greater, sometimes even enhanced by the supernatural.

These elements of her fiction were based solidly in her own

character and experiences. Dorothy Mackie Low (*RNA News*, Spring 1993), recorded that Anne Maybury had 'travelled widely and brought a sense of adventure into her books, often derived from bizarre personal experiences. She seemed to attract excitement, even danger, and said that she had met more than one murderer during her travels abroad.'

As well as her travels, she drew on family legend for her sense of history (she was born Anne Arundel and her ancestors were said to have come over with the Conquest) and her love of poetry, encouraged by her father, a distinguished poet. It was Low also, who said that Maybury 'developed early in life the profound interest in human behaviour and intrigue which was to prove a valuable asset in her writing'. She was also charming, interested in everything, very well read, great fun and she loved a good party—but she was a professional and she never missed a deadline, no matter what the social temptations.

Eventually Modern Gothics fell out of favour and her novels with them. However, Maybury remained a name to conjure with whenever the best of the genre was considered. *Romantic Times* (issue 173 August 1998) recommended her *Walk in the Paradise Garden* as a book by a master of the genre, to be read by all enthusiasts for the then re-discovered genre. And in 2000 her American publisher Bantam reissued it.

Above all, she wrote beautifully. Illustrating Anne Maybury's ability to delight the senses, intrigue the mind and grab the reader from the first moment, Dorothy Mackie Low quoted the first paragraph from *Ride a White Dolphin*:

'The shutters creaked as I opened them onto the fluid gold of the early Venetian morning. And as the quiet of the room met the stillness of the lagoon, I thought a voice behind me called my name.'

Who could resist?

Sheila Walsh Vice President and multi award winner

Many writers who come through the New Writers' Scheme find a publisher and move onto other things, leaving the RNA behind them. Shelia Walsh was not one of them. She did most jobs, on and off the committee, won both the New Writers' Award, (the Netta Muskett) and the Romantic Novel of the Year and nurtured the north-western chapter of the RNA like a mother.

Sheila Walsh first joined the NWS in the seventies and, after three years of writing, won the Netta Muskett Award for 1974 with her first completed full length novel, *The Golden Songbird* in 1974. Published by Hurst & Blackett, with the US paperback rights sold to Signet in 1975, it was a classic Regency: Miss Lucia Mannering's stepfather loses her in a wager to dashing Hugo, Marquis of Mandersley.

Sheila Walsh, RNA News, Summer 1974

She is what educationalists call a 'late developer'. She says she has always been an incurable romantic and an avid reader, being unable to remember a time when she was not making up stories and acting them out in her head, although she never had the urge to write them down.

She was born in Birmingham, spent a contented childhood there, with an elder sister, until wartime bombs forced them to leave the city. She then went to Southport, where she still lives, and completed her education at the Notre Dame Convent in Birkdale. She then spent three happy years at work in the local Art College, training as a singer and taking part in amateur dramatics where, incidentally, she met her husband. As a result of her mother's ill-health, she says she then became 'head cook and bottle-washer', a job she declares stood her in good stead when she married; she had been happily married for twenty-four years.

Eventually, she says, the writing bug bit her, but at the same time her sister died tragically, and she was responsible for looking after her own parents, who were not in good health, as well as her own family. She was suffering from claustrophobic frustration as a result of being tied to the house, when Joan Nicholson moved to Southport and started a Writers' Circle, which she joined. Sheila began to write seriously, being encouraged and stimulated all the time to greater efforts; she declares that she is overjoyed to know that her first attempt at a full length novel has won the

Netta Muskett Award and been accepted for publication.
   Sheila Walsh's husband is a jeweller and she has two
daughters — they are all overjoyed, she says, by her
success, only the autocratic Burmese cat signifying his
disapproval by sitting on her writing! She says she had
great fun writing her first book, and her mind is full
of ideas which, if they work out as she hopes, will push
dressmaking and gardening into second place, and keep
the skirting boards happily gathering dust for many
years to come.

Her ambition was realised. She wrote 30 books in 28 years. In 1984 she won the Romantic Novel of the Year Award for *A Highly Respectable Marriage*, published in hardback by Hutchinson and in paperback by Mills & Boon's historical imprint, Masquerade. (It had everything, an orphaned heroine trying to care for her two brothers, who tries to hire herself to a duke as a governess and gets taken on as a wife instead.) After the demise of Hurst & Blackett, Walsh was published by Hutchinson, Arrow and Severn House in the UK and Signet Regency Romance in the US.

She remained a great supporter of local writers and in September 1980 told the committee that the Northern Luncheon [at the Adelphi Hotel] was now becoming highly expensive; she offered to hold a Buffet Luncheon at her home in future years. She did so the following year and 24 attended; the committee thanked her at the November meeting. This eventually turned into a regular summer party at her house, and north-western members who were the beneficiaries remember with equal enthusiasm both the fabulous food and the warm welcome. She was also a shrewd and kindly critic, if asked, as Roger Sanderson (writing as Gill Sanderson for Harlequin Mills & Boon) recalls. Trisha Ashley (published by Avon) likewise appreciated her guidance: 'I loved her dry, sharp-edged humour and she was so very astute.' Sheila Walsh was also elected Life President of the Southport Writers' Circle in 1986.

She regularly attended the London meetings and in 1980 was made a Vice President of the RNA. She was Chairman 1985-87 and, hence, was holding the baton when beloved President,

Mary Burchell, died in December 1986. By that time negotiations were in hand to find a sponsor for the Main Award and the whole landscape of commercial romantic fiction was changing radically from the days in which she sold her first book.

The public's taste for sweet Regencies declined, but Walsh continued to write, albeit at a slower rate, trying her hand at various times at the then fashionable 'hot historical' (which she apparently found very amusing but seems not to have sold, or perhaps, finished) and, with more success, at Liverpool family sagas, the first of which, *Until Tomorrow* (Arrow 1993) was dedicated to son-in-law Andrew and daughter Fran, from whose old-fashioned bakery in Southport she had garnered much of the background.

The changing fashions of the romantic novel

Diane Pearson surveys the changes in genre and style over her long career in publishing and writing:

When I began my career as a rather nervous but hopeful junior editor with Corgi Paperbacks in the early sixties, I was originally given the science fiction list to handle. But of course, I was always dying to get my hands on the romance list and I would watch with avid interest the way my distinguished boss, Mike Legat, handled his romance authors. At that time the main thrust of the romance market, in paperback at any rate, lay with the hospital doctor-nurse genre. Yes, other romances were selling which had either period or contemporary settings, but undoubtedly the most popular were hospital dramas and we were lucky enough to have the Queen of hospital romances, Lucilla Andrews. Not far behind her were Claire Rayner and Kate Norway and the strength of these writers was that all of them were nurses. Lucilla indeed, had been a Nightingale nurse who had cared for blitz victims and the survivors of Dunkirk at St Thomas's Hospital. Their books had an authenticity and realistic quality that derived from their own experiences.

Kate Norway was the most prolific, writing under three names, her own, Bess Norton, and Hilary Neal. On one occasion, I recall, we got one name on the cover and a different one on the title page. We telephoned Alan Boon, from whom we had bought the paperback rights, to apologise and he confessed that they had once managed to get her third name on the back cover. Both he and Kate were most forgiving.

Hurst & Blackett was also one of the major hardcover publishers in this genre and many of their hospital romances helped to dominate the bookshop shelves. It is as well to remember that in the sixties and seventies Mills & Boon did not have the monopoly of nurse romances. At that time they were primarily a hardcover house and many paperback publishers were able to buy rights from them. As the marketplace changed over the years, Mills & Boon slowly took over the genre until now they are the primary publishers for this particular brand.

The strange thing about changing fashions is that there is always a prototype who writes long before the genre becomes mass market and popular but who somehow launches a new fashion in novels. Thus it was with the next wave of popularity, the gothic—and that's what they were called in the middle/late sixties although the title eventually morphed into suspense/romance, and later, women in jeopardy.

Of course the most famous and classic gothic is *Jane Eyre* followed by *Rebecca* by Daphne du Maurier. Then, in the 1950s Mary Stewart exploded into the marketplace with her own version of the genre—often minus the sinister house, but nonetheless the suspense of a romantic mystery was there. America took up the baton first and began to hunt for and publish 'gothics'.

The British market, in spite of having Mary Stewart, lagged a bit behind and then tried to catch up as the genre's popularity and sales potential became obvious. At Corgi we had nothing suitable at all, and Mike Legat wrote to our three 'stars', Lucilla, Kate and Claire, and asked them if they felt able to tackle the new and popular genre. He explained the plot in detail—a large dark house in a sombre setting, a brooding taciturn hero with a dreadful secret, and a young heroine who walks into the setting, solves the mystery, and marries the hero. Bless them, the three stars of hospital drama all took on the challenge and wrote their 'gothics'. What's more, so did I, for that letter from Mike to his authors started off my novel writing. I thought, well, I'll have a go too, and did, and got published. Many of our members did particularly well in this genre and one, Anne Maybury, a Vice President of the RNA, became a huge bestseller in America as well as in the UK.

For a while the genre boomed and blossomed. Then—for whatever reason, possibly a marketing and presentation problem—their popularity began to wane. Books by authors like Evelyn Anthony, who was hugely successful, began to be packaged as thrillers and the romantic element played down, at least on the covers. These days romantic suspense is still being published, and in some cases very successfully. Louise Bagshawe does very well but the packaging doesn't shout romantic suspense. It concentrates on the romantic aspect although in the content there is often quite a violent element, miles removed from Mary Stewart. The book trade still has to find a way of presenting these books that nearly every reader one talks to loves.

As the 'gothics' began to cease dominating the shelves, so the next big wave of popular romantic fiction took over.

Back to prototypes: *Forever Amber*, published in 1944, had had an outstanding success, not least because it was considered extremely naughty. Strangely, although the book was hugely popular, the genre did not really catch on until the seventies, when suddenly the 'hot historicals' or 'bodice rippers' exploded into the market place. Undoubtedly the leading imprint for this genre was Troubador, founded by Rosie de Courcy and Leslie Saxby. Between them, they launched a list of authors expert in the field; many other publishers followed and a great many American titles (where the cult had begun) were brought in. The popularity of the genre lasted for quite a time and certainly some of our members had considerable success with their 'hotties'. Rosie de Courcy, at the end of this section, gives us an interesting account of how the new genre came into being.

In the late seventies and early eighties the Georgian/Regency romances became popular. Georgette Heyer (and in some degree,

Jane Austen) was of course the prototype and imprints such as Troubador and Masquerade specialised in them. Most paperback publishers launched their own line. At Corgi we began our Georgian Romance series and featured quite a few RNA members on the list, Sylvia Thorpe, and Alice Chetwynd Ley among them. They never quite dominated the romance shelves as the hospital romances and the hot historicals had done, but they still made a lot of money for the book trade and were immensely popular. They also had a more promising history in that they survived in a smaller but more solid way and are still one of Mills & Boon's most successful brands.

Catherine Cookson had been writing for many years with modest success which gradually grew into tremendous success and proved the prototype for the next explosion of popular fiction—the regional saga. Catherine Cookson came to talk to the RNA in 1970 about her writing and here she spoke about the background of her books.

From RNA News Spring 1970

THE MAKINGS OF A REGIONAL NOVELIST
Report of the 28th January meeting at
St Andrew's Hall

Mrs Catherine Cookson gave a lively and interesting talk on 'The Makings of a Regional Novelist'. She admitted feeling at the start of her career as a novelist that the word 'regional' was some kind of stigma, and, aggravated by the comment of a local acquaintance, decided to shift the setting of her next books to her home town — Hastings. The result of this, said Catherine Cookson, was that nothing in the story had guts except the fish.

She has since written almost entirely about Tyneside. Three men, she said, had had a tremendous influence on her life — her grandfather, Lord Chesterfield, and her husband. Of the first she had many hilarious anecdotes and affirmed that his calling her a 'stinkin' liar' who

would make money one day was a prophecy of her future
career. In Lord Chesterfield's 'Letters to His Son' she
found a rich source of knowledge and the 'culture' she
yearned for.
   By way of a painful breakdown she came finally to
face the fact that not only had her writing to have a
regional background but that she herself must fully
accept the facts of her early life.
   She paid tribute to her husband — the critic on the
hearth.
   She writes three books a year, making use of even
the odd minute, and pointed out that six periods of five
minutes meant half an hour! Apart from its helpfulness,
Catherine Cookson's talk was a story of great courage
which could not fail to inspire us.
MAIR UNSWORTH

Even though sagas do not dominate the paperback shelves as
they did at one time, it is a genre which has not died. Although
their popularity always began in their relevant 'region', inevitably,
publishers found that sales began to spread nationwide. Cookson
was read everywhere, but so were Elvi Rhodes, Audrey Howard,
Josephine Cox and many others. Unlike the gothics and the
hot historicals which came into popularity first in America, this
particular genre grew and flourished in the UK.

Of course, one thinks of Cookson as the writer who launched the
hugely successful genre. At one time she was the biggest paperback
seller in the trade. But there were prototypes before Cookson:
the *Herries Chronicle* series by Hugh Walpole, the books of Arnold
Bennet, particularly *The Old Wives' Tale*, and *King Cotton* by Thomas
Armstrong. In some ways it is a formula which will always be
popular and, as Caroline Sheldon writes at the end of this
passage, rumours of the genre being dead are very untrue.

And so on to the Aga sagas (dreadful classification but one
unfortunately that seems to have stuck). What was it that suddenly
made middle-class, contemporary novels popular? Certainly they
were being written long before the cult began to dominate the

bestseller lists. I can remember reading excellent books of this type and style in the sixties and seventies but one couldn't really paperback them for the popular market as—well—they just weren't popular. One of our members, Maynah Lewis, wrote in this genre, very much before her time. She won the Major Award in 1968 and again in 1972 but, were her books published today, she would be a much bigger name than she was then. Perhaps it was the success of Mary Wesley and Joanna Trollope that set the pattern for the big trend towards what I prefer to call 'relationship novels' rather than Aga sagas.

And so to the latest and present 'big' fashion in romantic reading, chick-lit. Prototype *Bridget Jones* of course, books for a new young market with characters straight out of contemporary middle-class life (chick-lit characters rarely live on a sink estate on benefits) but withall a very popular genre that seems ready to stay for a while. They cover a huge range of styles and content, from Marion Keyes and Lisa Jewell, who verge on the serious novel market but who are packaged as chick-lit, to the enormous fun ones like Sophie Kinsella, possibly more akin to the original *Bridget Jones*. It is a hugely successful genre, and although its popularity will, one supposes, inevitably wane, certain authors will stay on the bestseller lists.

The less explosive genres have had their day too, and still do. The lasting fashions such as the quality historical, although never dominating the market place, survived through good and bad times and it is wonderful to see the historical, in all its guises, back in strength on the bookshelves after a longish period in the wilderness. Like chick-lit, the historical ranges from the highly romantic, mostly published by Mills & Boon, to the serious and literary (but still romantic) books by Tracy Chevalier and Sarah Waters. Georgette Heyer is back on the shelves, so are Jean Plaidy and Anya Seton. There's a revival and it is splendid to see this ever popular genre thriving again. And although there are some successful US writers in this field, it does tend to be dominated by British authors.

The 'sex and shopping' novels (stemming mostly from America) enjoyed a brief spell of success and morphed into 'bonkbusters' but are successful more as individual authors—that is, Jackie Collins et al rather than a huge genre.

Of course one genre, if one can call it that, has been and always will be forever hugely popular and successful—the giant, epic romantic novels which take time, effort, research and stamina to write but nearly always explode onto the bestseller lists and remain classics of their kind for a long time. I suppose the greatest of these is *War and Peace* by Tolstoy. Literature, yes, but also a classic romantic novel covering huge landscapes, huge subjects, and huge heartbreaking relationships at its core. *Gone with the Wind, The Thornbirds, Captain Corelli's Mandolin, The Far Pavilions, Penmarric* and many others follow the great tradition. Sometimes these epic romantic novels come out of a writer's one-off inspiration and they never write again—*Gone with the Wind* by Margaret Mitchell and *Zemindar* by Valerie Fitzgerald. Other writers such as Rosamunde Pilcher and Susan Howatch manage to perpetuate the genre. Rosie Thomas and Penny Vincenzi also manage, in some remarkable way, to keep producing epic-sized romantic novels which I always think of as operatic in style. They are, perhaps, the most splendid examples of the romantic novel.

If the chick-lit genre is currently the latest and most popular genre of romantic fiction, it is rapidly being challenged by the paranormal romance, a fashion beginning in the US, and quickly becoming immensely popular here. Read mainly by a young market—teenage up to early twenties—reports from the US say they are increasingly being read by older women. The time-slip novels are read by an older market—*The Time Traveller's Wife* by Audrey Niffenegger, and Michelle Paver's brilliant and wildly romantic novel, *A Place in the Hills*—but undoubtedly the big successes, backed and perhaps inspired by immensely popular TV series and films, are vampire romances, followed by werewolves, wizards, dragons and so on. I don't think at the moment we have had zombie romances but I could be wrong. I feel it may be difficult to make a zombie hero romantic. Although paranormal romance began its popularity in the States, many British authors are making good sales and some have had lucrative TV and film deals. It is a new and exciting genre.

I thought it would be interesting to have 'experts' in some of these genres giving their memories and views on just how and why they came into such waves of popularity. Here are some comments by those who either knew or have studied these hugely successful waves of romantic fiction.

Medical romances

Kate Hardy, author

Medical romances have been going for decades. Mills & Boon have published them for almost 100 years, and Harlequin chose Anne Vinton's medical romance *The Hospital in Buwambo* for the first Mills & Boon title in Canada in 1957. In the 1960s, medical romance author Ivy Ferrari was as famous as the Beatles; her daughter Lillie wrote a fan letter to George Harrison and received a reply from his mother asking, 'Are you by any chance related to a writer called Ivy Ferrari, who writes doctor-and-nurse romances?'

So what's the secret of their appeal?

In the early years, nursing was one of the few career opportunities open to women, alongside teaching and secretarial work; and as Mills & Boon novels tend to reflect their time, nurse heroines and doctor heroes were very popular. Nowadays, again reflecting contemporary career trends and attitudes, the heroine of a medical romance is just as likely to be a doctor as a nurse; if she is a nurse, the doctor hero will see her as his equal. He'll recognise that she's a professional, and that as a senior nurse she's far more likely to pick up on changes in a patient's condition than a wet-behind-the-ears junior doctor will—and she'll know exactly what needs to be done to help the patient.

Medical dramas have been popular on TV and radio, from the days of *Dr Kildare*, *Dr Finlay's Casebook* and *Emergency Ward 10* all the way through to modern dramas such as *ER* and *Grey's Anatomy*; and the BBC's *Casualty* (first aired in 1986) is the longest-running medical drama in the world, with a prime-time Saturday night slot. So it's unsurprising that readers look for something similar in a medical romance; one of the most popular settings is the emergency department, followed closely by maternity units, children's wards and family (GP) practices. The medical continuity *Brides of Penhally Bay* series, set in a GP surgery in a Cornish fishing village, was so loved by readers that a second series was brought out.

As with the other Mills & Boon lines, medical romance moves with the times. As well as the traditional settings that readers love, medical romances have been set in the worlds of forensic medicine and global aid organisations. Our characters include mountain rescue teams and firefighters; others work to make people's dreams come true in fertility centres; and we've even had a medical team working on the slopes of Mount Everest.

The medical romance hero is someone who can work on a mountainside—but he can do more than that. 'He's a man who will move mountains,' according to senior editor Sheila Hodgson, 'to save a life or resolve a medical problem—the kind of person who we all dream of having on our side in a medical emergency. He is strong, intelligent, successful and respected. He may struggle in certain areas of his life, juggling his work with his children, with his emotions. Generally the heroine will help him resolve his struggles; equally he will help her resolve hers. We almost always see his point of view, as well as the heroine's. He is a man of action and precision; he has high standards in his work and expects them of others. He can display wit and certainly oodles of charm. He may be the heroine's boss, or he may not, but they are equally matched and equally respected in their fields.'

One of the reasons I enjoy writing medical romances as well as reading them is that there's very much a 'real world' feel to them. The hero and heroine are centre stage, as they should be, but the romance takes place with a supporting cast of characters and patients. Add the warmth and caring nature of the medical world, emotional conflicts that are reflected in life-and-death situations, and you end up with a book that will make you feel that this could really happen. Medical dramas touch most people's lives at some point—that's actually how I started writing romances, at my six-week-old daughter's hospital bedside. There was a happy ending in this case: the book was accepted on her first birthday and published on her second. And although not all dramas have a happy ending, a medical romance always will...

Romantic suspense
Anna Lucia, author
I fell in love with romantic suspense reading Mary Stewart. For me, suspenseful, adventurous romances offer stakes that are greater than the relationship alone. This is not life and love—it's life and death.

When Charity and Richard make an emotional commitment in *Madam, Will You Talk?* there's more at stake than their hearts and future happiness. There's a child's life, murder and liberty in the mix. For contrast, when Linda tries to oppose Raoul, the hero of *Nine Coaches Waiting*, she does it to save Philippe, the young Comte de Valmy's life, and the desperate pain for both protagonists following that mistaken betrayal of trust has me crying through the last chapters, even on my ninth read. The life and death stakes may be high, but the emotion that balances it is equally deep.

Yet I remember vividly my first ever Romantic Novelists' Association conference. I arrived in a state of awe at my own nerve; I left with two strong messages: *write what you love*, and, *there is no UK market for romantic suspense*. Which left me in a bit of a pickle.

The romantic suspense market in America has been going strong for a while. Books abound with FBI, CIA, police, military, PI heroes and heroines, facing up to serial killers, kidnappers, spies, terrorists and sundry plotters and falling in love at the same time. At the time of writing, Nora Roberts is at number one in the paperback fiction list with *The Hollow Hills*. Romantic suspense is a common category in bookshops and libraries and in literary competitions. It's a classification the reading public recognises. I frequently have to explain the term to reading Brits.

So I'm a writer in exile. As I write this, my first novel has been out on shelves for its first week, on shelves 3,300 miles away. Because I write romantic suspense and editors say they can't sell it in the UK—nobody knows where to shelve it.

Which brings me, inevitably, to the subject of Nora Roberts. Romantic Suspense may not have its own shelf over here, but Nora Roberts frequently does. With around 300 million copies of her books in print and 147 *New York Times* bestseller listings to her credit, Nora Roberts is a US household name and a romance and suspense writing sensation. Her UK reissues did not, at first, perform as well as hoped. There has been much debate online and elsewhere about covers, marketing, and whether to package her books as romance or women's fiction. (Show some of Nora's UK covers to a US fan and they'll say, 'but that makes it look like women's fiction, not romance!' A UK marketer will reply, 'Oh, good'.) But that is in the past. She is not as big in the UK as the US yet but recognition is beginning to build.

With the advent of Louise Bagshawe's *Passion*, marketed as James Bond for girls and shortlisted for the 2010 Romantic Novel of the Year, I can only hope that the UK market is changing at last.

Hot historicals

Rosemary de Courcy, publisher

The craze for hot historicals, or bodice rippers, began, as so many crazes do, in America.

Peter Mayer's secretary at Avon Books in New York was a spectacular looking girl with a waterfall of long dark hair, called Nancy Coffey. One of Nancy's jobs was to sift through the slush pile and there she found a manuscript called *The Flame and the Flower* by a young housewife, rather splendidly named Kathleen E Woodiwiss. In her submission letter Kathleen Woodiwiss said that she had written the novel because she couldn't find anything really exciting to read any more. And exciting it certainly was.

The story was a vast, breathless romp, set in the eighteenth century, in which a young innocent girl (the flower) becomes the hostage of a dashing, rather wicked sea captain (the flame) with a well-concealed heart of gold. He takes her virginity against her will, and then ravishes her whenever he feels like it, while secretly falling in love with her. They fight and make love ceaselessly, through interminable adventures, before sailing off into the sunset and wedded bliss.

The Flame and the Flower was published as an Avon Spectacular in 1976 and became a *New York Times* bestseller with a million copies in print. It was followed by two more huge, bestselling Nancy Coffey discoveries: *Sweet Savage Love* by Rosemary Rogers and *Moonlight Madness* by Laurie McBain, and so the bodice ripper craze was born.

Meanwhile, in London, we had started a paperback imprint called Futura for BPC and at Macdonald & Jane's, our hardcover sister company, Lesley Saxby had launched a new romance imprint called Troubador. Lesley was one of the greatest editors I have ever known, with an unerring eye for quality romantic fiction. My job was to publish in paperback the novels which Lesley bought for her fledgling hardcover list. The first—and really only—hint of friction came when Anthony Cheetham brought back a copy of *The Flame and the Flower* from New York and told Lesley that he wanted to publish it as a Troubador Spectacular and then, if that worked, to follow with *Sweet Savage Love* and *Moonlight Madness*.

Lesley could see at once that these were very commercial novels, but she also thought they were pretty silly (why, for example, did those incessantly ravished girls never get pregnant?) and not the direction in which she wanted to take Troubador. In the end we agreed that there would be a degree of latitude with Troubador paperbacks, which would enable us to publish the bodice-ripping ladies, without contaminating the altogether classier list which Lesley was building over at Macdonald & Jane's.

Whether or not I would enjoy reading them now, I cannot say, but I must admit that back then I absolutely adored those hot historicals. Of course Lesley was right, they were silly and wildly over-written, but they were also sizzling with energy and great fun. At least, I thought so.

The first one I bought completely off my own bat was *Love's Tender Fury* by Jennifer Wilde (later revealed to be a man writing under a pseudonym) and it was also the first to come from

Warner Paperbacks, rather than Avon. It shot on to the bestseller list on both sides of the Atlantic and suddenly, of all the commercial fiction genres, male or female, the hot historical was *the* big category.

Anthony had always believed in commissioning original fiction for Futura. Two of our biggest successes were to be Ken Follett's *The Eye of the Needle* and *The Flowers of the Field* by Sarah Harrison. Now our New York scout and agent, Nat Sobel, said to us that we really ought to be commissioning British hot historicals and buying US rights for him to sell.

The first author I approached was one of Lesley's discoveries, Phyllida Barstow, married to Duff Hart-Davis, and author of a romantic suspense novel with a hint of sexiness about some of the love scenes. Lesley approved my choice. 'Yes,' she said, 'a very modern girl. She could do it for you.' The second was a short story writer of agent Carol Smith's called Annette Motley and the third, a well-established romantic novelist called Edna Dawes, who we re-invented as Emma Drummond.

Phyllida Barstow, under the pseudonym Olivia O'Neill, set her bodice ripper, *Distant Thunder*, in India. Annette Motley took an idea of mine about a woman going to find her husband during the Crusades, for *My Lady's Crusade* and Emma Drummond's *Scarlet Shadows* was set during the Crimean War.

The first to be offered to the States was *Distant Thunder*. I shall never forget Nat Sobel ringing me at Futura to say that the first editor to see it—Arlene Friedmann at Fawcett—was prepared to offer $25,000 on condition that the author did a great deal of rewriting under her direction. I cannot now think what possessed me, because it was downright foolhardy, but I indignantly replied that it was not nearly enough money and, with author and agent's blessing, told Nat to turn it down. Both he and Anthony were very annoyed with us, but reluctantly set about holding an auction and cheered up a bit when Fawcett agreed to leave their $25,000 in as a floor.

I still have the piece of yellowed paper on which Nat recorded the various stages of the *Distant Thunder* auction. At the time we were also bidding for UK rights in *The Thorn Birds* by Colleen McCullough. Anthony was in New York and rang me with an update. Did I want the good news or the bad? I wanted to get the bad news out of the way. The bidding was still on for *The Thorn Birds*, the money had got crazy, Harper & Row had removed Australian rights mid-auction, was I still sticking to my guns about how wonderful it was? And the good news? My Olivia O'Neill novel, *Distant Thunder*, had gone for $250,000 to Berkley.

A month later Nat sold *My Lady's Crusade* for $220,000 to Bantam, and *Scarlet Shadows* to Dell for $100,000. The last one to hit the big time was Julia Fitzgerald's *Royal Slave*, sold to Ballantine for $90,000. We were on the most extraordinary roll. I was interviewed on radio and television by feminist journalists who thought we were peddling dangerous romantic fantasies about rape and male domination.

But the truth was that these commissioned British bodice rippers did not hit the spot with the reading public, either side of the Atlantic. Whereas we were selling 250,000 copies of Rosemary Rogers, Kathleen Woodiwiss and Jennifer Wilde, 100,000 copy subscriptions on the others were invariably followed by heavy returns and diminishing sales on subsequent books. It really was an American genre and perhaps, too, the public sensed that those novels of Olivia O'Neill, Emma Drummond and Annette Motley were cooked-up jobs.

In any event, by 1978, taste was swinging towards great panoramic family sagas like *The Thorn Birds*, *Csardas* and *The Flowers of the Field*. The day of the hot historical was over quite quickly, but while it lasted was incredibly intense, heady and a lot of fun—just like the novels themselves.

Sagas

Caroline Sheldon, agent

Rumours of the death of the saga are greatly exaggerated. It's always seemed to me there's something about the saga genre that predisposes publishers to predict its demise. An editor just needs to get a whiff of a decline of sales for one author and the whole genre is declared moribund. But in fact, from the days of its earliest and greatest exponent Catherine Cookson, the genre has been remarkably resilient with new names springing into the bestseller lists and achieving huge sales in every decade.

I think the greatest gifts sagas offer readers are a gripping telling of an old-fashioned (in the best sense of the word) tale and a nostalgic feel for a time when there was a much greater sense of community. And this sense of community is tied in with poverty. The saga world is a world where misfortune was always at the door so neighbours helping each other was an essential part of survival. People went to each other's houses to borrow candle ends or a twist of sugar. People watched out for each other. Kids played barefoot in the street. No one sat home alone watching celebrity television.

The regional setting of the saga forms a part of its success. Grimy urban backgrounds have always attracted. Liverpool, the North East, Glasgow and the East End of London have all led the field and the more closely an author is associated with an area, its language and mores the better. Pity the poor author who wants to write a regional saga and whose links are in Essex, Hampshire or Sussex. Sagas and the Home Counties don't go.

But don't let me give the impression great sagas are all misery. At the centre there may be a woman who is repeatedly knocked down by the vicissitudes of fortune and who fights her fate, but there will always be some warmth and often humour in the writing. The warmth of friendship, family links and the love of children are at the heart of the genre. Cold characters do not a saga make.

Over the years the saga has more than bagged its pew in the broad church of romantic fiction. *Vive* the Aga saga, bodice rippers, the chick-lit and the mumlit, the rom com and the gothic, but *vive* the saga too.

The Aga saga

Elizabeth Buchan, author and reviewer

What is it exactly? Romance? *Bildungsroman*? Fantasy? Chronicle? The answer is that the Aga saga combines elements of all these things. It is sometimes spoken of with contempt but they who do so are unwise and are blind to its many pleasures and rewards. For these are novels which have been read, marked and enjoyed by thousands of readers—and not all of them have been women.

Why the sneers? The answer, perhaps, lies in the domestic arena which is generally, but by no means always, the locus for these novels. These are stories of married life, seen usually from the female point of view, and the plot's twists and turns frequently come up against difficult children, straying spouses and elderly relations, not to mention the unruly yearnings of the protagonist. Naturally the family and, by extension, the kitchen in which this mythical saga reposes provides a centre to these narratives. And why not? You do not have to venture down the mean streets, or gallop into battle, or shoot off into space in order to experience the profound and important shifts in sensibility and feeling which mark out our lives, and often change them. These can just as easily be experienced peeling potatoes or wrestling with a tin of soup which is the fate of the majority of us. In that respect, the Aga saga provides democratic reading—for it mirrors life as it pans out for most.

By and large, Aga sagas do not engage directly with politics and economics, nor do they aspire to be epic or sweeping. Rather they deal with politics of individual happiness and the constant changes of the internal landscape. The best purvey a well-mannered subversion and a willingness to confront the darker realities of life. Equally, they can be light and deliciously comic and life affirming. It is their characteristic quietness, observation, truthfulness and lack of showiness that give the Aga saga its special, trustworthy quality.

Chick-Lit

Kate Harrison, author: A girl's right to Jimmy Choos? The trouble with Chick-Lit

Mention the phrase 'chick-lit' to a writer of women's contemporary fiction, and the reaction is likely to be one of the following:

    a) a pained wince;

    b) a heartfelt speech about the complexities of genre definitions;

    c) a punch in the teeth.

Violence is clearly not the answer, but for many chick-lit writers, labels are an issue (and I don't mean not being able to afford a Prada handbag).

Women have been reading, and writing, about their own lives for centuries, of course, but the chick-lit label was born in the mid-1990s. According to Wikipedia, the term was first used in the *New Yorker* magazine article in 1996 and is 'a humorous reference to Chiclets, a kind of candy'.

So far, so sensible, though I have my doubts that a phenomenon with its roots in the UK and Ireland (with writers like Helen Fielding, Marian Keyes and Sophie Kinsella leading the chick-olution) is named after a sweet I've never tasted.

Fielding's heroine, Bridget Jones, was one of the first and is still among the best known chick-lit characters. She became the archetypal singleton heroine: she works in a glamorous industry (publishing) in a glamorous city (London), and worries about her weight, her booze/fag consumption, and, most of all, about the gaping man-shaped hole in her life.

So far, so funny. Bridget—who first appeared in a Jane Austen-influenced newspaper column—was a character women recognised worldwide (though she was also reviled for her 'fuck-witted' behaviour) and the novel sold in its millions.

Both readers and publishers were wanting more, and soon the shelves were groaning with hundreds of similar books. Many of the new chick-lit authors delivered exactly what *Bridget Jones'* readers had enjoyed so much: singleton romances with plenty of humour and 'bonking'. Sophie Kinsella's *Shopaholic* series celebrates the joy of retail, though many critics fail to spot the satirical edge and the message that, actually, shopping doesn't automatically equal happiness.

Other authors had broader agenda: Irish writer Marian Keyes has, at the time of writing, published ten novels dealing with love, but also with infertility, domestic violence, bereavement and, in *Rachel's Holiday*, addiction.

Keyes is not the only author who explores the dark side: in many chick-lit novels, difficult themes are explored through humour, mainly because life has a tendency to veer from tragedy to comedy and back to tragedy again.

But whatever the content, the packaging is almost always the same: a pastel cover (pink is the pastel of choice), a witty title, a cartoon or a picture of shoes on the front. It helps sell books, but it doesn't always reflect the wide-ranging content. So while the genre develops, the derogatory perception of it doesn't change. Maybe it's not surprising—there has always been something faintly sexist and condescending about the idea of 'lit' for 'chicks'.

Not that this attitude to commercial fiction is new. In a 2003 entry on the UK feminist blog *The F Word*, Cazz Blaze cites the example of the nineteenth century Penny Dreadfuls: 'cheap fiction purchased by the masses of varying subject and quality'. She says: 'It was argued that devouring novel after novel would actually make you morally degenerate.'

What critics fail to accept is that many readers have wide-ranging tastes—one day they might read a brilliant Lisa Jewell novel, the next an equally brilliant Booker nominee. There is no law that says readers of chick-lit will only ever read in the genre—and even if they do, it is their choice. The film industry celebrates the idea that a movie can make audiences laugh, cry and forget their problems. Yet in some literary circles, escapism is seen as shameful.

For those of us who are promoted as being part of the genre, it presents a dilemma. Arguing that chick-lit novels can be incisive, relevant or moving as well as funny could make us look arrogant, or dismissive of the earlier 'pure' singleton novels. Yet there's no easy replacement definition: women's contemporary fiction doesn't exactly trip off the tongue.

The truth about chick-lit is that it is like any other genre. Like crime, it encompasses brilliant books and so-so ones, original novels and derivative copycat stories. But when crime writers complain about their treatment by the critics, they might spare a thought for the 'chicks', who have to contend with sexism as well as snobbery.

So where is chick-lit in 2010? The problem of definition remains. If you click on 'chick-lit' on the Play.com website, for example, you'll find novels by Paul Coehlo, Vladimir Nabokov, Sylvia Plath, Kate Atkinson and even Ian McEwan (*Enduring Love*—well, it's got love in the title so it must be for girls!) as well as Keyes and Kinsella. Sub-genres have hatched, too: lad-lit, mum-lit, matron-lit (ugh!) for menopausal Bridgets, and even split-lit for the recently divorced. And chick-lit-style young adult fiction has been a massive success in its own right, with authors like Meg Cabot and Louise Rennison delighting both teen and adult audiences.

In America, after a period of huge growth, grown-up chick-lit is currently about as popular with publishers as swine flu, yet brand-name authors (including Candace Bushnell, Jennifer Weiner and many Irish/British authors) are still selling in their millions. In the UK, new writers continue to be published alongside the established ones, though the chick-lit gold rush is over (replaced by an avalanche of glamorous 'bonkbusters' to help us forget the privations of the credit crunch).

Interestingly, the big expansion is happening in countries where the single city girl phenomenon is also newer. India has a flourishing chick-lit scene and its homegrown authors are gaining publishing deals worldwide. On a recent trip to Vietnam, I saw a press article about the increasing popularity of the genre from Hanoi to Ho Chi Minh City. In Chinese cities, where thirty-something women face difficulties finding husbands due to their 'three highs'—high expectations, high levels of education and high incomes—chick-lit is also striking a chord.

And for the authors? I love writing in my genre because I want to reflect the contemporary lives of women: where else could I deal with phobias, thwarted ambition, bad customer service, nuclear proliferation and sex after widowhood? I also love other writers in my genre: intelligent women (and some men) with varied backgrounds and careers, who like writing with humour and verve. Just like our readers.

There are signs of progress. The Melissa Nathan Award for Comedy Romance, set up in memory of the bestselling author of *The Nanny*, celebrates the genre as never before. I'm doing my bit: with six other authors of contemporary women's novels, we've formed the New Romantics (www.thenewromantics.org) to champion the benefits of feelgood fiction.

But maybe there's another, better approach. Perhaps, fifteen years on, it's time to accept that the label is here to stay. Perhaps we must all embrace our inner chicks. After all, we have nothing to lose but our feathers...

Paranormal romantic fiction
Rosemary Laurey, author, with Jenny Haddon

UK taste often follows the US, as it did with the hot historical in the eighties. Paranormal romance may prove to be another, with Stephenie Meyer's *Twilight* saga topping the bestseller lists in 2009 for Little, Brown's UK Atom imprint. A vampire-human love story set in a Seattle high school, it is aimed squarely at teenage girls, with sales boosted by the movie, which opened in the UK in December 2008.

The paranormal genre is not one we readily recognise in the UK. It embraces elements of science fiction and pure fantasy, as well as romance. In the States, it can be argued that the first mega paranormal was Diana Gabaldon's time-slip *Outlander* series in 1991, which went on to be an international bestseller. Then Joss Whedon's television series *Buffy the Vampire Slayer* made vampires a huge hit with authors and readers alike. (*New York Times* Bestseller Jennifer Crusie writes about its characters on her website.) By 2006, *Time* reported that Christine Feehan was selling half a million copies of each of her *Carpathian* vampire novels.

Publishers like Avon produce paranormals as single titles while Harlequin Enterprises introduced two specific imprints: Luna (sub-Arthurian courts, magicians, fairies, stressing female power) and Nocturne (vampires, shape shifters, dark and sensual, urban fantasy).

In the UK, there has been a long tradition of distinguished time slip/previous life romantic novels such as *The Middle Window* (1935) by RNA founder member Elizabeth Goudge and the international bestseller Barbara Erskine's *Lady of Hay* (1986) but it has tended to be the choice of one particular author, never a general movement. Jane Gaskell's *Atlan* paranormal fantasy trilogy (1963-66), hugely popular at the time, was a coming of age adventure and hugely sexy. But romantic?

Publisher Judy Piatkus has brought several of the US bestsellers to the UK, including Feehan and Sherilyn Kenyon—and presented the RNA's 2006 conference with copies of the entertaining *Undead and Unwed* (comedy vampire revenge romance) by MaryJanice Davidson. Many have a loyal following. But it seems that, so far, while other worlds and strange creatures do phenomenally well for UK publishers when they appear in sweeping adventure (Tolkein), children's/teenage (Diana Wynne Jones, David Almond and, of course, JK Rowling) and satire (Terry Pratchett), they haven't yet migrated to a home-grown romantic genre.

Rosemary Laurey, author, writes:
Imagine werewolves, witches, elves, fairies, vampires, dragons and so forth as the heroes and heroines (and sometimes villains) of romantic fiction. These, and countless other fantastical creatures, populate the pages of paranormal romantic fiction: a definite niche genre now enjoying immense popularity and interest in the US.

Paranormal romance includes stories with fantastical, mythical, or magical elements, creatures of folklore and legends, fantasy and stories set in magical or future worlds as well as time travel and time slip. For the writer, it is a genre of near limitless possibilities: a wonderful venture into the realm of the unbridled imagination.

Some readers are avid fans; others seldom read the genre, dismissing vampires, humanised gargoyles and the like as too far-fetched and unrealistic.

From the publishers' point of view, paranormal and its various sub genres come in and out of fashion. As I write, most genres—with the possible exception of time travel—are eagerly sought after by editors in the US.

Ten years ago few editors in New York would glance twice at a vampire romance. Now it's one of the 'hot' genres. From vampires, publishers braved the topics of werewolves, shape shifters, magic, wizards and dragons and the occasional venture into fantasy or futuristic. So, at the present time, there is a wonderful selection of paranormal romantic fiction on the booksellers' shelves.

The mesh between reality and fictional worlds in paranormal books varies. Charlaine Harris's *Southern Vampire Mysteries* (now also a TV series) is set in an alternative contemporary Louisiana, where the existence of vampires is acknowledged if not totally welcome, and the heroine is a reluctant telepath. In Maggie Shane's *Wings of the Night* series, vampires conceal their existence and identity, partly to avoid the rogue terrorist Division of Paranormal Investigation. In my own *Forever* series, vampires stay safely under the radar of mortal existence, banding together for protection. Chelsea Quinn Yarbro's vampires live a solitary existence, apart even from those who made them.

Fantasy is identified as a story set in an entirely fictitious or alternate world. It gives the writer a very wide canvas and often includes magical or mystical elements, as in Catherine Asaro's *The Charmed Sphere* or Katherine Greyle's *Oracle.* Witch, wiccan, and druid themes appear in books such as Maggie Shayne's *Witch* trilogy and JC Wilder's *Shadow Dwellers* series. Futuristic romance is an outgrowth of traditional Sci Fi and Fantasy, and covers a wide spectrum from Catherine Asaro's *Skolian Empire* (with Hard Science) to Lois McMaster Bujold's space opera *Vorkosigan Saga*.

Paranormal romantic fiction has not, so far at least, achieved vast popularity in the UK, but give it time.

Harlequin Mills & Boon

When the RNA started in 1960 many publishers had romance lists and there were several dedicated imprints. These mostly closed during the sixties, with the demise of the commercial lending libraries. When Hurst & Blackett closed in 1978, Mills & Boon was left as the only publisher who specialised in romantic fiction.

In the ensuing decades their name was to become synonymous with romantic fiction in the mind of the public, as much as Barbara Cartland's. (It is a common misconception that Miss Cartland wrote for Mills & Boon; she never did.) It is not surprising that Mills & Boon was the only romantic survivor—right from the first they drew a good proportion of their sales from this type of women's fiction and it was probably due to their commitment to the genre that the firm survived the twentieth century's two World Wars.

In the RNA, roughly 15 per cent of published author membership writes or has written for HMB. The number of authors on the New Writers' Scheme who target HMB fluctuates but currently it is between 17 per cent and 26 per cent.

History
In 1908 Gerald Mills, Educational Manager at Methuen, and Charles Boon, General Manager also at Methuen, left and set up their own

imprint. Their early lists offered all genres of fiction and a wide range of non-fiction, from school textbooks and travel guides to politics and child care. Their early fiction list had included PG Wodehouse (*The Prince and Betty*, a novel which went through several incarnations and does, indeed, sound like a Riviera romance) Hugh Walpole, Jack London, EF Benson, and early Georgette Heyer (writing as Stella Martin—*The Transformation of Philip Jettan*, 1923; it was later re-issued by Heinemann in 1930, renamed *Powder and Patch* with the original final chapter deleted) and Denise Robins, another early star, though she left in 1935 when another publisher offered better terms.

After Mills died, Charles Boon headed the firm and decided to concentrate on 'light fiction' for women, recognising the demand from commercial circulating libraries which developed in the thirties. This enabled a print run averaging 7,000 copies per title. Authors were encouraged to be as prolific as possible, some writing seven novels a year, under different pseudonyms, as the larger libraries would not take more than two books a year under one author's name. In those early days, as Leila MacKinlay recalled in the 1973 Spring *RNA News*, books were often 70,000 or 80,000 words long. (55,000 was a good average by the seventies.)

Charles Boon died in 1943 and his three sons took over on returning from the war, with John Boon in finance and sales, Charles (Carol/Caryl) as head of production and Alan (see below) in charge of editorial, working very closely with the fiction editors of women's magazines and their sense of the times. Sometimes both got it wrong—Mills & Boon wrote to one author in 1959 that 'sheikhery' was dead in the water and would never be revived. Yet only ten years later Violet Winspear, heavily influenced by the Hollywood movies of her youth, published *Blue Jasmine*, her own take on *The Sheikh*, and in doing so opened the way to a sub-genre of 'sheikh' books, which took off in the seventies and is still going strong. Nearly all the new authors of the seventies and eighties wrote at least one 'sheikh' novel, including the brand leaders, Penny Jordan and Charlotte Lamb.

By 1968 Mills & Boon were publishing 130 hardback and 72

paperback romances a year. (Even so, they still on-sold some of the remaining hardback titles to dedicated paperback publishers like Corgi Books.) They published on a basic magazine schedule, monthly, with instantly recognisable company branding. Numbers of titles increased from six to eight and then twelve contemporary titles a month, plus two or three historicals.

From 1977, the company followed the example of their North American sister company's marketing and refined their UK branding to reflect, essentially, the increasing level of sexual activity within the stories (see Lines and Imprints, below). The historical line, however, was pretty much sex-free, mainly Regency, and called Masquerade until the nineties.

The authors might reflect the world they saw around them in their novels but editorial management was wary of anything too politically explicit and of feminism *per se*. Jay Dixon, author of *The Romantic Fiction of Mills & Boon 1909-90s* recalls, 'At my interview in 1985, when I said I was a feminist, I was immediately interrogated on the likelihood of hordes of protesting feminists arriving at the doors!' This was not just paranoia. In addition to the accustomed sneers, the publisher was having to contend with accusations of reinforcing outdated stereotypes and the subjugation of women.

Harlequin

In 1957 the Canadian company Harlequin approached Mills & Boon asking if any of their novels were available for Canadian reprint rights. The relationship strengthened and by the time Harlequin sought to take control of Mills & Boon, as John Boon recalled, 60 per cent of their profits came from subsidiary rights in North America and elsewhere, not from sales. Other publishers showed an interest and the brothers had preliminary talks with several, including both Hutchinson and Heinemann in the UK and at least one US company. But too much of their business was already tied to Harlequin and that company took over/merged with Mills & Boon in 1972. Within a couple of years, Harlequin itself was sold to the *Toronto Star* group and in the mid-eighties it acquired Simon & Schuster's Silhouette subsidiary, which gave the global company three acquiring editorial offices, in Toronto, New York and London, and a number of new lines.

Alan Boon

When the RNA started, one of the first people from the industry whom they invited to be a Vice President was Alan Boon. He personally directed the romance list which was by then the backbone of Mills & Boon.

Alan had been educated at Felsted and joined Mills & Boon in 1931, aged 18. Finances were rocky after the premature death of Gerald Mills and there was no money for Alan to go to Cambridge as John, his younger brother by three years, was to do later. Alan worked in editorial and always said that he learned everything he knew of romances simply by doing the job. He learned his trade in the first place from his father, and secondly from conversations and business with the powerful fiction editors of women's magazines.

He clearly had aptitude. If asked (and only if asked) he would recommend to his authors *The Craft Of Fiction* by Percy Lubbock (1921), which contrasted showing and telling, and said that a book was not a row of facts but a single image. Lubbock—who had been friends with Queen of the Victorian circulating libraries, Rhoda Broughton (*Not Wisely But Too Well, Dr Cupid* and so on)—held that the best fiction, such as Flaubert's *Madame Bovary*, succeeded in part because it was written from the heroine's point of view. So Alan Boon, from an early age, valued immediacy in writing and the woman-centred story.

After his return from the war, with his father dead, it fell to Alan to negotiate with and recruit authors for the romance list. Mills & Boon's terms, especially to first-time authors, were never generous but he made up for that with a mixture of taciturn dignity, occasional mischief, encouragement and dazzlingly lavish lunches. Basically, he made his authors feel wonderful and sometimes he made them laugh. It was a mixture that inspired great loyalty in a wide range of authors over five decades. It was said that if the firm ever got into trouble, Alan's authors would each have written a book for nothing to dig the company out of the hole.

Partly it was his manner—Anne Weale, a formidable woman not easily impressed, described him as a tall, blue-eyed ex-naval officer (he had served in the Navy during the War) who had great authority and presence. There was also genuine kindness, in the firm's paternalist tradition. (His father, after all, had sent Mary Burchell home to show the M&B contract to her own father before he would allow her to sign it.) Alan Boon was clearly a good listener and extremely courteous. Authors who wrote to him found that he replied personally to every letter.

But courtesy and kindness stopped a long way short of social intimacy. Any author developing a crush on him, as at least one of the firm's star names did in the sixties, found that he took evasive action when it was possible, and simply refused to see her when it was not. He hated rows. Occasional authors who stormed into the office looking for blood (like a 1950s signing, fulminating over typographical errors in one of her titles) found that Mr Alan had just slipped out—if he was lurking in the broom cupboard, the staff never gave him away. And, when stuck with taking uncongenial overseas visitors to his beloved races, he was not above landing them on a colleague from another publishing house and slithering off into the crowd.

Author Ida Pollock, in her memoir *Starlight* (2009), gives an interesting assessment, both of his skills and his personality, when she first met him in the fifties:

'M&B's triumph was to swell the list of publishing legends, and to a very large extent it was designed and crafted by one remarkable man, Alan Boon himself. Alan's brothers, John and Caryl, played their part, but Alan had an extraordinarily analytical mind and, taken together with common sense and a wide understanding of literature, this spelt out a recipe for publishing success. Unemotional—on the surface, at least—and certainly not over-chatty, he could be quite difficult to understand, but it didn't take me long to gauge the level of his ability, or to realise that I would be wise to take any advice that he cared to offer.'

She was also the recipient of one of his sudden, unsolicited acts of kindness. Struggling with acute money worries—she had been working as a cook/housekeeper to make ends meet—and a chronically asthmatic child who needed to go to Switzerland, she was wondering how many books she needed to write to pay their travel expenses. Maybe two books, maybe three, but that could take another six months. She aired the issue, in passing, over lunch with Alan. He looked thoughtful and talked about dessert. But just before they parted he said, 'When I get back to the office, I'll see you're sent a cheque that will cover five advances. Stop worrying, and take her to Switzerland.'

As an editor he had a remarkable ability to spot potential. He did not sweat the small stuff and was never a fact-checker by temperament (which led to unpleasant exchanges with Harlequin's Editor in Chief, who was) but he could see when a book had a strong, in Lubbock's phrase, 'single image'. He cared about style and grammar. He steered a careful course between the demands of the important, socially conservative markets like Ireland, and the racier, more sexually relaxed stories that were gaining popularity elsewhere. And, when Harlequin was unconvinced, Alan Boon backed his judgment with his personal guarantee of the new, sexier, Presents line.

Above all, he gave the authors only the lightest of guidelines. If they took a direction which he thought might disturb their regular readers he suggested a new pen name. But otherwise he trusted their own vision and urged them to stay true to it. The late Jane Donnelly, a wonderful writer much respected by her fellow authors, remembered him saying, when sexier books were proving big sellers, that she might like to think about introducing more explicit sexual congress—but only if she felt comfortable and if it was right for her characters Mills & Boon would continue to publish her, whatever she decided.

Similarly, he published and continued to publish, the doctor-nurse romances of Betty Neels, whose books already looked old-fashioned when he took her first title in 1969. But he said she had a unique voice and remained loyal to her, even when the books were regularly among the slowest sellers, month after month. A high proportion of readers who bought Neels, he argued, would not buy anyone else on the list as a substitute, and would be lost if she were dropped. Besides, there was something special about her sweetness of tone, her resilient, honest, well-mannered heroines and the Dutch surgeon heroes with their integrity and kindness. One day she would find the readership she deserved. His judgment was finally justified when, in the nineties, she became a bestseller, attracting reprint after reprint, while younger authors danced for joy if they found they had been put in a two-in-one with a Betty Neels because it trebled their sales.

He had great business sense but, inevitably, he bore a lot of teasing about selling romance. It must have hurt. At Alan's memorial cocktail party in the Ritz, Larry Heisey, former chairman of Harlequin, recalled seeing Alan at Frankfurt, trying to sell the books pretty much out of a suitcase. Alan knew that they were well written and deserved respect, he just did not know how to convince a resistant world. He knew that romances with a happy ending could bring readers out of the Slough of Despond without recourse to habit-forming chemicals. Only when he said it, some demon prompted him to add, 'They ought to be prescribed in every doctor's surgery, like valium.' The quote everyone picked up was the last two words, alas.

Between the ribbing of his UK peers, editorial clashes with Harlequin and demand for ever more titles and authors, his last decade at Mills & Boon cannot have been easy. It never showed to the authors. Sara Craven remembers the sheer fun of being summoned to lunch with Alan. 'We giggled and gossiped and drank too much and talked about books. He was a voracious reader and was always pinching manuscripts off editors' desks. They would have to rummage through his office while he was out, to get them back.' But she also remembers Alan dragging her off to Selfridges after lunch, where he approached browsers in the book department with a cheery, 'Would you like to meet one of our splendid authors?' He then drove them towards the shrinking writer and slapped a signed copy of the latest Sara Craven into their alarmed hands.

Authors who met him at this stage were taking their editorial guidance from the editors he had brought in, notably Frances Whitehead and Jacqui Bianchi. Alan Boon, however, continued to host the Lunches and tell the authors what wonderful books they wrote. He was much loved, the last of the Gentleman Publishers.

The publisher and the fiction editor

For many years, Mills & Boon worked closely with magazines, earning well from on-selling serial rights. In the fifties and sixties it was a major source of income, for both Mills & Boon and the authors. So the magazines' fiction editors' word was law. By the eighties this had become a less important source of income, but it was still Alan Boon's habit to entertain the relevant fiction editors to a sumptuous lunch at the Ritz, to discuss what their mutual authors were doing and where, if at all, the magazines' and Mills & Boon's requirements diverged. Did they need another rural doctor series? Should they have another go at a historical mystery? That sort of thing.

The late Brenda McDougall, then an Associate Vice President of the RNA and Fiction Editor of *Woman's Weekly*, often recalled one prolonged and bibulous meal in the early eighties when, after the last raspberry had been consumed, Alan suddenly leaned back in his chair and went into his best *sotto voce*. What that actually meant in Alan Boon's case was that he got even growlier and more clipped than usual. The volume pretty much stayed the same, but was accompanied by a conspiratorial mien that would attract the attention of the most self-absorbed diner.

'Tell me Brenda . . .' he said, *sotto voce* Boon-style.

'Yes, Alan?' said Brenda, conscious of a slightly swimming head —few people could hold their drink to rival Alan Boon—but alert to the fact that this was the business he had been leading up to through the last five courses. 'Yes?'

'Grateful for your advice ...' said Alan, writhing a little, clearly reluctant to come to the point.

'Of course, Alan. If I can help ... '

'Professional opinion ...'

'Naturally.'

Alan leaned forward confidentially. 'What line are you taking on oral sex these days?' he boomed.

Now Ritz waiters are too polished to drop trays or even clatter spoons. Not so Ritz diners. Brenda said you could hear the collective intake of breath like a force ten gale.

'If only,' she mourned, 'if only he had not said *professional* opinion.'

Frances Whitehead

The RNA first heard of Frances Whitehead when Nancy Sawyer, then Public Relations Officer, sent extracts from a thesis on the attitude of various public libraries to holding romantic fiction in their stock. (The north was better than the south, but there were pockets of resistance everywhere.) Whitehead joined Mills & Boon as Alan Boon's PA initially and ended as Editorial Director. In 1974 she addressed the RNA's January meeting.

RNA News Spring 1974

Helen McGregor's report on talk by Frances Whitehead of Mills & Boon

Mills & Boon novels provide 'romance by proxy' and in them women can escape from the kitchen sink and read of strong masterful men who, nevertheless, make good husband material — the type of man with whom the reader who has not yet met her ideal could imagine herself in love. The heroine should be under thirty, have a job if possible and be articulate. In a difference of opinion with the hero she must be able to say the things that most women wish they could have said!

The setting is important because the reader likes to read of a place she has already visited or which she

hopes to visit, but care must be taken not to make the
description read like a travel brochure. The plot should
be uncomplicated. The author must be involved with her
characters — no cardboard characters wanted.
   Although studying Mills & Boon novels is advisable,
a carbon copy is a danger. Originality is wanted. The
heroine must, of course, get her man and the hero
should be impressive. Dialogue must read naturally.
The writing of a successful novel for Mills & Boon
involves intelligence, dedication, and hard work — and
fresh talent, which can come out of the blue, is always
wanted.
   A lively discussion followed on such topics as what
constitutes a romantic hero, why he is usually older
than the heroine, the inadvisability of using dialect.
The really important qualities a novelist needed were
sincerity and the power to tell a compelling story.
From market research, the firm knows what their readers
want and aim to satisfy that need.

From the mid-seventies Mills & Boon editorial began to detach itself from the symbiotic relationship with the women's magazines, and to trust their authors' imagination to lead in new directions. In contemporary stories, this tended away from domestic backgrounds and heroes who were, in Brenda McDougall's phrase 'a good provider' towards heroines who could provide for themselves and men who were darker and more troubled, more Mr Rochester than Mr Darcy.

It was Alan Boon who told the late Charlotte Lamb (joining the RNA in 1974, on the strength of rather gentle romances, often Regencies) to try a sexier approach; but it was Frances with whom she worked to produce dark, Gothic stories of sexual power struggles which turned her into an international star. Like Alan himself, Frances turned out to have an exceptional ability to spot a writer who was naturally in tune with the genre and to steer them along the right path.

Mills & Boon authors of the seventies and eighties explored not only the implications of more sexual information and freedom, but also the problems the 'sexual revolution' held for women, along with their fight for equal working conditions. Charlotte Lamb's *Man's World* (1980) featured a junior editor heroine who has been carrying a pre-retirement colleague and is then beaten to his job by a big name journalist. Her professional frustration steams off the page, but there are darker elements to her conflict with the hero, for this is a divorced heroine whose family is in denial about the violence of her former marriage. Independence and a good career, in fact, could be just another source of pain with the wrong man and had to be carefully negotiated with the right one.

Another of Frances's star authors, Sara Craven, remembers:
Like many Mills & Boon authors in the seventies, my first contact with the company was through Frances Whitehead, in the first instance a cool clear voice on the telephone inviting me to London to discuss the acquisition of my first novel which she'd discovered in her slush pile.

I met a tall girl with pale skin, long dark hair and glasses, but this potentially dreamy appearance concealed a razor-sharp mind and a highly-honed perception of women's fiction as a whole and the Mills & Boon phenomenon in particular.

I apologised for my lousy typing. She gave me a surprised look and said, 'It's not that bad and at least you used a new ribbon,' producing a manuscript from a drawer which appeared to have been written in Braille, to prove her point.

At our first lunch at the top of the Post Office Tower, she shook her head over the souvenir tea towel presented to me by Alan Boon. 'She won't have time for drying dishes,' she told him with her keynote crispness. 'She'll be writing. Give it to her husband.'

Over the next 19 years our relationship flourished, personally and professionally, with a judicious use of the editorial carrot and stick.

The PO Tower had closed, alas, but the Ritz took its place, and the carrot was being invited to long lunches there with Mr Alan, fuelled by the office tonic (champagne) which Frances herself detested, being strictly a G&T girl. She was also a conviction vegetarian, although she told me once that she sometimes wavered when staying with her aunt in Blackburn and the aroma of frying bacon came drifting upstairs.

Authorial lunches cannot have been much fun when she was so often presented with little more than a plate of the vegetables of the day with a cheese sauce. Once, when she came to spend a weekend with me in Yorkshire, I was able to redress the balance a little.

An advance telephone call to the Pool Court Restaurant and the understanding owner produced a main course of a whole pineapple, its flesh diced and mixed with every kind of fruit imaginable, then glazed, the entire thing framed by a display of tiny carrots, green beans, tiny tomatoes and asparagus spears. It was like a still life painting, and when Frances had finished she said simply that it was the best vegetarian meal she'd ever eaten.

There were also the (encouraging?!) letters. 'Where's this script? Are you sunk in rural lethargy? Stir yourself.'

And there was the stick—popularly known as the Star Chamber Treatment. The Hapless Author (me) was met at the lift by Frances, now glamorous and sophisticated in scarlet with matching lipstick, her hair cut into a glossy black bob, and the glasses replaced by contact lenses (a formidable sight), and conducted not to Mr Alan's office and a fridge full of Moët, but to an editorial room, where the file on recent sales figures was opened and the sudden unwelcome decline in those of the Hapless A pointed out with a stab of the finger.

'Out of ten titles you came ninth. Disgraceful.'

Useless to protest, as I did, that some of my writer friends thought it was the best book I'd written so far.

'Just shows how little they know,' returned the relentless inquisitor across the desk. 'Besides you're writing for the readers who love you, not your peers.

'As I told you when I read the script, it was two books in one, and far too long. But you insisted on it going through. The readers agreed with me, and because you've disappointed them, the next book has wobbled too. Now you have to trust me and start the climb back into favour.'

One such session was usually quite enough to ensure that, in future, one's eye would stay firmly on the ball, helped along by Ms Whitehead's pithy, 'That's more like it, thank God,' when the next book went in.

Her instinct was sure and her judgement serious. Once, stuck over the tension points in a narrative, I asked for advice, and she referred me to one of my earlier books, *The Devil at Archangel*, accepted without much comment from her at the time, but which she now said had 'almost perfect structure'.

In January 1994 when my life was falling in bits around me, she rang to wish me a Happy New Year and said consolingly, 'Things can only get better.'

They didn't. In a matter of weeks, she had gone too, and a Mills & Boon era was over.

Jacqui Bianchi

In the eighties, expanding the editorial department, Alan Boon brought in an ex-librarian who had thought she was going to be a great artist until she was 16 (when somehow it died on her), with a passion for the theatre and a considerable reading habit. She loved Mills & Boons and was thrilled to work with the names she had read and loved, no matter how difficult. She and Violet Winspear traded competing impoverished backgrounds—Jacqui's family came from Newcastle, where the docks had been as badly bombed as Winspear's London—until the notoriously sensitive author agreed that Jacqui *understood*, in spite of her comparative youth.

Jacqui was also brilliant at encouraging the faltering steps of new novelists, boosting them when they needed boosting, challenging them when they needed that, too, and giving the Australian husband-and-wife phenomenon who turned into multi seller Emma Darcy a masterclass in how and where to cut a slug of 50 or more pages out of an over-long novel. 'Jacqui went through the whole manuscript,' they recalled, after she died. 'What was most fascinating for us was that she didn't cut 30, 40 or 50 pages. She cut a paragraph here, a phrase there, a sentence here. On practically every page there was a cut. In doing that, she showed us how to tighten up the writing, and move forward more quickly. We learned so much from her on that first book.'

She died horribly young, leaving many of her authors bereft. Three whose hands she held remember her.

Penny Jordan writes:
My first contact with Jacqui was via the telephone when she rang to invite me down to London to discuss my first submission to HMB. (What I didn't know then, and didn't find out for many years, was that Linda Fildew had picked my book out of the slush pile.) Jacqui had the most lovely mesmerising voice, instantly soothing and reassuring and yet at the same time able to inject confidence into the person with whom she was speaking.

I was, needless to say, filled with 'shock and awe' but Jacqui put me at ease the minute we met. She had that knack of making you feel that whatever you were saying was genuinely important to her. I was very much an amateur and an outsider in the world of publishing, and Jacqui was always at pains to make sure I felt comfortable and never gave so much as a hint that she knew how awkward and not really a proper writer I felt.

She was, I think, a writers' editor. She knew and understood us and she was very protective of us. I learned so much from her about the art of being gracious and kind and understanding the needs of 'the newbie writer'. She was a terrific mentor and teacher.

Her quiet confidence helped me to feel confident. If Jacqui believed I could write then I must be able to do so.

She had a passion for reading and such a feeling for the work of her authors that it never seemed necessary to explain what you were trying to achieve—she knew and was there ahead of you. She was tremendously giving, and endlessly patient. She used her hands a lot when she spoke but slowly and carefully, in a measured manner rather than one that was busy.

It was Jacqui who urged me to write longer, more complex books and who helped me towards my one and only *Sunday Times* bestseller status. She was a great 'hand holder' when the need arose.

She was a writer herself, of course, writing passionately about dark alpha heroes who gripped the reader's guts. I envied her that talent. I'd wanted to write historical books myself but reading Jacqui's made me realise how much I had to learn before I could be anything like good enough.

She was fun and warm and I remember she always used to encourage me onwards in a book with the words 'what if…' to take a book forward, followed by 'but why' to explain the back story.

A still unanswered personal 'but why' moment came to me thanks to Jacqui via the purchase of a dress from Parkers, an expensive dress shop close to Brookes Mews. Jacqui had bought a diamond patterned jacket there—her Harlequin jacket—and for reasons that now escape me I ended up buying my 'but why' frock there. I still have this frock—and it is 'a frock'. A monstrosity in black and silver swirly patterned fabric, ruched, stretchy and tight fitting in diva style from bust to knee and from there flaring out in a fish tail over net petticoats; if that weren't enough it also has tight ruched full length sleeves and has a full-on diamante snake running down the front.

Nope, I never wore it, but every time I look at it I think of Jacqui and I give a big wide smile.

I owe her so much. Just typing this piece has brought back so many happy memories of her and all that she did for me. She was a very special person. I still miss her.

Sally Beauman recalls:
I first met Jacqui through the theatre—she was a great fan of my husband, Alan Howard's, work and used to attend all his performances (quite a feat). She was then a consultant editor at Mills & Boon and we used to discuss M&B romances in the intervals at the Royal

Shakespeare Company in Stratford. I was then very arrogant about them, thought they were laughably simple etc etc—and as a result, took on an amiable bet that I could write one in two weeks, no problem … Well, of course, there were a *million* problems, and the project did not turn out to be the easy journalistic assignment I'd imagined. I found it horribly hard, realised that I had absolutely no idea how to write fiction of any kind, even genre fiction with tight, learnable rules—and was duly taken down several pegs, as I deserved to be. Jacqui, who had foreseen this outcome I'm sure, used to tease me gently on this score for ages afterwards.

Some years later, when I was bogged down on a biography of Ellen Terry for OUP, Jacqui encouraged me to try romance again, and this time—with a great deal of help from her—I managed it more successfully. I then became fascinated with genre fiction for a while, and over the next three years or so wrote about ten M&B titles under a pseudonym—in every case working closely with Jacqui from initial idea to completed ms.

She had by then become the senior executive editor at Mills & Boon and she was brilliant at her job—one of the best, most intelligent, intuitive and quick-witted editors I've known in England or America. All the writers who worked with her will attest to this, I'm sure: she found and nurtured some of the most original M&B authors in the early eighties, writers who were prepared to alter, adapt and reinvent the previously rigid M&B format. She also wrote historical romances herself—and very interesting, rather Jacobean, they were. I especially remember one that was ingeniously based on Tourneur's *The Revenger's Tragedy.*

She died tragically young: having recovered from breast cancer, which she had fought with characteristic fortitude, she was knocked down and killed in a traffic accident near her home in 1987 or 1988. (I know because it was not long after Bantam published my novel *Destiny*.) I still miss her.

Jenny Haddon (Sophie Weston) remembers:
I first met Jacqui after my agent, Diana Avebury, rang me and announced in a Voice from the Crypt, 'You've got a new editor and She Wants to See You.' She added helpfully, 'They're all scared of her.' Later, I came to the conclusion that it was Diana (never a woman's woman and, hitherto, running my career on the basis of cheerful champagne-soaked lunches with Alan Boon) who was scared of her. But it wasn't a promising start.

Jacqui, it turned out, was small, dark, emphatic, weird, funny and totally inspiring. She didn't pull her punches. 'You're holding back,' she told me that first time, tapping my manuscript with a pointed nail. 'Don't.'

Jacqui herself wrote historical melodramas, with Machiavellian fallen-angel heroes, deeply politically incorrect. Try *The Silver Devil*. She used to dress up in a long, embroidered kaftan and bathe in scented oils to put herself in the mood to write. (I know because she recommended the method to me. It works.) Mind you, she was never po-faced about her own work. Her pen name was Teresa Denys, after Denis Quilley's character in *Privates on Parade*, equally dark, equally funny, equally incorrect.

But from her authors' point of view, Jacqui was our first, best reader, with absolutely no urge to shadow-write our books. She just wanted you to give her an electrifying read. And she clearly loved Mills & Boon.

Always she wanted me to go further than I thought I could or than I thought the conventions of Mills & Boon would allow. 'Try it,' she'd say. 'If it doesn't work, you'll know.' And when it didn't, she told me. She turned down a book that had been through three rewrites. 'Each time you change it, you make the first three chapters more painful,' she wrote, 'so that now it is impossible to give [the heroine] a happy ending in 55,000 words. Take a quarter of a million words if you have to. But it's not an M&B.'

After I told her about the old Girls' Guide to Guys (that is, NSIT—not safe in taxis) she gave me back a manuscript with NORD written in the margin. I rang her, panicking.

'NORD? What's NORD?'

Jac snorted coffee. 'Not Our Readership, darling.'

When she died I lost a friend and an inspiration: informed, enthusiastic, appreciative—and full of insights that I still return to.

'Luxuriate; romantic fiction is life with texture added.'

'If you don't love your characters, who else will?'

And, when she was yelling at me for not making a scene dramatic enough, 'Screw the punch; you want a knock out, don't you?'

Anne Weale

Anne Weale was one of Mills & Boon's most distinguished authors and a founder member of the RNA. She lived a great deal of her life abroad but served on the committee and was Editor of the *RNA News* for a brief period in the sixties.

Early Years

She often said that she felt she was destined to be a writer. An only child, brought up in a house of books, she told herself stories before she could write. She reacted against the examples of her mother and aunt. 'Neither was capable of supporting themselves,' she said, adding, 'Not surprising that I grew up determined to pay my way ASAP.' It was a determination she held to all her life, and continually urged upon younger writers. Aged 18 she talked herself into a job on the *Norwich Evening News*, as their first female reporter. She clearly adored it and learned a great deal, including her incisive style and a certain free-wheeling willingness to have a go at anything.

On her *Bookworm on the Net* blog she said in 2007, 'In my day, one of the pleasures of staff journalism was that it wasn't a 9-5 job.' She never forgot the provincial newspaper virtues of fact checking and accurate quotes, and often defended the profession when wounded romantic authors were fulminating against some media misrepresentation. Pleasingly, the *Eastern Daily Press*, sister paper to the *Norwich Evening News*, ran an article about the HMB centenary in 2008, in which Norwich-based author

Kate Hardy says she was 'very proud to share a page with her'.

But, as Anne Weale wrote in a biographical note for her publisher: 'When she was 21 the man she was wildly in love with announced that he was off to the other side of the world. He thought they should either marry or say goodbye. At the time, Anne was a newspaper reporter with a career plan. But she felt that wonderful men were much harder to find than good jobs, so she put her career on hold. What a wise decision it was!'

So these were the qualities she brought to her books: a lucid style, a wide interest in whatever came her way, impeccable research methods, determination, discipline, and the bright courage to follow her heart. She was clear-eyed, original and never, ever, sentimental.

RNA News April-May 67

In her own words...

Born in Liverpool of Cornish/Spanish/Irish origins. Childhood a succession of removals, new schools. From 18 to 21 was a newspaper reporter, then married — but did not settle down! In their first 12 years together, she and her husband had a dozen impermanent homes, five in the Far East. Today, still in their thirties, with a country house and acres of wooded garden, they can laugh at their early reverses. Their first English home was a dreary furnished room in a London suburb. Anne failed to get a job in Fleet Street (and was turned down by all the women's magazines) so had to sell hairbrushes at Boots in Regent Street. Her husband, now a director of a Norfolk furnishing company, toiled in the stockroom at Woolworths in Oxford Street. 'So much for our dreams of a gay London whirl of theatre-going etc. We were almost reduced to pawning our one valuable heirloom, and oh! the misery of those tired-out, sardine-packed tube journeys back to dismal Finsbury Park!'
    Penniless, but youthfully optimistic, they tried Bristol. The dour landlady of some more uncomfortable rooms (we were forbidden to fry onions for fear the smell would impregnate her hideous rust moquette suite) had a surprising passion for romantic novels,

```
devouring half a dozen weekly. Anne borrowed and
studied some, particularly those of the late Rosalind
Brett. Reporting for the 'Western Daily Press' by day,
she wrote 'Winter is Past' at night. A year later,
having moved again to York, she was astounded by a
telephone call from Alan Boon. Not only would Mills
& Boon accept her book, but it was to be serialised
before publication. That was 24 books, four more homes,
and one seven-year-old son ago. Twenty books have been
serialised. 'Terrace in the Sun' [runner up for that
year's Major Award] appeared in 'My Home' and has since
sold to France, Italy and Germany. The Italian hardback
is in a collection of classic romances, including such
exalted names as Bronte, Dumas and Dickens.
```

Weale and category romance

Alan Boon and her mentor at *Woman's Weekly*, Miss Biddy Johnson, at once recognised a sparkling modern voice. Weale's backgrounds were authentically international, her heroines energetic, independent and competent, though less career-minded than their creator, her heroes enigmatically sexy. Both hero and heroine always had integrity. The heroine was often untried and/or facing huge practical difficulties and the hero was to some extent her mentor, even rescuer. Her heroines were always brave and the heroes came to respect them— and recognise that they were complementary characters. Weale was particularly good on emotional solitaries who blossomed into their full potential only when they found their soul mate. Often her exotic settings, frequently the Caribbean, were part of the heroine's trial: young Charlotte Martin losing the island she loved in *Sullivan's Reef* or Amalie, returning from exile to the West Indies to find her grandfather's charter business is nearly bankrupt. And then there's Cassie in *Antigua Kiss* who is deeply out of her depth in the Caribbean in the first place and only went there to take care of her orphaned nephew.

By the eighties she was by no means the steamiest writer on Mills & Boon's books, but her novels crackled with sexual tension and she was a pioneer of realistic sex scenes in the genre. *Antigua Kiss* (1982) became famous for it. Partly as a result of this truthfulness, her stories are timeless, slightly to her own surprise. Her early books returned under new covers ten years or more later, in the Mills & Boon Classic and similar imprints. In 2007, the last year of her life, she reported that Germany had just reprinted *Lord of the Sierras*, which had first been published in 1975. 'For a romance to survive for 32 years is rather fun,' she said.

Weale and the longer novel

She had always wanted to write a longer book and in 1983, approached by Mills & Boon to write at greater length, she produced *Flora*, described by the blurb as the story of 'a delicate Eurasian child-woman who moved between two worlds but was shunned by both. An innocent beauty whose unawakened fires could be ignited by only one man. A sensuous tale of love, heartbreak and searing passion that sweeps from a remote village in western China to the teeming decadence of old Shanghai, and reaches its heart stirring conclusion in the opulent mansions and lush estates of turn-of-the century England.' It was to be the start of a saga set around a stately home, Longwarden. She took the sequel, *All My Worldly Goods*, to Century Arrow, either because Mills & Boon were discontinuing their single title line or because they were not attracted to a book which was a saga (in the way that *Flora* had not been) covering four heroines, two continents and twelve months. It did well and she sold Century a third, *Time and Chance* (1989). But she wasn't entirely happy with the result and hesitated over a deal to sell the fourth, *Past Forgetting*. Realistic as always, afterwards she said that its non-appearance was partly her own fault. While she hesitated, the editor who was interested in Longwarden left and a new one did not like the proposal. So she put Longwarden on hold and stuck to category romance—though at the time of her death she was considering publishing the fourth volume herself. She always thought that the Longwarden saga was the best thing she wrote, and went on receiving correspondence about it from readers—many of them saying it had moved them to tears—right up to her death.

Weale and the RNA

Anne was one of the world's natural correspondents. She really came into her own with the advent of email and, particularly, the RNA's internet group, to which she posted regularly. She had strong opinions and not much truck with wishy-washy consensus-building, so her ideas often provoked robust arguments, still remembered wistfully by many.

A great advocate of professional standards, she was also convinced that writers were born not made. 'I have nothing against born writers writing for money rather than literary acclaim,' she said in the nineties, 'but I don't approve of the thousands of not-born writers who are currently cluttering the market with largely second-rate stuff.' Increasingly she locked horns with the many RNA members who were committed to educating aspiring authors, but her position was based on long-held beliefs. For instance, back in 1967 she had conducted a survey as Editor of the *RNA News* and offered some pretty terse comments on the answers:

QUESTION: Which do you want most? To write books which please you, or to make as much money as possible?

ANSWERS: Six probationers were emphatic about pleasing themselves. None wanted, above all, to make money. One was 'not terribly interested in money'; another had turned down 'hack work for very good money.' The aim of one was to write a book that a publisher wanted to publish. Several said 'a bit of both'. Only two mentioned pleasing readers.

COMMENT: A trap question. The answer separates the born professionals from the idealistic Amateurs. Writing to please themselves is something only proven mistresses of their craft can afford to do, and then only with discretion. Please yourself if you must— but it's not the way to the top. Top RNs [Romantic Novelists] are pleased by pleasing others— publishers and readers or, in the case of serialists, editors who represent readers. Wanting money is not unworthy. Money is proof of popularity. Full members whose earnings are disappointing might pause to wonder if less self-indulgence might lead to a leap of income.

There was always a lot of sense and considerable thought in Anne Weale's arguments and they generated interesting discussion—and personally she was kind and unfailingly courteous. But you can see why sometimes she could get up some people's noses.

On the other hand, in private bilateral correspondence she was generous, interested, willing to share what she had learned (including from her mistakes), never bearing a grudge and surprisingly undogmatic except about the need for authors to keep emotion out of their career planning. 'Never forget this is a business,' she would say, time and again.

She could also paint a word picture of those early days, recalling the first Awards dinner, with everyone in evening dress and furs (she had hired her own), Barbara Cartland sparkling with diamonds and Denise Robins elegant in dark velvet. As a talented needle-woman and Oxfam-shop-rummager herself, Weale recalled in 2007, 'I still have a dazzling memory of a grey tulle ball gown worn by Dorothy Black at one of the early RNA dinners in the sixties or seventies. The second layer of tulle was sewn with crystal drops. I think it was a Dior but whether new or second-hand, who knows? Possibly new, as Dorothy Black was very successful at the time.'

What she didn't say, because she was modest about her own achievements, and what none of us knew until we started to scour the archives for this memoir, was that she was runner up for Romantic Novel of the Year 1967, with *Terrace in the Sun*, published by Mills & Boon. She wore white lace and gold lamé.

Harlequin Mills & Boon today

From 1993 the UK operation became wholly integrated for management and marketing purposes into what had become a multinational enterprise.

From the authors' point of view the fully realised merger had mixed results. For instance, editorial guidelines became more prescriptive. That was a shock to the authors of the day, although today's writers take it in their stride, well aware that they are writing for a global market. (Mind you, even in the seventies editors were warning authors, 'Don't talk about *The Archers* if you want to sell abroad.') Today's titles will be offered to the editorial offices of Harlequin's foreign language ventures and authors may receive copies of their work in 28 languages (including Chinese, Russian and Arabic). The company says they are sold in more than 100 overseas markets.

Centenary

The lively centenary celebrations in 2008 demonstrated clearly that the genres covered by Harlequin Mills & Boon—now generally referred to as category romance in the publishing trade—are thriving. There were talks at leading literary festivals, an exhibition which started at the Central Library in Manchester and travelled round the country, and two linked television programmes—author Stella Duffy trying her hand at writing a Mills & Boon, mentored by an author and editor; and a one-off drama *Consuming Passions*, written by Emma Frost (of *Shameless* fame) interweaving the stories of three women—Mary Boon, wife of the co-founder, an imaginary author of the sixties and, again imaginary, the love story of a modern day lecturer in literature and feminist studies.

Lines and imprints

Today, Mills & Boon publish 50 new titles a month, still on that magazine schedule. At the time of going to press there were ten products (their word) in the Mills & Boon series, five of which are edited out of the UK office in Richmond (authors may come from anywhere in the world, including Europe, North America and Australasia) *viz:*

- **Modern**: the UK label of the line which is sold in north America as **Presents** – glamorous, sophisticated, passionate, maybe a touch of modern gothic feel to the plots.
- **Modern Extra**: sexy but buzzy urban backgrounds and a lot of style.
- **Romance**: warm and tender, some sexier than others, the only line where you will find the beta hero, along with a fair smattering of untraditional sheikhs and tycoons-with-a-conscience.
- **Medical**: a direct descendant of the hospital romances of Mary Burchell, Betty Neels and Lucilla Andrews. Caring is a strong element and research is meticulous.
- **Historical**: any love story set in the past, from the Roman Empire to the roaring twenties, with a heavy preponderance of the popular Regency. Longer than the contemporary stories, they are described by the publisher as 'rich and vivid, capturing the essence of times gone by'. Many historical writers are passionate about their periods, as you can see from their postings about their research on the eHarlequin message boards. This is the one line where the bad-boy/rake is going to be a sure fire winner. Political correctness is not an issue in your historical romance.

Commitment to new authors

Right from the start, Mills & Boon was innovative in its search for new authors. Charles Boon, always a good publicist, inaugurated the 'June 15 Novel', which was advertised as a search to discover a major new author. The winner was *The Veil: A Romance of Tunisia* by

ES Stevens and sold 7,000 copies. The second title they published under this banner was IAR Wylie's *The Rajah's People* in 1910, which sold out all 14,000 copies and printed more than ten editions in two years. Perhaps because of this success, in 1912 Mills & Boon received one thousand manuscripts, 75 per cent of which were from women, with 95 per cent from new authors. Competitions to find new authors have remained a feature throughout the company's history to the present day—as has the massive slush pile.

In 2010 Mills & Boon's latest competition is called New Voices. It is web-based and uses reader feedback for the first time, along with a dash of X-Factor public voting, which will be interesting.

For most publishers, the slush pile is a penance and a purge and these days most of them say they won't read unsolicited material. By contrast, the Mills & Boon slush pile has always contained a high proportion of stories from people who are already readers and have a real feeling for the genre and over the years HMB have found a number of their most loved writers there. These days guidelines for all their imprints and writing tips are available at dedicated sections of their website.

To appreciate the magnitude of this undertaking, you have to understand that in 2009 they received just under 1,400 unsolicited submissions and judged 1,350 contest submissions. Editorial Director Karin Stoecker says, 'From those we took on 11 new authors. We remain one of the few publishers to accept unsolicited submissions and now of course accept these electronically via the link on our web site.'

Sex

It is impossible to talk about romantic fiction for long without falling over the issue of sex. There are so many conflicting assumptions that it is only fair to try to unpick at least some of them. Reviewing the archive for evidence of what the authors thought at various times, the editors have found much of it tantalisingly elliptical. Clearly the authors knew what they were talking about in the context of their own times and were certain that their RNA fellows would know too, without it having to be spelled out. So we have done our best to put their comments in context.

The romantic inheritance in 1960

While some of the RNA's founder members, like Alex Stuart, Lucilla Andrews and Anne Weale were first published only after the War, many of the most successful founders, including President Denise Robins and Vice President Barbara Cartland, had been writing since the twenties. They had grown up with the middle European royalty-and-adventure romances of Elinor Glyn and Anthony Hope (*The Prisoner of Zenda*), the bucolic chivalry of Jeffrey Farnol, the swashbuckling historical adventures of Baroness Orczy (*The Scarlet Pimpernel*) and Rafael Sabatini, and the high excitements of love in outposts of empire by Ethel M Dell. (A cover flash on one of Dell's books proclaimed 'When Mrs Dell speaks, an Empire listens'.

George Orwell loathed her, PG Wodehouse sent her up as Rosie M Banks and Barbara Cartland always cited her as a role model.)

Some of these authors introduced terrific sexual tension in their books. Elinor Glyn's *Three Weeks*, with its sexually predatory Balkan princess who seduces an innocent young British hero, was considered so shocking that Edward VII, that great moralist, forbade any mention of it in his presence. Yet one of the first prizes offered by the RNA in 1960 was named after Elinor Glyn, a writer much admired by Cartland, and the prize itself was a leather-bound presentation volume of one of her novels.

For all the steaminess of some of the plots, in all these books sex, if it occurs at all, takes place off the page. What is more, the protagonists are consciously principled, indeed sometimes heroic, in sexual matters. Even Glyn's Balkan princess doesn't jump on our hero out of lust, or not lust alone. And Farnol's manly heroes treat their ladies as if they are untouchable goddesses. Sabatini is less respectful, notably in *The Sea Hawk* (1915), where the hero kidnaps the heroine and eventually forces her to marry him in order to save her from the vile Basha, but the details are left to the reader's imagination.

For the next generation of writers, the role models were cooler, more sophisticated and a lot less given to sexual dramatics. In 1967 the *RNA News* Editor conducted a survey of the most influential authors on whom RNA members modelled themselves. The winners by far were Mary Stewart and Georgette Heyer, with Victoria Holt/Jean Plaidy as a distant third. Their characters, if less heroic, are sexually better behaved than the earlier generation, on solid principle and a sense that superior behaviour demands restraint. (Heyer's heroes, too, of course, would never want to 'make a cake of themselves', though one or two of her heroes, like the Marquis of Vidal, can get a bit Sabatinian when strongly moved.) In the best of Heyer and in Mary Stewart's romantic suspense novels, the sexual tension between hero and heroine is transmuted over the course of the story into deep emotion and real mutual understanding, so that the reader can readily imagine them having a happy marriage after the book ends.

1960

When the RNA was formed in January 1960, it was a time of huge change in the western world, both socially and for literature. Writing to the Society of Women Writers and Journalists magazine, *The Woman Journalist*, Spring 1960, Alex Stuart, the RNA's strong-minded first Chairman said that, while she had found enthusiastic reviews of romantic fiction in the *Times Literary Supplement*, the *Sunday Times* and the *Scotsman* as recently as 1938, these days the genre was ignored; 'yet *Lolita* and *Return to Peyton Place*—which I should have thought an apology was called for—are treated with enormous respect as works of art.' She went on, 'It is fashionable to write dirty books, I am aware: sex and sales are synonymous these days and Colin Wilson would have the romantic novelist write of perversion and lust, according to his recent article in *John o'London's*, and he treats what we do write with the contempt the majority of reviewers accord it, because we avoid such unsavoury topics.'

But actually, authors like the hugely successful Netta Muskett were already addressing 'unsavoury topics', including female sexual frustration and disappointment, not generally on the agenda for the male authors of that first wave of the sexual revolution. Her publisher quoted Robert Pitman in *The Daily Express* on the back cover of her paperbacks, 'While most books on the romance shelf are stronger on sentiment than sex, you can be certain of realism every time you pick up a Muskett'. Even so, though the problems she wrote about were realistic, the situations painful and the heroines by no means all sympathetic or innocent, sex as such still took place off the page.

And then came *Lady Chatterley's Lover*. In January the RNA had its inaugural meeting in London; in October Penguin published the full (banned) text of *Lady Chatterley*, resulting in a headline-grabbing six-day trail for obscenity. The jury cleared it and when Foyle's opened on 10th November they sold out of copies in 15 minutes, taking orders for a further 3,000. In the States, Grove Press went to the Supreme Court to defend *Lady C* in 1960 but Australia held out until 1963, until when it was a prohibited import, along with two of Alex Stuart's bêtes noires, *Lolita* and *Peyton Place*.

The courting novel/light romance

Alex Stuart, like many, but not all, those early members, wrote classical romances (in her case about doctors and nurses for Mills & Boon). They were serialised, sold well and gave much pleasure to her readers. Essentially they were about the courting dance, with hero and heroine both members of a caring and largely middle-class profession and with impeccable personal standards. In practice, at the end of the fifties, that meant sexual restraint by both parties. These were the standards of behaviour which readers had recognised and approved for three generations. In her memoir, *No Time for Romance*, Lucilla Andrews said that such standards might be a strain but they also provided a 'reassuring social armour'. Having been to watch the moon on Salisbury Plain with a young Cavalry officer during the War, she returned home, after lights-out but unscathed. She explained, 'When too emotionally immature to handle one's sexual emotions, it was often a great relief to know that all one was expected to do was control them.'

Alex Stuart claimed that her books did 'a great deal more good, especially where the impressionable reader is concerned, than *Lolita* or *Peyton Place* or *Room at the Top*.' A *Sun* reader, writing from Cardiff in 1965 seems to confirm this, contrasting romantic fiction with thrillers and whodunits and finding 'the level of writing higher and their outlook a great deal more wholesome.'

But this social climate was shifting as education improved, more and more young people left home before they married and female control of contraception became possible. What is astonishing is the speed of the change. In 1959 Anne Weale was removing a grandmother's extra-marital affair from one of her Mills & Boon novels, at the request of the editors. By 1961, she was writing to Alan Boon worrying that her plots were 'a shade old-fashioned'. She was 32. She had just read *Song in my Heart* by Rachel Lindsay (who also wrote as Robert Leigh) in which the (virginal, just) heroine falls in love with a married man and does her best to seduce him. He resists. But then his wife turns out to have been a bad lot, and is murdered by her lover, so there are no impediments to the happy-ever-after ending. Weale, who had been brought up on the strict requirements of Miss Johnson, Fiction Editor at *Woman's Weekly*, was staggered by 'the Muskettish goings-on'. However, encouraged by Alan Boon, she took the brakes off her own plots and became one of the sexiest authors of her era, with novels like *The Sea Waif* (1967) and *Antigua Kiss* (1982). It was the latter which gave rise to Alan Boon's discussion with Brenda McDougall, by then Fiction Editor at *Woman's Weekly*, about the acceptability of oral sex to the modern reader (see Chapter on Harlequin Mills & Boon).

Publishers of the courting novel, or 'light romance', like Mills & Boon, Ward Lock and Hurst & Blackett had a dilemma. They still looked to magazine serialisation for a big contribution to profit and, while many authors wanted to test the boundaries, the magazine editors were conservative. Miss Johnson, for instance, would not have strong drink, swearing, divorce or sex outside marriage. (As a result she invented the MINA or marriage in name only, which led to plots which often strained credibility but kept the stories acceptable to morally conservative readers.) Some authors, of course, remained quite content with restraint, including RNA founder member, veteran Constance M Evans (first novel 1932, last novel 1974). In Spring 1973 she sent the *RNA News* a progress report: 'a very exciting year—two interviews in newspapers, a seat on a National Book Week Panel. Somebody asked if it made any difference to my writing now that the permissive age was here. I answered that although the outward veneer has changed the basic material hasn't!'

Sometimes, it was simply a matter of temperament. Born in 1910, Betty Neels's first book was published in 1969 but she was still more comfortable with ladylike heroines, steady responsible heroes and sex after marriage, a long way after the book ended. Sometimes, it was because authors thought sex was just not romantic enough. Lillian Peake told the *RNA News* Spring 1975 that the *Southend Evening Echo* had published a letter from her on 3rd March in which she answered a critic who thought her books ought to reflect reality (that is, have more sex): 'But if so,' she wrote, 'then the readers would not want to read them. These books are escapism ... they offer millions of women a dream world in which they can leave reality behind.'

Renée Shann, another veteran who published her first book, *With All My Heart*, in 1936 and went on to clock up a total of one hundred and forty-eight titles for various publishers, was more frustrated. She told the *RNA News* in 1968 that she was 'not altogether in favour of keeping sex out of romantic novels but readers insist on it.' She herself would have loved to move with the times and pointed out to her publishers, Collins, that courtship had changed. 'But no, a girl in my books has to be pure as the driven snow.' Michael Brennan in the *News of the World* expressed surprise but commented that Renée Shann had been a big seller all over the world. So that was what the market wanted ...

Mills & Boon, with the largest list of purely romantic titles, was able to spread their risk and soon found that the sexier titles were the most popular. A stable of new, steamier authors boosted their sales in the second half of the sixties—Anne Hampson, Roberta Leigh, Anne Mather, Violet Winspear. These new stories were led by the hero, the classic alpha man, charismatic and powerful, often older than the heroine and always more sexually experienced. This was the heyday of the 'waif' story, with the hero graduating from guardian to lover (*The Seventh Veil* was said to be the iconic movie for Mills & Boon editors of the time) and sometimes skirting violence in the process. Violet Winspear, indeed, interviewed in *Radio Times* before the BBC *Man Alive* programme, announced that her heroes 'must be the sort of men who are capable of rape; men it's dangerous to be alone in the room with.' It was too crude a description, but it had enough truth for Brenda McDougall, when Fiction Editor of *Woman's Weekly* a generation later, to tell a new author, 'Heroes must be strong and know their own mind and be madly in love with the heroine, of course. But we don't want bullies. It's important not to give the reader the idea that rapists make good husbands.' And she told an RNA meeting in Autumn 1977 that she preferred to avoid violence, sensational permissiveness, and divorces, smoking, drugs and swearing. So the hero wasn't going to be that much of a wild man, if his story was serialised in *Woman's Weekly*.

But no matter how demanding the hero, there was no sex before marriage until the mid-seventies. The hero might have sowed his wild oats but the heroine would be, it was assumed, virgin and stay that way until she married the hero. Author Sara Craven remembers being told of discussions at a Harlequin Mills & Boon sales conference about whether the readership was yet ready for pre-marital sex—and the editors saying that actually they already had such a ms in Craven's *Flame of Diablo*, published 1979. There were extenuating circumstances—the heroine thinks the hero is going to die the following day—and there is no doubt, either, that it is she, not he, who drives their sexual encounter. Afterwards, since he does not die after all, the hero insists on marriage and behaves with positively 1950s restraint and respect.

From this time on, waifs began to fall out of favour and heroines became more self-determining with decent careers and some experience of life, as exemplified in the work of the two bestsellers of the decade, Penny Jordan and Charlotte Lamb. Sometimes they had clearly had sexual experience too—giving rise to the popular theme of the 'secret baby'—but it was not always spelled out. It is really only in the twenty-first century that heroines of category romance, as it is now called, are expected to have had a sexual life before they encounter the hero.

The influence of the magazine editors

Editors of serials proved to be more conservative even than publishers. During the sixties it was not unusual for the Fiction Editors to edit out or tone down some aspect of the story which was then reversed when the book went into hardback and paperback. But that did not mean that they didn't move with the times at all. In 1973, Patricia Brougham, then Associate Editor for *Woman*, warned against a heroine who 'was too naïve to tell the cad from the hero' or 'meekly accepted everything and never stood up for herself'. *Woman* was not looking for the straight little romantic story or anything too sentimental any more. It needed 'tougher' fiction. But Mary Howard, a *Woman* regular, paused to reflect at the age of 70 in the *RNA News* of Winter 1977, 'The magazines seem to reflect the restless world we live in and no one seems to know what anyone wants. Their policies shift and change, frantically trying to keep level with the changes of fashion and the trends of public opinion. At one moment there is a cry for *strong* fiction, more *realism* and greater *frankness*, but half-a-dozen letters from elderly readers will send them into reverse, scaling everything back to what they think is acceptable. No one seems to have the courage of their convictions, and so many opinions have to be asked, that no guide for the unfortunate writer ever seems to appear.

'The features pages are dominated by sensationalism on newspaper lines: the love life (or lives) of film stars; the private agonies of the wives and girlfriends of defaulting public figures. Fiction swings about in a bemused manner alternately shocking or shushing as the case may be, and no editor issues posters promoting her authors, rarely gives them advances or cover by-lines, and some would like to get rid of it completely.'

Sex books

The explosion of permissiveness in fiction of the early 1960s produced a different problem for the writer of mainstream romantic fiction. It was not a question of broadening their scope by gently pushing at the boundaries, as in light romance. They were faced with a completely new set of competitors on the commercial fiction shelves. In 1961 Harold Robbins's *The Carpetbaggers* was published and went straight into the bestseller lists, despite (or perhaps because of) the *New York Times* calling it 'a collection of monotonous episodes about normal and abnormal sex.' In the UK, Nicholas Monsarrat, who had written *The Cruel Sea*, turned his hand to sex-and-money in *The Nylon Pirates* (1960), but the 'sex novel' was generally considered to be a US invention. The prejudice received another boost in 1966, though, when Jacqueline Susann published another instant international bestseller, *Valley of the Dolls*, the semi-autobiographical story of three women in the New York theatre scene of the fifties which embraced drugs, drink, insanity, abortion, promiscuity and suicide.

Anne Maybury, who worked very closely with her American publisher, found herself defending the whole New York publishing industry in *RNA News* Summer 1970: 'A note in the *News* with regard to America prompts me to an immediate protest. The inference seems to me to be that sex is Number One on the list of interests in the American fiction market. Nothing could be further from the truth.'

She contrasts 'sex books, written quickly and for the most part without literary merit' with books 'concerned with the deep and controversial problems where sex is a necessary part of the whole social or economic pattern and is therefore inseparable from the plot.' (Incidentally, unlike Alex Stuart, she defended *Lolita*.) What American publishers wanted, she said, was 'strong plots, good writing, speed— these are the ingredients that will pay in the long run; not sex.'

Romantic fiction and the sexual revolution

However, criticism that romantic fiction was trivial was now augmented by the accusation that it was hopelessly old-fashioned and failed to reflect the realities of contemporary relationships. In the mid-seventies Rachel Anderson published *The Purple Heart Throbs: the Sub Literature of Love*. Reviewing it in the *RNA News* Spring 1974, founder member, former Chairman and Regency novelist Alice Chetwynd Ley wrote, 'Ms Anderson sees the formation of the RNA as confirmation of the fact that romantic novelists saw themselves as a restraining, conservative influence on society. … She urges us to be rebels. But aren't we? The Victorian and Edwardian novelists had good cause to remind their society that sex was a part of love. Today's romantic novelist serves to remind the permissive society of her time that sex is indeed a part, but not the whole. It is not, of course, as shocking a message as the earlier one; but it is none the less valid.'

But actually, both Anderson and Chetwynd Ley were looking at relatively small areas of the landscape. In other parts of the forest, romantic writers were already exploring contemporary issues and pushing literary boundaries. Very soon the books short-listed for the Main Award started to reflect the dilemmas of greater sexual freedom and wider opportunities for women, which sometimes did not expand fast enough to keep up with them.

The second Main Award winner in 1961, *The Witches' Sabbath* by Paula Allardyce, is a dark story about a love affair which went wrong before the book opens, sending the man off into a bad marriage which ended in murder. The woman, Tamar, is a writer investigating a witch trial, who finds parallels between seventeenth-century Abigail, hated and accused of being a witch, and her own position as an independent career woman in the twentieth. And the second-time-around love affair is startling in its intensity. Trisha Ashley (*Chocolate Wishes*, Avon 2010) writes, 'It was violently passionate stuff—sometimes physically so—which surprised me from a novel in this era. They had done everything except have sex in their previous relationship, so a lot of this passion was sheer frustration. The heroine is very liberated in every way except this one, being young, independent and earning a living as a writer. (Very bohemian!) It is a very sexy book, even though they don't actually have sex.' Allardyce (real name Ursula Torday) was a fascinating writer who repays study. The daughter of explorer anthropologist Emil Torday, she travelled widely in spite of movement problems as the result of childhood polio, and wrote dark, intense, intelligent novels which never received the attention they deserved.

The subject matter of Award winners expanded with the times, but Anne Maybury, who told a local chapter in 1968 that the public would soon get tired of sex books, was right in one way: novels about sex *per se* became less important in the bestseller lists after the sixties. There were flurries, of course. The vogue for hot historicals meant that publishers looked for authors able to write a good steamy relationship with plenty of sexual encounters, and the sex and shopping blockbusters of the eighties demanded not only sexually explicit writing but also a good deal of sexual inventiveness. So does the twenty-first century invention Romantica, described as erotic romance, and a major genre in e-publishing.

Sensual writing

President Mary Burchell's take on this was typically down-to-earth. Definitely one of the more traditional writers in the RNA, she went to the *Romantic Times* convention in the US in 1983. She told the Summer *RNA News* of that year, that her invitation to this had resulted from an American writer in the UK asking her, 'Do you believe in sustaining sensuality?' to which she had answered, 'If you mean soft porn, no! It means he's unsure of himself if he's young, a D.O.M. [Dirty Old Man] if he's old and both are to be ignored in fact and fiction.' She was promptly asked to come to the convention!

It did however, present an interesting new problem for writers, as more and more readers wanted to follow characters beyond the bedroom door. Publishers began to press writers to satisfy the demand. By 1986, Elizabeth Harrison, deploring some gratuitous sex scenes in New Writers' Scheme submissions, advised, 'Certainly there is a place for sex in today's romantic fiction, but only as a part of a growing and meaningful relationship.' She wrote for Harlequin Mills & Boon.

In a talk full of good advice reported by Nina Lambert, Caroline Upcher, successful author and then Editorial Director of Century fiction, told the *RNA News*, Summer 1990: '"Either don't write about sex at all—it's not obligatory—or do it properly." A lot of people feel uncomfortable writing sex scenes and, although Caroline found that these caused her no problem, she does regret bowing to pressure and inserting an extra sex scene in her book at the request of her American publisher. This was written during a plane trip from London to New York, with a male fellow passenger peering over her shoulder, and she now finds it artificial and wishes she had cut it out. She advised us never to write a scene against our own better judgement; editorial changes only work if the author does them willingly.'

There were, of course, still those who felt that a veil should be drawn, as a letter from Anne Vinton, published in the *RNA News* Autumn 1991 illustrates: 'As a Founder Member of the RNA—and how many of us are left?—may I address the subject of our being, and our aim, which is to use all the means in our power to *raise the prestige of Romantic Authorship*. Nothing could be further from our original aims than the admission that sex, tacitly hygienic and explicitly anatomical, is totally fulfilling, nor from the Romance we founders promulgated. Why have the arch romantics submitted to this greed for sexual explicitness?'

But there was a time when she was ahead of her publisher in such matters, as she admitted ruefully: 'Old fogeys like me lived through days when Mills & Boon would blue-pencil out love scenes as not being suitable for sales in Ireland!'

In 2004, Julie Cohen, then a newly published author, discussed the subject at the RNA Conference (using chocolate and strawberries as teaching aids) and, in particular, how to deal with the risk of embarrassment. 'Create distance between ourselves and our characters,' she advised. 'Sex scenes aren't about us. Get into the characters' heads and stay there. Make the scene about emotion, not mechanics.' But always remember that a sex scene is an action scene. Oh, and turn off your inner mother.

But cool and sophisticated as the twenty-first century may be, *sex* is always good for a headline. The *Daily Telegraph* (4th July 2004) picked up Julie's seminar under the headline, 'Explicit Sex now used to lure young women readers'. The conference organiser wrote to correct a couple of impressions: 'Hot stuff has been around the drawing room since at least 1907 when Elinor Glyn wrote *Three Weeks*. Also, it's a long time since romantic novels stopped at "chaste clinches by moonlight". In Harlequin Mills & Boon, for example, there have been full docking procedures since at least the mid-seventies.'

All credit to them, they printed it.

Moi? A Romantic?

Moi? Read romantic novels?

At the 2010 Conference in Greenwich, David Shelley, Deputy Publisher at Little, Brown, giving some personal reflections on the genre, mused that romantic content was popular, nay essential, but the romantic label was a turn off. Thrillers and mysteries sold better if they contained an element of romance. But that was after readers had discovered for themselves that it was there. Nobody wanted it to be called romantic on the cover.

Why? Has the amazing durability of the Cartland brand attached dukes and breathless prose to the word 'romantic' for ever? Or is it that seeking to read about love, the risks and rewards of relationships, makes us feel needy? Or, even worse, uncool.

Whatever the answer, it is not new.

In Winter 1974 author Brenda Castle was telling the *RNA News*: 'Recently I have given two talks on writing romantic fiction to ladies' groups and, although they have all been tremendously interested and have eagerly noted titles of my books to obtain, not one person amongst them would admit to being a reader of romantic fiction! In fact it is rare to find anyone who will admit to reading it. I wonder if other members have come up against this kind of prejudice?' To which the *News* Editor said, 'They have indeed!'

Moi? A romantic novelist?

Diane Pearson writes:

What is it about the word 'romantic' that makes so many authors, methinks protesting too much, declare vehemently that their romantic novels are not romantic?

It happens all the time. There was the bestselling historical novelist who left the shortest possible time between accepting the £10,000 cheque for winning the Romantic Novel of the Year Award, and rushing onto radio to say she did not write romantic novels. Mike Legat relates in his autobiography that 'Ursula Bloom was nothing if not a romantic novelist, but she always refused to join the RNA. When I asked her why, she replied frigidly that she was not qualified to join since she wrote novels, not romances.' Mike succinctly sums up this conversation with a sardonic 'H'm'. I have observed over the years, both as an editor and an author, that it is nearly always the really romantic novelists who deny their roots.

There was the guest speaker, an actress who makes cakes, who finished her address to us with the statement: 'I do not read romantic novels myself, but I like to think there are people out there who do.' What? I thought, never read *War and Peace*, *Gone With The Wind*, the Brontës, Jane Austen, Sir Walter Scott, huge tranches of Dickens and Trollope (Anthony Trollope's *Miss Mackenzie* is one of the most charming, funny and tender romances I have ever read), to say nothing of the big bestselling contemporary novels like *Bridget Jones's Diary* and the epic novels of Rosamunde Pilcher, Penny Vincenzi, Rosie Thomas, Maeve Binchy and Susan Howatch?

Only once, to my knowledge, has a writer asked to be removed from the Award's shortlist. This was a male author whose romantic novels were astoundingly successful and one could only respect his decision. It is more than possible he would have won the prize.

It is extraordinary that the word 'romantic' produces such vehement reactions, but only in the world of novel writing. Refer to the romantic period of art, poetry, music (although I do have a cousin who doesn't like Brahms because he is 'too romantic') and it just means a huge body of work that has created a recognisable period and style. But call a novel 'romantic' and writers bristle and protest.

Some of the fear of being labelled 'romantic' may come from self-doubt and insecurity in the quality of one's writing. When AS Byatt's *Possession* was published she had no such self-doubt and allowed the publishers to put 'A Romance' on the front cover. It was indeed a romance, beautifully written, engrossing, and with wonderful literary undertones, but still a romance. It won the Booker Prize and was a great triumph for the genre—but why did the bulk of romantic novelists not take pride in this accolade?

Perhaps because not all of us have the literary reputation and talent of AS Byatt. Indeed, some romantic novels are quite badly written, but there is no reason why the whole genre should be judged by these, any more than bad novels should define any category of fiction. Even so, perhaps some romantic authors are terrified of being downgraded and automatically associated with bad writing.

Of course, some part of the problem lies with the 'lady in pink' who was very much on the scene in our early days. An individual, slightly eccentric 'celebrity', Barbara Cartland, while establishing herself as a worldwide name also somewhat damaged the image of the serious romantic novelist. She was professional, but she also gave us a certain reputation especially in the early days when the media, particularly TV, were only too happy to seize upon us as objects of ridicule. This has, thank goodness, died away over the years as our financial importance to the book trade became apparent. When publishers, agents, and booksellers had to admit that we were a huge section of their trade turnover (at one time romantic novels accounted for 62 per cent of paperback turnover) the sneers abated. No one wanted to kill the golden goose.

There is also the fear that—oh horror!—one will be associated with Mills & Boon, a particularly unpleasant piece of literary snobbism. As has been stated elsewhere in this book, Mills & Boon romances (one must understand that in trade terms the M&B publications are known as romances as distinct from romantic novels) are professionally, skilfully written books which have to obey clearly defined rules. They are not easy to write. Some of them transcend their restrictions and produce examples of moving sincerity, elegance and style. A great many 'epic' romantic writers began their careers with Mills & Boon. Sally Beauman, who writes warmly of her M&B editor elsewhere in this book, learnt her craft at M&B and eventually morphed into a giant, bestselling romantic novelist of literary merit. Rosamunde Pilcher also began her writing career with Mills & Boon and, indeed, quite a few big names came from that highly professional stable.

But why, when one says the word 'romantic', is the immediate association Barbara Cartland and Mills & Boon? Barbara Cartland is one name among many and her books are not as popular now as they used to be. And the Mills & Boon category is only a comparatively minor strand in a huge body of work that encompasses the romantic novel. It is like saying all crime writers are the same as Micky Spillane—crime covers a range of books from Raymond Chandler and Agatha Christie through PD James and Frederick Forsyth to CJ Sansom, some popular and perhaps downmarket, some violent, some deductive puzzles, and some quite literary. But even the crime genre, huge though it is, does not encompass such an enormous breadth of work as the romantic novel: Mills & Boon, Cooksonesque sagas, chick-lit, Aga sagas, comedies, historicals, epics, literary greats, literary classics and so on.

I don't know how we can, once and for all, stamp out the fear and recoil from the word 'romantic'. What we romantic novelists, in all our guises, write are novels of human relationships and emotional aspirations, sometimes varnished with a veneer of glamour and glory and a heroic grandeur of the spirit. The Crime Writers, with whom inevitably we are often compared, and who indeed have their own problems to contend with, are supposed to deal with action and violence and intellectual deduction. But even those definitions aren't written in stone. Some romantic novels include action and violence, and some crime novels encompass emotional relationships (think of poor old Morse) and human aspirations. But, so far as I know, no crime writer has denied the genre in which he writes. But then, they never had a Barbara Cartland equivalent to contend with.

We have to stand firm by our standards and accomplishments. We have to try and explain to those who protest what a huge school of work they are condemning. We have to get up and make our declaration—'My name is Diane Pearson and I am a romantic novelist'. And my final advice to those who shrink from the word 'romantic' is just to say *War and Peace*, possibly the greatest romantic novel ever written.

Romantic fiction—whence and whither?

Joanna Trollope, recipient of a Lifetime Achievement Award this year and, in the words of Chairman Katie Fforde, the RNA's Koh-i-Noor, addressed the 50th Anniversary Conference at Greenwich on 11th July 2010. This is what she said:

Ladies and gentlemen—
It's a huge pleasure to be here, and an honour to be asked to speak to you on such an occasion—and in this wonderful place.

I want to start with the reason we are all here together today, in the first place. And that reason is fiction. The writing of fiction. Let's think about it for a moment, and what we mean by it. For our professional purposes, we could say it means telling stories as a branch of literature. Or we could amplify that and say that it means telling stories as a product of the imagination.

There is a considerable difference between the two. To begin with, the idea of telling stories as a product of the imagination is as old as the history of articulate mankind. Stories as poems, or plays, or songs, go back to the dawn of sentient time. Greek drama alone is over two thousand years old—vibrant evidence of humanity's desire to explore itself and record itself and its emotions and hopes and fears, as proof and validation of having lived and breathed in the first place.

But storytelling as a recognised branch of literature is very young, less than 300 years old when, about 1740, men like Samuel Richardson, a printer and professional letter writer, who had had insights into the workings of the female heart through writing love letters for illiterate servant girls, decided to use his writing skills and his psychological knowledge to write a long story, in letter form, about a girl called Pamela, who did not exist in life—although she might have done.

The subsequent genre, building on all those centuries of poetic and dramatic stories, flourished. Richardson was joined by the now familiar eighteenth-century roll call—Henry Fielding, Tobias Smollett, Laurence Sterne, Walter Scott—and then Jane Austen, and we were off. In a hundred and fifty years, fiction was acknowledged and established. A hundred and thirty years further on, and we would not be sitting here together without it. The writing of fiction isn't just how we earn our livings, it's how we identify ourselves, how we shape our thinking and our being. We are novelists— novel—members of the new breed of writers.

One of the reasons, I think, that fiction has been so vastly successful as a genre is because of its intense connection to humanity. It is a fundamental aspect of human nature to be absorbed by the story of our own lives, and the novel is the perfect vehicle to recognise that and to reflect our stories back to us through created character and situation. In *Northanger Abbey*, Jane Austen, after describing a girl putting down a book dismissively saying that it was 'Only a novel ...' retorts ... '*Only* some work in which the most thorough knowledge of human nature, the happiest delineation of its varieties, the liveliest effusions of wit and humour, are conveyed to the world in the best chosen language ...'

Good for Jane.

As fiction took hold, and expanded, it also quite naturally diversified, and Samuel Richardson's interminable exchanges of letters were joined by the picaresque (*Tom Jones*), the comic (*Humphrey Clinker*), the intellectually wacky (*Tristram Shandy*), the Gothic

(*The Mysteries of Udolpho*), the historical (*Rob Roy*) and, for our purposes today, the romantic—enter Miss Austen.

I would like us all to reflect upon this category of Romance for a moment. The word itself has origins that have nothing to do with the vagaries of the human heart. Unsurprisingly perhaps, we have to go back to the name buried in the word—Roman. Many things, of course, pertained to Rome in the ancient world, but perhaps the two most lastingly influential were its empire and its language.

Its language was called Latin, because the district around Rome, of which Rome was the heart, was called Latium. So the language of this powerful city and its subordinate surroundings became known as Latin, and as the influence and empire spread inexorably across Europe and the Mediterranean, this language spread too, and, as it spread, became inevitably involved with the native languages it encountered on the way, and a whole new breed of vernacular tongues grew up—part Latin, but also part French, part Provençal, part Italian or Spanish or Portuguese or Romanian. And these languages and their dialects, because of their connection to the mothership in Rome, became known as Romance.

I only emphasise this because it's interesting to know how ancient and important the roots of the romance genre are, even if fiction itself was only given the seal of official literary approval quite recently. Those roots weren't just about language either, because they were all tangled up with the old stories of all the cultures the Romans swept up into their empire, notably the tales of magnificent human conduct, both in battle and in the recognisable territory of human relationships. They are stylised to our eyes, and formal, but the tales of chivalry that flourished in the outposts were a reflection of what those populations wanted, stories that told of something wonderful, stories that lifted people out of the mud of ordinary life. It is very, very early in cultural history that romance came to mean a story redolent of the adventurous, the chivalrous, the—in the best sense— glamorous, something that was completely remote from the scenes and incidents of the humdrum and everyday. Indeed, the peasant woman working in a turnip patch in twelfth century Romania was in as much need of an imaginative escape from her daily life as the weary girl stuck behind a supermarket check-out till today.

I think, when considering romance, that the word adventure is important. We may not think about it consciously, but what adventure involves—the chance, the remarkable incident, the excitement, the risk, the daring, the tension—is very much at the heart of romantic writing. Because—and I think this is the reason that people go on writing and reading romantic fiction—falling in love is essentially an adventure. It is probably the biggest emotional adventure that happens to any of us, and it happens irrespective of gender or sexuality or race or creed or age or intelligence or looks or prosperity. It is possibly, and apart from breathing, the one element of the human condition that unites us *all*—even if the object of our love varies from a motorbike to Jesus. No wonder it is so important.

Indeed, the early practitioners understood that it had to be preserved by leaving it at a moment of fleeting perfection, the way the Japanese celebrate cherry blossom because they know it cannot last. If you look at the novels of Charlotte Brontë or Jane Austen, you will see that they knew when the sheer adventure of an excitingly complicated romance was over. We do not follow Lizzie and Mr Darcy into a marriage bedevilled by prolonged visits from Mr Darcy's mother in law. We leave Jane Eyre at the height of her triumph, the adored young wife of a subdued and blinded Mr Rochester, with no hint of how the transfer of control might affect the dynamic between them—sex god turned stumbling patient ... the subject for another novel of a very different kind ...

It is perhaps the essence of good romantic fiction that the writer pulls back at the moment of attainment, of surrender, because that is the moment when the heady rush of adventure stops and loading the dishwasher begins. There may be sober satisfaction in the latter, but there is, quite rightly, little romance. And romance, as a genre, has a specific job to do, as its long history so powerfully demonstrates, a job that we all have a strong instinct for, which is to give everyone who reads the chance to dream and to aspire.

I have nine grandchildren, five of whom are girls. The middle one of those girls is three, and she is currently obsessed with the princesses of fairy tales. Of course she loves what she calls their dancing dresses, and their Disney tiaras and waist length hair, but what she really loves is the romance of their adventures. As a result, one often finds her draped over the arm of a sofa, eyes closed, waiting to be woken from a century of slumber with a kiss. Or she will run away from you, very slowly, carefully dropping a shoe as she goes, and you have to retrieve the shoe, exclaim, 'Oh! Her glass slipper! Will I *ever* find the girl whose foot this fits?' and put it on a cushion, and set off in hot pursuit. My granddaughter knows that this is fantasy—that is, not real life—but she also believes in the reality of the possibility of such magic. And she is right.

Romance is not escapism, in the sense of trying to avoid what must be faced, and it is not trivial. It is, instead, crucial for the richness of our imaginative lives and for the optimistic health of our hearts and minds. Hormones and physiology may dictate that a boy fantasises about physical exploits and achievements in a way that girls reserve for human connections, but both are essentially romantic because both lift the imagination out of the habitual and, if you like, re-boot the brain to give it energy for all the banal areas of life which have to be attended to for the most pragmatic of reasons. What you personally find romance *in*, is not of consequence: what matters is that there is something, somewhere that makes you believe that round the corner waits a possibility of some kind that will give your life a whole new dimension. For huge numbers of people, especially all those wonderful women who make up over 65 per cent of the book buying public in this country, that something is to be found between the covers of a romantic novel.

And now we come to the present. The present state of romantic fiction. I looked at the *Sunday Times* bestseller lists this morning, and in the hardback fiction top ten, there are six crime or thriller novels, and in the paperback list, there are another six. That's twelve of a single genre out of twenty. Romantic fiction has four out of twenty—warm congratulations to Katie Fforde, Jane Green, Maeve Binchy and Jill Mansell. But that is a third the number of crime novels. Why?

We may have a good idea of why crime fiction sells in hard times. As the wonderful PD James says, crime novels are 'small celebrations of order', so that you can understand that when the world seems in such deep and insoluble trouble, the satisfactory solutions and plot conclusions of a crime novel not only reassert a moral order, but also console with their finality. But romantic fiction, with its emphasis on the possible, its promise of adventure and a turning luck, should be equally apposite, if for different reasons, in a belt-tightening, anxious time. Yet, it isn't. It isn't selling in the quantities that it could, or even deserves, to sell. Or, to put it more optimistically, it isn't yet.

There are, I think, a number of reasons for this. The first is the most obvious—the look of the thing. I am sorry to say this, but, by and large, romantic fiction, as a section in a bookshop, looks—awful. For some reason, publishing art and marketing departments have got stuck in an infantile rut of pink. And more pink. And pearlised embossed lettering, and cartoon drawings of cocktail glasses and handbags and ditsy girls falling off their designer heels. There is a section, in branches of Accessorize, familiar to all of you I'm sure, dedicated to little girls. The stands are packed with sparkle and glitter and spangle and pink. The items are simply charming, no doubt about it, but they are not meant for grown-ups. They are meant for my princess granddaughter. The average current romantic novel book jacket looks as if it is meant for my granddaughter too. I don't think it's deliberate. I think it's a marketing habit, treating a reader as if she was three going on four. I also think it wouldn't be too hard a habit to break if agents and writers insisted upon a change. I mean *insisted*.

I also think the genre suffers from a snobbery. It arises, as all snobberies do, out of fear—a fear of emotional display, a fear of emotional vulnerability, and also a terror of humiliation and rejection—all of which are entirely human and perfectly understandable. But the effect of this snobbery in publishing terms is to dismiss a whole genre of writing which actually has some important things to say about the human heart—common to every person on this planet—as well as encouraging in readers exactly the imaginative ambition that I have already described.

In recent times, both *Bridget Jones*, and *Sex and the City* were significant books, then television and cinema films. I know they both started as newspaper columns but it was in book form that they both had their first impact, picking up, as they did, on the very real and urgent *zeitgeist* of their times, which was what were young women to do with their natural and valid emotional and sexual needs in a society which had delivered them a long overdue independence—but also its unforeseen but inevitable loneliness and lack of intimate connection? The author of *Persuasion* and the author of *Villette* would have relished such a topic, and even if they would have treated it differently both from now, and from each other, they would have recognised it instantly as the issue of the day for modern girls, just as marriage was the only real career option for girls for their own.

But they were writing in a relatively empty writing world. Modern writers are writing in a very overcrowded one, and the consequence of these two seminal modern books in a crowded world with everyone battling for a share of the market was—constant cloning. The formula that Helen Fielding and Candace Bushnell developed—a slightly breathless, musing, self-deprecating, funny, autobiographical voice, as if inside the heads of Bridget Jones and Carrie Bradshaw—was taken up and taken over, in so many forms and guises that an essentially strong and original message became drowned out by an almost infinite chorus of twitterings—in the old sense!—that could of course just be dismissed by the media in the manner of a Victorian doctor telling a seriously unhappy female patient that she was merely hysterical.

And then the media got stuck. It got as stuck as the publishing art departments seem to be. Rather than look to romantic fiction for important messages about what is happening in the hearts and minds of contemporary womanhood, there is a tendency to toss aside anything with the R word in the press release, as if the intelligent mind might somehow be diminished by engaging with it.

This is, I'm sure, more than evident to all of you. But—and this is the hard part to say to this audience—the media, the reviewers, the publishers, are not wholly to blame for the place that romantic fiction finds itself in. You can, after all, only promote and market and sell the material you are provided with in the first place.

For the last four years, I have been on the judging panel of the Melissa Nathan award. You will remember Melissa, who was just coming good, professionally, with novels such as *The Nanny*, when she was tragically afflicted with cancer, and died of it. The prize, set up in her memory, is for a romantic comedy, a category which is fiendishly difficult to write, but which she profoundly believed in, as her own considerable achievements testify.

So, every year, Melissa's agent, Maggie Phillips, plus Jo Brand, Sophie Kinsella, Morwenna Banks, Lisa Tarbuck and I sit down to choose a winner. And it isn't easy. Not easy at all. Not because we are snowed under with good books, but because, to our yearly disappointment, we aren't. And these are published books, not hopeful manuscripts.

It's not really that the writers can't write. There's a lot of good writing. But it's more the poverty of ambition and subject matter that distresses us. Too often, it seems, romantic writers have succumbed to the preoccupations of *Closer* magazine rather than tackle—even with jokes—the very real, abiding and profound importance of how our emotional and imaginative lives in these disturbed but interesting times, affect not just our relish of this world, but our capacity to live in it usefully and richly.

Don't get me wrong. Shopping has its place in every sane life, and few things cheer like a pair of new, not sensible, shoes or an unexpected martini. But these are sequins on the dress, not the dress itself, let alone the body under the dress. Think of the history of this wonderful genre, think of where it came from, who its early practitioners were, and how it has faithfully recorded— better than any non-fiction social history—the   extraordinary changes that have come upon men and women and love and marriage and sex and work in the last two hundred years.

And think of those readers out there, patronised by the book jackets, dismissed as airheads by the media, but who need and value good romantic fiction now probably more than they ever did.

We are living now in a world where books are going to have to fight for their place more than ever, in the face of the new technological diversions and distractions tempting the young, in particular, every day.

Books in their printed form won't die, unless we let them, but they have to offer something that can't be found anywhere else, something apart from reliable quality. The thing is—romantic fiction writers have a particular advantage because they have a magic ingredient that no iPad can match, because it's something that eludes technology by its very nature—and it's something that can get romantic fiction back where it belongs in the bestseller lists. And that quality? Which has been the essence of the romantic culture since its beginnings in the days of the Roman Empire?

Why—it's hope. Of course. And I urge you all to go home— and write about it.

Ladies and gentlemen, thank you very much.

Index

Note: Pen names of authors appear in italics.